# The Social Construction of Management

From cultural studies we understand that the relationship between text and reader is not passive but that each one works upon the other, and that text is active in forming the identity of the reader. This book is the first to discuss how management textbooks construct their readers. It analyses management textbooks published since the 1950s and shows they construct a world in which chaos is kept at bay only by strong management, and in which strong management is based upon the rationality of modernity. This book exposes and analyses such claims to truths, and theorizes their arguments using the work of Butler and Foucault, the sociology of scientific knowledge, critical legal studies, art history and queer theory.

By revealing a post-modern turn in management textbooks, *The Social Construction of Management* is both a critical and empirical study that explores the constitution of managerial identities in the age of mass education in management. An exciting contribution to the growing body of knowledge within critical management studies, this book challenges the way we think about organizations and their management, and about management education as a whole. This is thought-provoking reading for anyone studying management, or working in the managerial organization.

**Nancy Harding** is Senior Lecturer in Management at the Nuffield Institute at the University of Leeds. She has written widely on the subjects of critical management, social construction and health-related topics.

# Management, Organizations and Society
Edited by Professor Barbara Czarniawska
*Göteborg University, Sweden*

and

## Professor Martha Feldman
*University of Michigan, USA*

**Management, Organizations and Society** presents innovative work grounded in new realities, addressing issues crucial to an understanding of the contemporary world. This is the world of organized societies, where boundaries between formal and informal, public and private, local and global organizations have been displaced or have vanished, along with other nineteenth-century dichotomies and oppositions. Management, apart from becoming a specialized profession for a growing number of people, is an everyday activity for most members of modern societies.

Similarly, at the level of enquiry, culture and technology, and literature and economics, can no longer be conceived as isolated intellectual fields; conventional canons and established mainstreams are contested. **Management, Organizations and Society** will address these contemporary dynamics of transformation in a manner that transcends disciplinary boundaries, with work which will appeal to researchers, students and practitioners alike.

**Contrasting Involvements**
A study of management accounting practices in Britain and Germany
*Thomas Ahrens*

**Turning Words, Spinning Worlds**
Chapters in organizational ethnography
*Michael Rosen*

**Breaking Through the Grass Ceiling**
Women, power and leadership in agricultural organizations
*Margaret Alston*

**The Poetic Logic of Administration**
Styles and changes of style in the art of organizing
*Kaj Sköldberg*

**Casting the Other**
The production and maintenance of inequalities in work organizations
*Edited by Barbara Czarniawska and Heather Höpfl*

**Gender, Identity and the Culture of Organizations**
*Edited by Iiris Aaltio and Albert J. Mills*

**Text/Work**
Representing organization and organizing representation
*Edited by Stephen Linstead*

**The Social Construction of Management**
Texts and identities
*Nancy Harding*

# The Social Construction of Management
## Texts and identities

Nancy Harding

Routledge
Taylor & Francis Group

LONDON AND NEW YORK

For Brychan James Harding and Dylan Thomas Harding
And, especially, Clare Harding
With thanks for the magic and the joy

First published 2003
by Routledge
11 New Fetter Lane, London EC4P 4EE

Simultaneously published in the US and Canada
by Routledge
29 West 35th Street, New York, NY 10001

*Routledge is an imprint of the Taylor & Francis Group*

© 2003 Nancy Harding

Typeset in Sabon by
Florence Production Ltd, Stoodleigh, Devon

Printed and bound in Malta by
Gutenberg Press Ltd

*British Library Cataloguing in Publication Data*
A catalogue record for this book is available from the British
Library

*Library of Congress Cataloging in Publication Data*
A catalog record for this book has been requested

ISBN 0–415–36942–8

# Contents

# Acknowledgements

This book has been a long time in the writing, and in some ways it originated in the long discussions with Peter Anthony, back in the mid-1980s. I've never had a chance to thank him properly so here is that thanks.

In the meantime, many people have borne with fortitude my incoherent arguments, the incandescent furies when the ideas wouldn't come, rages against tyrannies, imagined, real or socially constructed, and the sodden mess that emerged from tear-filled hours of pillow-hugging during the dark hours of lost confidence. Colleagues at the Nuffield Institute have taken the brunt and listened (sometimes incredulously) and coaxed, cajoled and challenged – thanks especially to Tony Burton, Jane Shaw, Laura Stroud and John Lawler. Viv Sercombe has taken the brunt of my absent-mindedness. Kahryn Hughes made me sharpen my sloppy use of concepts and is a founder member of the Foucault and Lipstick (not to mention babies) discussion group. Jim Connelly, *bricoleur* and *flaneur manqué*, introduced me to Fredric Jameson and has helped me sharpen my arguments. Mark Learmonth and Kavi Vadamootoo, doctoral students and also friends, have introduced me to new ways of thinking, new theorists and many hours of stimulating discussion. There are two people I owe most thanks to. Jackie Ford has given me years of strong colleagueship, support, friendship, mentoring, stimulus, laughter and discussion and is the icing on the cake of a very enjoyable job. Hugh Lee has contributed so much to the sheer joy of life, inside and outside academia, and all in the name of friendship, that I don't have sufficient words to give thanks. Both ensured this book finally reached some sort of completion.

It is a huge, huge pleasure to be able to say 'thank you' in print.

# 1 Introduction

## Management and the manager as social constructions

Much of this book is devoted to exploring management textbooks and how they construct management and thus the subject positions into which managers step. I will thus begin in the way that a textbook does, albeit that these first two sentences make explicit the parodic intent of this beginning.

This book argues that (*here we must bring on the bullet points*):

- Management is a subject position into which the person known as 'the manager' steps, to be saturated with the meanings and identities of management; so the discovery of how managers construct their identities requires first that we understand how management is constructed.

It proceeds from the following assumptions:

- The subject position of management requires of managers that they both oppress others (the 'workers' whom they 'manage') and are themselves oppressed.
- Improvements in the experience of our lives as workers in organizations, including rights to be treated with dignity and respect, require changes in the ways in which management, and thus managers, is constituted.
- If we are to work to bring about these changes, we first need to understand the deep processes of constitution and construction of management and managers, for as the metaphors of construction and constitution imply, the bedrock upon which the current oppressive identities are built serves to uphold them and make them impervious to change. It is only by exploring that bedrock that we can begin to identify ways of bringing about meaningful change.

*And now we must bring in the summary.*

This book is therefore an analysis of how management as a subject position is constituted and how managers construct their identities as managers. Its title, *The Social Construction of Management*, conflates this doubled process, of the constitution of *management* and the social construction of *the manager*. It focuses in large part upon management textbooks and explores the relationship between the textbook and the reader, arguing that each mutually contaminates the other, that each is mutually implicated and mutually engaged with the other. The reader of the textbook, as Best (1999) argues of readers of novels, desires in this coupling of self and other to be given an identity and to be read by the other. Having explored the textbooks, this book then turns to an analysis of empirical research undertaken into the construction of managerial identities. This intrusion of 'the real world' is designed to inform the analysis of how textbooks construct the subject position of management through discovering how persons occupying that subject position construct their managerial identities.

*And now we must bring in the objectives of the chapter, including the learning outcomes.*

This chapter explains first the perspective of management which informs its arguments, i.e. why I see management/managers as oppressive, and draws upon arguments from the subdiscipline now known as critical management studies (Fournier and Grey, 2000). The larger part of the book explores the constitution of management through the pages of management textbooks, which could lead to the accusation that my arguments are therefore not *social* constructionist. To allay that charge I will then outline the perspective of social constructionism which informs the pages of this book, i.e. one which argues that the dissolution of the boundaries between the social sciences and humanities allows us to explore the mutually imbricative dynamic between cultural artefacts, in this case textbooks, and the social.

*And now I must abandon this parody, or is it pastiche, of a management textbook, lest I fall unthinkingly into 'management speak' and the certainties contained within management texts which believe that what is ordained will come to pass, so long as there is good management.*

## Management as object, rather than subject, of study, or studies *of* management rather than *for* management

I was introduced to management as both a subject and object of study in 1980, when I enrolled on one of the few management degrees then available in the British university system. In those early days of studying management at degree level, the curriculum could offer only four management subjects, i.e. half of a degree. For the other half of my degree I studied the topics offered by the staff in the other half of the department, the Industrial Relations side, and so tripped happily from a lecture on how to manage strategically, or one on the niceties of marketing tactics, to one on how Marxist thinking had influenced Harry Braverman, or another on the philosophy of work (in my memory I see Peter Anthony walking into the first lecture, standing with both hands on the lectern, and announcing that this year we would be exploring *why* we worked. My mind exploded – bloody hell, wow, what a question!). Today, management degrees are the most popular in the British university system, at both undergraduate and post-graduate level, and numerous other subdegree courses, short courses, training courses, etc., induct the learner into theories of what management is and what managers do. For the vast majority, the study of management is the study of a *subject*, i.e. how to do something, rather than the more traditional mode of study of British higher education institutions, of a critical and questioning approach to understanding of the *object* of their intellectual interest (Anthony, 1986).

I am acutely aware of how the process of studying for a degree and subsequent inculcation into academic life wrought huge changes in my identity, and will expand upon it tediously to anyone who will listen – at the bus stop, over tea or whisky with friends, in the check-out queue at Tesco's – my story of how I used to be a miner's wife and factory machinist and typist, but turned into a leftish-inclined, struggling to be feminist but never quite making it as a good feminist so hooray for queer theory, academic. What is still tediously and clumsily called 'the post-modernist/post-structuralist turn' (and which not only allows but almost demands, in the spirit of reflexivity, the insertion into this text of this personal, first-person narrative that explains 'where I'm coming from') has made the exploration of the constitution of identities into an academic endeavour. The decentring of the subject has replaced humanism and the concept of the universal human being with the individual who is involved perpetually in processes of identity formation, and it is those processes which fascinate and inform much of our current theorizing and research practices.

In this context, I am led to ask: What is the impact upon identities of inducting vast numbers of our most highly educated citizens into theories of how to do management and how to be a manager? I answer myself thus: the formation of identities that are diminished by the removal of possibilities of freedom and pleasure in work, for management as it is presently imagined serves to maintain oppressive systems of control over the workplace, the worker and the manager. Those very managers who have read the textbooks, attended the courses, and have never, ever, been challenged to think critically (Grey and Willmott, 2002) help in the maintenance of their own oppression and that of those whom they 'manage'.

This, of course, is not a new thesis. I deviate from Thomas and Anthony's argument (1996) that such teaching results in poor management, for I argue that the very existence of management implies that others need to be corralled, watched over, ferociously 'motivated' if they are to work sufficiently hard, and that this very implication brings about the existence of workers who seek every opportunity to work less efficiently. Indeed, I quarrel with the assumption that work should be about maximizing production, for workplaces are to the twenty-first century what villages or communities were to previous eras and so when we imagine 'work' as about nothing but production we diminish its importance in our lives and facilitate, in our lack of imagination, a form of post-modern feudalism where managers have taken over the rights of dictating how the many should live lives of debased servitude. Contributors to French and Grey (1996) have provided critiques of management education that have influenced the arguments in this book. However, such critiques have not explored how management *as a subject of study* serves to construct managerial identities or, in the terms used in this book, the subject position of management into which the manager steps.

Indeed, although the concept of identities has been brought to the forefront of much intellectual endeavour under the influence of post-modernism/post-structuralism, it is only recently that some tentative studies of identity in the workplace have appeared. Paul du Gay (1996), for example, in a very interesting discussion has argued that organizations display a new rationality of government and a novel regime of subjectification which is built on a conception of the individual as an 'entrepreneur of the self'. The result is a 'responsibilized, autonomized individual' who is given a compulsory autonomy which must be 'exercise[d] ... continuously in order to guarantee one's own reproduction' (du Gay, 1996, p. 183). Everyone now becomes an entrepreneur of their own lives, and the 'ethos of the enterprise form' inscribes all aspects of individual lives, each of which becomes 'structured as the pursuit of a range of different enterprises' (ibid., p. 184).

A perspective on workplace identities that may prove most influential, given the status of its authors, is that of Alvesson and Willmott (2002). They argue that managerial interventions are designed to influence employees' self-constructions so that they become congruent with managerially defined objectives. Identity-construction thus should be seen as a dimension of organizational control. I disagree with their arguments, and also with Paul du Gay's, on two grounds: first, the presumption that identities can be so easily manipulated, and second, in their reification of 'the organization'. On the first of these, I suggest that although

Alvesson and Willmott argue that members of organizations cannot be reduced to 'passive consumers of managerially designed and designated identities' (Alvesson and Willmott, 2002, p. 621), the model they develop of the relationship between self-identity, identity work and identity regulation betrays their avowal. In their model, 'regulation is accomplished by selectively, but not necessarily reflectively, adopting practices and discourses that are more or less intentionally targeted at the "insides" of employees, including managers' (ibid., p. 627). This is a model which can be seen as ahistoric, and which presumes that employees, when they arrive at work, leave other aspects of their identities in the glove compartment. Furthermore, the core metaphor they appear to use is that of the amoeba, absorbing into itself everything that is put in its path by nature or, in this case, the manager. Similar presumptions of an uncomplicated causal relationship between interpellation and becoming can be found in several disciplines, for example in psychotherapy (McLeod, 1997), and some cultural studies theorists who presume that what appears on the pages of a novel or in the flickering images of the film camera reflect, straightforwardly, what is happening in the social world. Within the social sciences such a failure of analysis of the causal processes involved should be avoided. With regard to the reification of 'the organization', I worry that continuing to think of this entity 'organization' as some monstrous overlord that watches our every move while it remains invisible to us, and that seeks ever-more insidious ways of controlling us, has the opposite effect to that intended, for it provides us with a monster that is too big and too scary to challenge (Ford and Harding, 2002).

However, I follow Alvesson and Willmott closely in many of their other arguments which, along with the contributions to critical management studies of an increasing number of theoretically informed academics and researchers, seek to critically interrogate management, with the aim of eventually transforming management practice (Grey and Willmott, 2002). This is not the place for a summary of thinking within critical management studies, one already more than admirably undertaken by Fournier and Grey (2000): suffice to say that in my reading it comes from a somewhat left-wing academic tradition which feels more or less comfortable with exploring the 'continuing reproduction of capitalist employment relations' (O'Doherty and Willmott, 2001). Its intellectual antecedents are those where knowledge is pursued for its own sake, and where education's aims are the provision of conceptual understanding, a breadth and depth of knowledge, a capacity to synthesize within a sustained intellectual framework, where 'theoretical grounding and the experience of critical dispute encourage the active pursuit of challenge' (Thomas and Anthony, 1996, p. 31). It is thus concerned with unsettling that 'pretence of indisputable and unproblematic techniques and skills to enhance managerial effectiveness' (French and Grey, 1996, p. 10) which dominates the business of business schools. Ultimately, its aims somewhat revolve around achieving different kinds of organizations in which work is carried out without destruction or debasement of individuals, although since the collapse of Marxism's promise of a utopia that followed upon revolution, the ultimate ends remain somewhat vague (Wray-Bliss and Parker, 1998).

This book is, in its adherence to traditions from critical management studies or, more broadly, from the sociology of organizations, an exploration of how we socially construct mechanisms of power which speak through managers. It is thus a study *of* management, which seeks explanation of why we have a supposed need for management, rather than a study *for* management, which attempts to teach people how to manage. Managers, who are the materialized metaphysics, so to speak, of capitalist power, are in this perspective a social construction in that they belong in a social world wherein lies the possibility for thinking, and thus practising, things differently. In order to bring about change we have to understand the mechanisms by which current pillars of power are maintained. Marxism had too simplistic an assumption about how change could be achieved and, indeed, about how the new utopia could be built. Market managerial utopianism sadly has been more successful in imposing its own vision of utopia (Parker, 2002a). Postmodernism/post-structuralism, while it has not yet helped us dream the design of the utopia we desire and has, indeed, in a peculiar reverse brought pragmatism to the discussion about utopias, helps us discern and understand those mechanisms. As Laclau (1990) has pointed out, it helps us open the possibilities repressed in the taken-for-granted and seemingly 'objective' social relations and identities. One of these mechanisms is a language of management which is now so dominant that it crowds out alternative ways of thinking of, speaking about and working in organizations. The language of management is materialized in and through managers. But it is too simple to think of the language of management as nothing more than a language of rationality, autonomy, entrepreneurship, etc. Both Derrida and Foucault have taught us to explore more deeply into any language, to discover the languages which make possible that language, and thus not to presume that the ideology spoken through the language is all that informs and sustains that power/knowledge formulation signified in writing and speech. Judith Butler, in taking forward Foucault's ideas, reminds us that the languages that inform our thinking, speaking and writing both subjectify and subjectivize. In the opening paragraphs in *The Psychic Life of Power* (1997), in a lucid style which belies the infamous difficulty of her writing, she brings the reader up short with the power of her discussion about power:

As a form of power, subjection is paradoxical. To be dominated by a power external to oneself is a familiar and agonizing form power takes. To find, however, that what 'one' is, one's very formation as a subject, is in some sense dependent upon that very power is quite another. We are used to thinking of power as what presses on the subject from the outside, as what subordinates, sets underneath, and relegates to a lower order. This is surely a fair description of part of what power does. But if, following Foucault, we understand power as *forming* the subject as well, as providing the very condition of its existence and the trajectory of its desire, then power is not simply what we oppose but also, in a strong sense, what we depend on for our existence and what we harbor and preserve in the beings that we are. The customary model for understanding this process goes as follows: power imposes itself on us, and, weakened by its force, we come to internalize or accept its terms. What such an account fails to note, however, is that the 'we' who accept such terms are fundamentally dependent on those terms for 'our' existence. Are there not discursive conditions for the articulation of any 'we'? Subjection consists precisely in this fundamental dependency on a discourse we never chose but that, paradoxically, initiates and sustains our agency.

(Butler, 1997, pp. 1–2)

Foucault, she points out, does not elaborate on the specific mechanisms of how the subject is formed in submission; he explores neither the psyche nor the double valence of power as subordinating and producing. That is Butler's task, and it is an example that is taken up in this book to analyse the power of the language of management, and how it brings into being subject positions that depend for their existence, ultimately, on abjected and subjugated others. In other words, it is a study of how power, first, impregnates the language of management that is found in textbooks, of how readers interact with the textbook and, seduced by the language, absorb it to some extent into their identities and thus come into being as managers. Second, in its empirical section, it is a study of how managers' identity is permeated through and through with and by the organizations in which they work. It is thus a study of how management is a social construction.

## Social constructionism

To adopt a social constructionist stance is to use a perspective which would appear to be in somewhat of a mess, not least because of the impossibility of definition. Yet many of those choosing to read a book entitled *The Social Construction of Management* will have a definite idea of what theoretical stance to expect in a text bearing such a designation, and the theoretical perspective offered will undoubtedly convince some that my arguments are not 'social constructionist'. But what is social constructionism?

First, it is a perspective which has been challenged by critics who, it can be suggested, prefer to refuse reasoned argument. Hacking, for instance, writes:

> Most constructionists have never heard of constructivism in mathematics. Constructivists, constructionists, and constructionalists live in different intellectual milieus. Yet the themes and attitudes that characterize these isms are not so different. From all three we hear that *things are not what they seem.* All three involve iconoclastic questioning of varnished reality, of what the general run of people take for real. Surprise, surprise! All construct-isms dwell in the dichotomy between appearance and reality set up by Plato, and given a definitive form by Kant. Although social constructionists bask in the sun they call post-modernism, they are really very old-fashioned.
>
> (Hacking, 1999, pp. 48–9)

He has his own definition of constructionism:

> It seems to me that in ethics, Kant, Rawls, and Foucault ... tell us how to build, and why. I urge (social) constructionists to keep the same faith. Anything worth calling a construction was or is constructed in quite definite stages, where the later stages are built upon, or out of, the product of earlier stages. Anything worth calling a construction has a history. But not just any history. It has to be a history of building.
>
> (ibid., p. 50)

Foucault is not included in his bibliography, and had he been (and indeed had his works been not only cited but read), then Hacking may have recognized the impossibility of using Foucault to support teleology.

There are other critics, of course, whose analyses are more considered, but always the dichotomy between realism and relativism, and debates about what is 'real' that lie at the heart of even the most considered critique, prevents either understanding or accommodation.

Second, social constructionism is a perspective which is challenged for its understanding of 'reality'. Burr (1998) has identified a confounding of three dimensions in the debate between pro- and anti-constructionists:

(a) reality defined as truth, versus falsehood;
(b) reality defined as materiality, versus illusion;
(c) reality defined as essence, versus construction.

The third of these, she suggests, is too often mapped on to the first two, so that constructionism is taken to mean 'illusion and/or falsehood'. We need to be able to understand, she argues, that things are 'at one and the same time socially constructed *and* real', a claim to be found also in the work of Judith Butler and articulated there in much more depth, and whose perspective will inform much of this book.

Assailed from without, social constructionism also suffers from disagreements between practitioners. All authors working in this field are anti-objectivists, anti-realists, anti- (rather than post-) positivists, and are thus subjectivists, interpretivists and idealists (Burr, 1995; Gergen, 1999). There are undoubtedly those who would classify themselves as fitting every category in that list, but who would deny that they are social constructionists. There are many who call themselves social constructionists who are involved in other forms of intellectual activity, as Hacking (eventually) shows (1998, 1999). There is thus a danger of nominalism: that social constructionism becomes whatever people who call themselves social constructionists claim to be doing.

Such a danger is reinforced by the difficulties of definition. At its most basic level, attempts to define social constructionism are bedevilled with the problem of designation, for there is disagreement among and between those who would apply to their work the label, albeit loosely, of 'constructionism' or 'constructivism'. For example, whereas Lynch (1998) sees one of the more prominent features of *social constructionism* as an incredulity toward master narratives, Spivey (1997) refers to *constructivism* as a metatheory. She sees social constructivism or social constructionism as one of the different forms within the metatheory.

Then there are differences between constructionists who believe that there is no 'reality' external to the self so everything is constructed through social interactions, discourses, etc., and those who argue that there is an external 'reality' consisting of matter, but that that matter is apprehended and interpreted through social means.

Although some social constructionist work is ahistorical, much else follows Foucault and is premised upon the importance of understanding the history of the ways in which social constructions develop. It would therefore appear to be appropriate to explore the history of the concept to elucidate understanding. However, social constructionism by its very nature abhors the writing of an 'official' history of the concept (Velody and Williams, 1998), although there is perhaps some consensus about the major theorists whose works have influenced social constructionist thinking. G.H. Mead is often cited as one of the earlier influences, and few accounts of the evolution of the perspective are complete without reference to Berger and Luckmann's (1967) seminal *The Social Construction of Reality*. Foucault and Kuhn are two writers most often thought latterly to be influential in providing resources for social constructionists, although many authors refer to their works neither directly nor indirectly (for example, many of the papers in the text edited by Sarbin and Kitsuse, 1994).

The concept is multidisciplinary, although many of the authors who publish consistently on the subject appear to be drawn from social psychology, notably the two textbooks offered by Gergen (1999) and Burr (1995), and the texts offered by Gergen (e.g. 1991, 1998), Potter (e.g. 1996), Shotter (1993), Shotter and Gergen (1989) and Parker (e.g. 1997).

Amid all this babble, most constructionists today are united in 'a reconsideration of the representational duties traditionally assigned to language' (Gergen, 1998), for language is at the heart of the ways in which we make sense of ourselves, what Gergen (1998) calls our 'accounting practices', which help in the creation and maintenance of our social worlds and ourselves as beings participating in that social order. In other words, such accounts 'work to structure our mental capacities, our psychological makeup, as the persons we are' (Shotter, 1985, p. 170). There is debate as to whether social constructionism underpins discourse theories or vice versa. Vivien Burr (1995) suggests social constructionism is a theoretical orientation which underpins discourse analysis, deconstruction and post-structuralism and that it is multidisciplinary in nature, but this, to me, is to equate social constructionism with the whole of an interpretivist theoretical perspective. Guba and Lincoln (1998) meanwhile see constructivism as occupying a separate paradigm from post-modernism and post-structuralism. It is thus difficult often to differentiate between post-modernist/post-structuralist and social constructionist perspectives. Further, whereas Lynch (1998) sees as a feature of the field the conflation of constructionism with a 'panoply of avant-garde radical intellectual movements', a longer view of social constructionist perspectives suggests that at any period in intellectual history there are schools of thought which are anti-realist, anti-positivist, anti-essentialist, idealist, etc., and those schools draw upon whichever intellectual perspectives best explain the constructed nature of the social world available to theorists at that time.

It thus seems open for anyone using the term 'social construction' to define the perspective for themselves. The definition I am offering here, based on the foregoing, is that social constructionism can be defined as an interpretivist epistemology which, at any point in intellectual history, draws upon the panoply of whatever interpretivist intellectual movement is seen as avant-garde and radical. The emphasis here is upon interpretivism. Thus, rather than agreeing with Hacking (1998) in his statement that the very word 'constructionism' is now worn out beyond its telling 'whose side you are on [rather] than of describing the content of your analysis' (ibid., p. 55) I see social constructionism as constantly renewing itself through its absorption of new theoretical perspectives. It is vainglorious to deny the continued dominance in many fields, and in much US social science, of positivism, so the need for constant renewal and constant reaffirmation of an anti-positivist stance is vital, and this is one of the functions of social constructionism – to gather under one label work which pits itself against the ever-dominant positivist stance.

There is, however, one further concept that must be included in this definition and which serves to distinguish social constructionism from other anti-positivist methods of analysing the social world.

Burr (1995), drawing upon Gergen (1985), has identified a set of key assumptions in social constructionism, one or more of which will form the foundations of the work of all social constructionists, i.e.:

- a critical stance towards our taken-for-granted knowledge;
- the historical and cultural relativity of knowledge;
- constitution and maintenance of knowledge through social processes;
- the interrelationship of knowledge and social action.

In this she in many ways is summarizing the work of Michel Foucault, notably in her emphasis upon knowledge and in her focus upon discourse as constitutional of the individual and our worlds. However, and crucially, she has omitted the concept of 'power', so influential in Foucault's analysis that he of course linked it irretrievably in the coupling of power/knowledge.

This emphasis almost solely upon language without a recourse to power is typical of much work in what authors call social constructionism at the end of the twentieth and beginning of the twenty-first centuries. However, in its omission of power, it is questionable as to whether much that currently claims to be social constructionist is not symbolic interactionism with a discursive turn. Symbolic interactionists, writing in an American tradition, shared a concern to explore the 'symbolic meanings' within which humans interact, assuming meanings emerged out of those shared interactions. Human behaviour here, in this American model, was

> not a unilinear unfolding toward a predetermined end, but an active constructing process whereby humans endeavor to 'make sense' of their social and physical environments. This 'making sense' process is internalized in the form of thought; for thinking is the intra-individual problem-solving process that is also characteristic of inter-individual interaction. In thinking, then, there occurs an interaction with oneself.
>
> (Meltzer *et al.*, 1975, p. vii)

In this perspective, society is 'constructed out of the behavior of humans, who actively play a role in developing the social limits that will be placed upon their behavior' (ibid.).

I have argued previously (Harding and Palfrey, 1997) that whereas symbolic interactionism primarily focused on the ways in which individuals built self-identities from the meanings they bring to categories of experience (such as gender, sexuality, male and female), social constructionism examines how meanings are formed and then used by individuals in their constituting of themselves and their worlds. An understanding of how meanings are formed *must* include an analysis of power. Both Burr and Gergen include, in their invitations or introductions to social construction, discussions about power, but there are writers who call themselves social constructionists whose focus is primarily upon discourse analysis and its use in social interactions between people who omit any reference to power. For me, these writers are not social constructionists. They ignore social constructionism's powers of ideological unmasking which assist in challenging the dominant regimes of truth, by demonstrating the linguistic and rhetorical devices that sustain the dominant ideologies and the contingency, both historically and culturally, of their truth claims (Gergen, 1985).

I thus reject such definitions of social constructionism as that offered by Sarbin and Kitsuse (1994), where they write that constructionists 'focus on how ordinary members (and sometimes professionals) create and employ constructions, on observing how others interact with those constructions, and on interpreting and sometimes proposing alternate constructions' (ibid., p. x) and their further argument (ibid., p. 2) that human beings are 'agents who process information in the context of cultural practices, purposes, beliefs, sacred stories, etc. They construct, negotiate, reform, fashion and organize social objects in their attempt to make sense of happenings in the world'. To me this is symbolic interactionism.

Rather, the definition of social constructionism I will use in this work is one that is very much of its time, i.e. it is first highly Foucauldian and is concerned with exploring how matters of legitimation and truth-telling are achieved through processes of construction which are irredeemably social in that they take place in the social world, and further how what is legitimated and regarded as truth serves to constitute identities. It is also Derridean in its exploration in that it studies how the 'grand discourses' identified by Foucault can be identified through close analysis of texts, but also in that it draws upon Derrida's later work to explore how the languages which speak through us colonize us (Derrida, 1998), and perform for us our psyches (Derrida, 1995). Rather than being feminist, it is a work that draws upon queer theory which, in its contestation of gendered identities, allows more sophisticated understanding of the formation of identities in general.

In particular, this work draws upon Judith Butler's contributions to queer theory.

Of importance to this text is that it is written at a time when the dissolution of the boundaries between the social sciences, arts and humanities is much heralded, so it explores how cultural products, here management textbooks, inform the social world, using ideas opened for us by theorists working in cultural studies. This allows, as Fuery and Mansfield (2000) point out, cultural practices such as book production to be used as material for investigating 'the broad construction of meanings and truths with all their social and political interconnections' (ibid., p. xix). They refer to 'the gaze' as something that is not simply a mechanism for perceiving, but is more fundamentally concerned with formations and operations of subjectivity (ibid., p. 71). From Lacan comes the theory that when we read we want the gaze of the text to see us, so that we know of our own presence. But the relationship with the text involves a two-way flow, so that our subjectivity becomes 'a text for the text', where reader and text are caught up in one another and where, through *suture*, the reader enters into the text while simultaneously operating from the place of the gaze. Suture comes from film theory, but is, in Silverman's (1988) formulation, equally applicable to literature. It refers to procedures whereby cultural texts confer subjectivity upon their viewers or readers (Silverman, 1988, p. 195), through building upon Freudian and Lacanian notions of how individuals use speech and discourse to represent themselves to themselves as they wish to be seen and how they wish the other with whom they are interacting to see them. The speaking subject 'I', Silverman observes, drawing upon the work of Benveniste, is activated through this ideal image rather than through reference to an actual speaker. However, cinema reminds us of a speaking subject always located at the site of production and a spoken subject who occupies the site of consumption which, in my interpretation, allows us to see the reader as someone who is involved both in constructing imagined identities for themselves and also actively consuming those identities. Theorists of suture can therefore explore several possibilities of being, the one that is of most interest for an exploration of interaction with textbooks being the connection between the reader and the fictional character (i.e. the imaginary manager implicit in the textbook) with which the reader is persuaded to identify, and in identifying sees an image of her/himself as the ideal manager who consumes that imagined identity. This, of course, leads to 'the inscription of lack', or a desire for that which is absent and always beyond reach.

The thesis of this book is therefore this. Management textbooks are cultural products (cultural studies) which inculcate generations of students into the body of knowledge known as 'management'. They serve to legitimize a body of knowledge (Foucault) and to organize a language

(Derrida) which constructs the subject position (Butler) of management. Subject positions serve in the social construction of identities of their occupants (Butler; Derrida). To understand the subject positions so constructed it is necessary to deconstruct management textbooks (Derrida) to identify the ways in which power works through them (Foucault), the ways in which this process has developed and changed in the 50 year history of management textbooks (Foucault) and how it has evolved as modernism gave way to post-modernism (Jameson). Further, a straightforward relationship between the cultural and the social cannot be presumed, so it is also necessary to explore managers themselves so as to identify the interaction of the cultural and social, and the third section of the book includes an empirical study of managers.

## Development of the arguments

Following the introduction, this book is divided into three parts.

Part I, 'Construction', which shows, through discovering the languages which coalesce at the nodal point of the management textbook and give management language its power, how a language of management has been constructed and come to power. This part has only one chapter, which traces the evolution of the language and their coalescing into the familiar language of today over a period of almost 40 years. To this end I have chosen one textbook that covers this period, that written originally by Harold Koontz and Cyril O'Donnell, the first edition of which was published in 1955 and the tenth in 1993. Following Cyril O'Donnell's death Heinz Weihrich became Koontz's co-author; later Harold Koontz died and Weihrich wrote the later editions only with the ghost of Koontz as his co-author. This first chapter reveals that the writers of management texts make the following claims to truth. They 'demonstrate' that without management the world will descend into anarchy and chaos. That management is capable of undertaking the role of superhero is due to its status as art, as science and as modernity. Management's right to manage in the earlier texts appeared somewhat frail and necessitating of legitimation, so in the earlier editions justification was sought in a recourse to law. By the mid-1970s management appeared more secure – it had now achieved its earlier aim of becoming a science, remained as always an art, and was until the 1980s secure in its position of modern, masculine rationality, so the recourse to law was dropped from the textbooks, an action that necessitates further plumbing. By the 1980s there were changes in the discursive style of the texts, and the 'dumbing down' of the textbooks proceeded apace. Students were discouraged more and more from thinking, from questioning, from critical analysis. Instead they were urged to accept the texts as biblical documents, speaking the one true word. The ugly phrase 'dumbing down' encapsulates most aptly the discursive changes precipitated then that continue into the latest management textbooks. I will argue that the changes which occurred in the 1970s heralded the inauguration of a post-modern turn in management textbooks, in that rather than seeking to define management they now sought to constitute the identities of managers.

Part II, 'Deconstruction', has four chapters each of which explores one of the four claims to truth on which the textbooks have rested. In keeping with the catholic tradition encouraged by social constructionism, and in order to avoid that sterility of thought that can come from using arguments from only one narrow discipline dominated by one theoretical perspective, I have used sources from several disciplines in order to explore the textbook's claim to truth. The eclectic claims to truth of the management textbooks requires this freedom to borrow from whatever discipline has developed the method of deconstruction most appropriate for the task in hand. Further, and perhaps more importantly, the narrowing of possibilities for thought engendered by remaining strictly within the territories of one subdiscipline become very evident when exploring how textbooks develop over the course of half a century. Textbook writers rely upon texts whose reference lists are drawn predominantly, or often solely, from within management studies, perpetuating a positivism that is not only stale and redolent of clinging to the caregiver's skirts, but also generative of a reductive language that inhibits possibilities for thought, exploration and reflexivity. I would be as guilty as textbook writers were I to remain within similar disciplinary boundaries. I thus attempt to apprehend Bourdieu's advice (1988, quoted in Fitzpatrick, 1992, p. 13) to the social scientist studying her own world that she should not, 'as the ethnologist would, domesticate the exotic, but, if I may venture the expression, exoticise the domestic, through a break with his [sic] initial relation of intimacy with the mode of life and thought which remain opaque to him because they are too familiar'. This I have read as requiring that the researcher moves outside her own discipline when seeking enlightenment, which in this case justifies my moving outside the field of critical management studies. I have thus, when examining management's claim to be an art, turned to art history for methods of deconstructing that claim; when they allege legitimacy in the law it allows me to turn to critical legal studies for illumination; I wander into the sociology of scientific knowledge for guidelines when exploring the managerialist claim to scientific status; and at some point in my journey I find geographers offering inspiration. Both Foucault and the Lacanian phallus prove ubiquitous, for no matter to which discipline I turned I found one or the other, often both, informing the arguments and offering the bridges between the developing arguments.

I begin the deconstructionist endeavour in Chapter 3 by exploring management's claim to be a science. Using perspectives from the

Sociology of Scientific Knowledge, I show in this chapter how the claim to be a science is made but not supported by the textbooks themselves, which, notably since the 1980s, elevate anecdote, gossip and unattributable quotations as the fount of credibility, and indeed surreptitiously denigrate science. Now this is fascinating, for we have a simultaneous lauding and denigration of science. I argue that the contradictions this involves provide a means of control over managers.

Law, I show in Chapter 4, disappeared from the management textbook as a claim to truth, but reappears in the workplace which, I argue, has become juridified, with management acting as judge, jury, law-maker and police service. I use examples from disciplinary procedures as the foundation for my arguments, and draw upon feminist theorists and those who use Lacan's theory of the phallus to provide links with the previous chapter.

Chapter 5 analyses management's claim to be an art. Here I found it apposite to explore art history. Koontz and O'Donnell's first textbook was written in the era when the US had, for the first time, secured from Europe dominance in the arts, and notably in painting. The abstract expressionists who had achieved this feat, and especially the work of Jackson Pollock, allow me to contrast management's claim to be an art with artists' claims about what art means. In the second part of the chapter I turn to Griselda Pollock for insight, for her work as an art historian allows an analysis of the meanings of the photographs of Taylor, Fayol, Weber and others which now feature prominently in management textbooks, and thus an exploration of what I term the managerial canon. This chapter continues the analysis of the change from modernism to post-modernism in the textbooks, i.e. the imagined reader changed from the ontologically fixed monad of modernism to the culturally constituted, decentred subjects of the post-modern.

The claim that management is modernity in motion, written upon the bodies of managers, is explored in Chapter 6. Here feminist and queer theory is drawn upon to analyse the photographs, charts and diagrams, and notably the organization chart, which take up much of the space of management textbooks. The maintenance of management as masculine, a gender identity which floats free of biologically inscribed bodies, is argued to be part of the logic of modernity. To develop this understanding I continue borrowing from art history, and delve also into social geography.

Part III, 'Reconstruction', offers an alternative understanding of management to that offered in textbooks. It begins with a chapter based on empirical research carried out to expand the understanding developed in the previous chapters, for I explore with a sample of managers how they construct their managerial selves, using a new model of discourse analysis, based upon use of personal pronouns, to explore the data. Chapter 8 concludes this part and the book. I here draw all the threads together, using Judith Butler's theories to argue that management in post-modern capitalism is an epistemological performative endeavour, where management is the discursive space within patriarchal managerialism into which the manager climbs to be subjectified and subjected.

# Part I

# Construction

Part I, 'Construction', consists of one chapter. It analyses, using techniques drawn from discourse analysis, a series of management textbooks published between 1955 and 1993. Its aims are the discovery of their claims to truth, the ways in which they have constructed management and the shifts in the discourses that have taken place in the four decades of publication. By its end the reader should be aware of the reasons why the next part, 'Deconstruction', has four chapters exploring each of the four claims to truth identified. By stating these aims and objectives here at the beginning of the part, I am imitating the style of management textbooks. Were I at this point to briefly summarize its arguments, thus suggesting that the reader could absorb its arguments merely through the brief, no doubt bullet-pointed summary I could give, I would be undertaking an even closer act of mimicry.

# 2   Management as text

Eve Kosofsky Sedgwick, in *Epistemology of the Closet* (1991), proposes 'that many of the major nodes of thought and knowledge in twentieth-century Western culture as a whole are structured – indeed, fractured – by a chronic, now endemic crisis of homo/heterosexual definition, indicatively male, dating from the end of the nineteenth century' (ibid., p. 1). She argues that virtually any aspect of modern Western culture can only be understood if it incorporates a critical analysis of modern homo/heterosexual definition. Grey (1999), meanwhile, explores a somewhat similar thesis, but in relation to the identity of 'manager'. He shows the constructed nature of the divide between manager and non-manager, and analyses a turn in language which equates manage-ment 'with any form of social co-ordination'. We thus appear to have two universal imperatives in identity formation, two discourses which will intersect at various nodal points to produce subjectivities. One aspect of Grey's argument, on the constructed nature of the divide between managers and other groups of workers, is the subject matter of this book, and his thoughtful and insightful paper has stimulated some of the ideas I will develop here. However, Kosofsky Sedgwick had the luxury of the word length of a book in which to develop her ideas, using a methodology, familiar within cultural studies, of using novels to explore and explain aspects of the social world. I will here therefore interrogate Grey's notion of the construction of management through the lens offered by Kosofsky Sedgwick, so as to anticipate the arguments which will evolve in this chapter.

Let us begin by exploring the similarities between the two theses. Grey is critical of the thesis that 'we are all managers now', arguing that all people may undertake management tasks, but not all are 'real' managers, and so the question becomes, importantly, 'how are we to understand the development of management not as a general activity that all humans engage in but as a specialist activity associated with a particular group within the work organisation?' (Grey, 1999, p. 565). In Kosofsky Sedgwick's analysis, sexual acts were undertaken poten-tially by all adults, and from the late nineteenth century the general activity that all humans engage in came to be so designated that one's object of sexual choice would furthermore determine the possibilities of identity. Identities were thus colonized by the objects of sexual choice. Both are concerned with the power of language: Grey warns that the 'use of words is not innocent, and in the case of management its use carries irrevocable implications and resonance which are associated with industrialism and modern Western forms of rationality and control' (ibid., p. 577), so that to argue that 'we are all managers now' is to facilitate an oppressive colonization, by management, of all human activities.

These two writers are thus exploring colonizations of lives through particular discursive formations which have occurred a century apart: Kosofsky Sedgwick's exploration of the establishment of the heteronormative society traces its beginnings to the late nineteenth and early twentieth centuries, and Grey explores theories circulating at the very end of the twentieth century. Each explores how possibilities for identity are constrained and limited by certain social constructs. Let me now introduce one concept from Kosofsky Sedgwick's work which is implicit in Grey's argument. Kosofsky Sedwick, in a nod to Derrida, explores how the heterosexual norm depends upon homosexuality, its Other, for its identity, opening the need for us to acknowledge that it is only possible for management to exist if it also has its Other, the worker. The analytic move which underpins Kosofsky Sedgwick's thesis is

> that categories presented in a culture as symmetrical binary oppo-sitions – heterosexual/homosexual, in this case, actually subsist in a more unsettled and dynamic tacit relation according to which, first, term B is not symmetrical with but subordinated to term A; but, second, the ontologically valorized term A actually depends for its meaning on the simultaneous subsumption and exclusion of term B; hence, third, the question of priority between the supposed central and the supposed marginal category of each dyad is ir-resolvably unstable, an instability caused by the fact that term B is constituted as at once internal and external to term A.
>
> (Grey, 1999, pp. 9–10)

If 'we are all managers now', managers by definition will have no Other, no workers whose very existence gives them identities as 'those who are not workers', and managers, or rather the function by which organization is achieved through the subordination of some to others, cannot continue to exist.

Now to methodologies. Grey talks of opening a space 'for the construction of forms of subjectivity which are not conceived in terms of the discourse of management and manageability' (ibid., p. 578), which both begs the question as to the forms of subjectivity which are available within the terms of the discourse of management and opens the way to thinking about alternatives. Kosofsky Sedgwick's methodology offers one of these ways. She uses novels of the era to explore how literary texts both captured and assisted in the circulation and absorption of the new, modern homo/heterosexual definitions. The equivalent for the purpose of understanding managerial subjectivities at the turn of the twenty-first century, for opening the space to understand managerial subjectivities, is, I suggest, management textbooks. Kosofsky Sedgwick shows that what was new from the turn of the twentieth century was

> the world-mapping by which every given person, just as he or she was necessarily assignable to a male or a female gender, was now considered necessarily assignable as well to a homo- or a heterosexuality, a binarized identity that was full of implications, however, confusing, for even the ostensibly least sexual aspects of personal existence.
>
> (Kosofsky Sedgwick, 1991, p. 2)

I suggest that what has occurred in the twentieth century, and is fully in place at the turn of the twenty-first century, is another world-mapping whereby, in the English-speaking Western world, every employed person is now categorized by the binary identity of manager or worker, with manager depending upon the subordinated term, worker, for its identity.

Thus, management textbooks should be seen not as bland aids to the teaching of a body of ideas but rather, just like the novels Kosofsky Sedgwick analyses, as 'sites of definitional creation, violence, and rupture in relation to particular readers, particular institutional circumstances' (ibid., p. 3), whereby their performative aspects, or their capacity for bringing into being that of which they speak, must be explored. They are a link between the cultural and social worlds, and they allow us to understand the processes by which we are constituting ourselves, each and every one of us, as managers of our own lives.

The question arises of how to analyse the management textbook. Kosofsky Sedgwick's book, now regarded as a seminal text in queer theory, follows a tradition of analysing influential texts in order to understand the present. She is heavily influenced by Foucault, whose influence is also heavy within this chapter. Derrida, however, perhaps comes closest to exploring the performative aspects of texts, notably in his more recent works and especially in *Archive Fever. A Freudian Impression* (1995). Throughout this book Derrida weaves together issues of writing and issues of the psyche, of memory and of inscription, so that the two so overlap and intertwine that 'our lexicon' becomes both the lexicon of the language available to us, and the lexicon of the self. He explores the 'power of consignation', by which he means both consignation or 'the act of assigning residence or of entrusting so as to put into reserve (to consign, to deposit), in a place and on a substrate' but also 'the act of *con*signing through *gathering together signs*' (Derrida, 1995, p. 3). The documents we archive occupy their place by virtue of a privileged topology, a place intersected by law and authority, and it behoves us to analyse how the archontic, or patriarchal principle, becomes instituted, and how legalities or legitimacies depend upon it. In this reading, the textbook becomes a house or museum in which are *con*signed knowledges, practices and institutions; these, importantly, simultaneously occupy the psyche, but the characters and traces of the textbook will follow complicated 'linguistic, culture, cipherable, and in general ciphered transgenerational and transindividual relays, transiting thus through an archive, the science of which is not at a standstill' (ibid., p. 35). Indeed, the archive will contain things that are repressed, things repressed both in the culture and in the individual.

Thus, when exploring management textbooks, it is necessary to go beyond Fineman and Gabriel's (1994) analysis of how organizational behaviour textbooks use rhetoric to structure a world. Each of these books, their analysis shows, is much of a muchness, sharing similarities of appearance, weight and content with its counterparts. Each has a sober cover that registers symbolically the concepts of order, precision, unambiguity, economy, etc. Their structures reflect 'the managerial presupposition that people and organizations can be separated, atomized and, ultimately, controlled', and their most striking feature is a text that is fragmented. 'The main tenet of textbook discourse appears to be', they suggest, that 'there should not be a full page of uninterrupted text' (Fineman and Gabriel, 1994, p. 380). Photographs, bullet points, framed case studies, typographical devices and graphs break up every page. Bland definitions reduce complex phenomena into simple ones and disallow any other definition. Case studies and vignettes have become ritualized learning devices, and in their managerial value stance they further close off possibilities of alternative analyses. The textbook is replete with lists, and these serve to substitute argument and to elevate memory and routinized learning. Knowledge, in these textbooks, 'is presented as distinct parcels piled tidily on top of each other, like boxes of shoes in a shoe-shop, each with its own label' (ibid., p. 384), and each label, or authority, is invoked by all, or nearly all, the authors. This convergence means that 'learning OB has come to mean associating the names with the theories and the theorists with lists of key terms' (ibid., p. 385). These texts, cultural commodities that embody the assumptions of their discipline, show how learning shall be achieved, and represent a rite of passage to their student readers (ibid., p. 379).

Those arguments are, of course, apposite, but they are embedded both temporally and spatially in the local space of understanding. They corral the textbook from the wider society, and ignore how it got to be the shape it did – in Derrida's terms there is no exploration of the institution of the archontic, in Foucault's of the text as a nodal point of fluctuating discourses into which the student may enter. It is these issues that concern me and are the subject of this text. I am exploring, given that many millions of people have now read management textbooks, the performative nature of these readings.

First, I must qualify the word 'performative'. In management studies, critical or otherwise, it tends to refer to the search for knowledge about how to maximize output for minimum input (Fournier and Grey, 2000). That is not the way in which I am using the term. Rather, I draw upon Judith Butler's reworking of Althusser's notion of interpellation through a Foucauldian and Saussurian lens so that:

> Performative acts are forms of authoritative speech: most performatives, for instance, are statements that, in the uttering, also perform a certain action and exercise a binding power.
>
> (Butler, 1993, p. 225)

It would, of course, be a major error to presume a direct correlation between reading and performance, as the empirical work explored in the penultimate part of this book demonstrates.

Further, in addition to the performative nature of textbooks, I suggest that without a close reading we refuse ourselves an understanding of the claims to truth suppressed within the texts which, through the processes of readerly relations, hypnotize the reader much like the snake, through its incessant and sybilant repetition of 'trust in me', hypnotizes Mowgli in *Jungle Book* (the Disney version). What passes between text and reader while the latter is in that spasmodically receptive state wherein memory becomes imbricated with inscription? What powers of resistance does the reader have, and is the resistance real or is the rhetoric seeping in through the cracks in conscious awareness? In short, what is it within these texts that may contribute to the performative? It is this last question that forms the core of this chapter, which consists of an outlining of an in-depth reading of one series of a management textbook. It is based on a paraphrasing of a question posed by Foucault, where I have substituted the term 'management' for Foucault's original term, 'science', i.e. the reading seeks to discover 'the politics of the [managerial] . . . statement, where knowing what external power imposes itself on [management] . . . is not the main question, but "what effects of power circulate among [managerial] . . . statements, what constitutes, as it were, their internal regime of power, and how and why at certain moments that regime undergoes a global modification"' (Foucault, 1980, pp. 112–13).

In order to avoid ahistoricism, I am using for this analysis one management textbook, written originally by Harold Koontz and Cyril O'Donnell, and later, following the death of O'Donnell, by Harold Koontz and Heinz Weihrich, and most recently by Heinz Weihrich who continues to share authorship with the now-deceased Harold Koontz. The textbook was published originally as *Principles of Management* in 1955, and, in its tenth edition in 1993, as *Management*. The Koontz textbook[1] is invaluable in exploring the world constituted within and through the management textbook because its various editions span these four decades of management thinking, thus making it possible to explore how management discourse and claims to truth have changed and evolved. In addition, the texts are influential, being widely used in Britain and the US and, having been translated into 16 languages, around the world. Finally, in being similar in its most recent texts to most management textbooks, a loose claim can be made that the Koontz text may in some ways represent all mainstream management textbooks.

Such a reading can make for tedious reading. To save many the burden of ploughing through the reading, I am summarizing the arguments, much in the style of management textbooks, in Box 2.1. What follows is a lengthy discussion of the processes which lead to those conclusions.

## The textbooks

These textbooks are weighty tomes, in terms of pounds and ounces. They are some 600 pages long, and until the 1970s they contained close-argued text relieved by few illustrations or diagrams. (That later editions changed fundamentally their style of presentation is a significant point that will be explored later.) Their index suggests little change over the years, for each has a preface and six parts. Part I in all editions provides chapters that discuss the basis of management, and argues that the management task universally can be broken down into five functions, each of which forms the following five parts for each book. Parts II–VI deal with planning, organization, staffing, directing/leading and controlling. The chapters contained within each of these subparts break the function down into its own constituent parts and discuss these in depth. These chapters have varied in content and layout over the years, but the overall structure of the book has remained constant, with the exception that the 1988 edition included a Part VII, which referred to international management, and in 1993 (the tenth edition), leading and controlling were subsumed within one part, so that the Part VI became 'Closing. Global Controlling and Global Challenges'.

This apparent immutability belies subterranean earthquakes. It is not, however, necessary for, nor will space permit, an exploration of

**Box 2.1  Summary of conclusions**

1   From its instigation, the textbook's implicit warning is of the anarchy and chaos that ensues wherever there is no management.

2   The world is divided into two: the managers and those who are managed.

3   There are three major 'epochs' in management thinking, i.e.:

  • To 1968 – an attempt to legitimize management through staking its claim to the status of both science and art, embedding its position within a legal framework, and elevating the rational and logical (modernist era).

  • The 1976 edition – a major break with the previous two decades, with management now regarded as having achieved its status as a science, and having like other sciences a long history of smooth development. From this base a universalizing imperative evolves.

  • The 1988 edition – evolution of a discourse of management, one based on such simple principles that it bodes the erosion of the faculty for critique and analysis (opening to the post-modernist era).

4   Throughout the claims-to-truth of the texts rest on assertions that management is:

  • art;
  • science;
  • law; and
  • the materialized metaphysics of modernity.

the evolution of all these chapters. An exploration of the prefaces and the first parts of the texts will suffice. I have chosen to analyse the prefaces because they create a point of entry to the 'world' of the texts, as they select and arrange participants, events and circumstances (Stillar, 1998, p. 28). The arguments in the first of the textbook's six parts show what has been thought significant at particular times, and demonstrate evolution in thinking over time.

The methodology of this chapter is, it follows, a genealogical trek (Prior, 1997) involving an eclectic selection of methods of discourse analysis and close textual reading of the various sections (Martin, 1990; Stillar, 1998). The prime interest is not in what the texts might mean to a thinking subject but in the origins, nature and structure of the discursive themes that have allowed the production of the text. Following Foucault, I will search for the dominant discourses that have governed what can and cannot be thought, and how these possibilities for thought have changed over the years.

This analysis will reveal that there have been three major 'epochs' in management thinking, i.e.:

1   To 1968 – an attempt to legitimize management through staking its claim to the status of both science and art, embedding its position within a legal framework, and elevating the rational and logical.
2   The 1976 edition – a major break with the previous two decades, with management now regarded as having achieved its status as a science, and having like other sciences a long history of smooth development. From this base there is the evolving of a universalizing imperative of management.
3   The 1988 edition – 'the' discourse of management is now fully fledged, one based on such simple principles that it bodes the erosion of the faculty for critique and analysis.

Throughout, the textbooks are informed by both a suppressed fear of anarchy and chaos, staved off only if management remains strong and in control, and claims to the truths of art, science, law and modernity.

## Analysing the prefaces

'Perhaps', the very first sentence of the preface of the first edition of the textbook in 1955 states, 'there is no more important area of human activity than management, since its task is that of getting things done through people.' 'Modern civilization', the authors write, 'is increasingly one of cooperative endeavor' where people work together in organizations 'toward the attainment of their joint goals', and the effectiveness of this joint working is largely determined by the ability of those who hold managerial positions (Koontz and O'Donnell, 1955, p. v). This statement is largely repeated in the 1964 edition, with the addition of the sentence 'It is to little avail to have scientific knowledge, engineering skills, technical abilities, or vast material resources unless the quality of management in organized groups permits effective coordination of human resources' (no page number). Having established this basis for the analysis, this statement is excluded from the prefaces of succeeding editions of the book, but it is to be found in the opening sentence of the first chapter of all succeeding editions. This statement reveals a presupposition upon which the whole foundation of management is arguably built, i.e. that people are incapable of organizing themselves and their work without the efforts of a group of people, labelled 'managers', who carry within themselves the authority of the organization's power structure.

From where does this presupposition arise? Jacques (1996) finds its location within American (or more specifically US) history, and the fear of an unregulated immigrant community from Europe. The last two decades of the nineteenth century saw the appearance of mass production technologies, a great increase in the amount of capital invested in industry and the development, a century after it had occurred in Britain, of a reliance upon steam power. These developments occurred simultaneously with urbanization and a mass influx of immigrants desperate for work. These new Americans were not married to the 'Yankee ideology of self-sufficiency' and indeed they had a higher degree of class consciousness and experience in industrial conflict. Traditional America was gripped by panic at the supposed threat of anarchy the immigrants brought with them, and the threats of labour with its 'evils of oppressed European peasantry'. The absorption into factories of the seeming revolutionaries offered the prospect of their being controlled by the emerging managerial class, and thus respite from fear of both capital and labour.

In Jacques' terms, it is possible to see Koontz and O'Donnell's opening statements as referring back to that earlier fear, seemingly embedded in the American psyche, of an anarchy and chaos that must be controlled. Furthermore, Koontz and O'Donnell were writing within a decade of the end of the Second World War and at the beginning of the seeming threats from the Communist world. Chaos, it seemed, was all around. Management offered a means of control, a means of holding back the chaos.

Could there perhaps be a longer history for this thinking that things, including people, always have to be controlled? Indeed, could it not be a fundamental, and deeply unchallenged, concept within Western society, one whose roots can be traced back to ancient Greece? Protevi (2001) certainly thinks so. He starts with the term 'hylomorphism', used most famously by Deleuze and Guattari. Hylomorphism is 'the doctrine that production is the result of an (architectural) imposition of a transcendent form on a chaotic and or passive matter' (Protevi, 2001, p. 8). This is an 'arche-thinking', i.e. one of the fundamental philosophical issues in the West, which assumes that 'a simple unchanging commanding origin is responsible for change in others' (ibid.), i.e. there can be no order without the conscious intrusion of an organizing intelligence. Tracing its inscription to Plato, and its subsequent imbrication within philosophical and political texts, Protevi argues that

Plato's disregard for artisanal and slave labour, and indeed for the ordering of matter, reverberates today through Western patterns of thought. Koontz and O'Donnell can thus be seen to be working blindly within a Platonic tradition where architectonic vision and philosophical command are vital to the establishment of form and meaning. 'The architect', like the manager or the organizational theorist, is blind to the possibility that matter may impose its own order; i.e. that workers, like slaves, may be utterly involved in organizing their own work without the intervention of management.

Such a possibility must remain in the realm of the speculative – this book is not attempting to replicate Foucault or Derrida in showing in some detail how ancient Greek ideas continue to inform twenty-first century lives. Suffice it to say that this opening statement of an early management textbook, that continues to live through all succeeding editions, closes off the possibility of ways of organizing. Alternatives undeniably exist. The NHS, for example, until recently was 'administered' by a class of functionaries who facilitated the organization's smooth running; factories and coal mines had long been run by teams of workers reporting to their own team leader who 'sold' their output to the mine or factory owner. Nowhere in Koontz and O'Donnell's statement is there a question that managers could function as the *servants* of the scientists, engineers and technicians working in organizations – it is explicit from the first sentence of their textbook that the manager should have power over others. There may be forms of organization we have not yet been able to dream off, for we do not have the words through which to articulate other alternatives.

However, when we look at the binary opposites within the text we see that the texts bespeak of an originating myth (Jeffcutt, 1994) that is far older than Jacques imagines, and indeed Protevi's argument may have more support, for the narrative underpinning the prefaces is as old as humankind.

### Binary opposites

As is well known since Derrida's earlier works were translated into English, identification of the binary opposites in texts makes explicit what is implicit and shows upon what assumptions a text's arguments rest. The binary opposites within the prefaces include (with the suppressed term coming second):

> management/chaos
> cooperation/fighting
> facts/fictions
> principles (meaning 1)/immorality
> principles (meaning 2)/disorder

logic/illogic
manager/worker
truth/untruth
science/myth
art/work of the lumpen proletariat
intellectually challenging/easily assimilated
global/parochial

The dominant terms throughout the prefaces refer to managers and management and the world that will exist if it is a managed world – one of law, order, art and science, a world that is stimulating, comfortable, prosperous. Without management we have the world of the lumpen proletariat, where myths and other fictions are believed, where chaos and disorder abound and rule is by the bovine. Here we have the nightmare world from ancient myths, a godless world, we have heaven and hell. The text's implicit story is that without large corporations (and thus without managers) we will return to the penury of the days before the Second World War, where diseases of poverty were rife, and lives were short and miserable. The world we would have without managers is far worst than that world. It is the world perceived by Americans in the late nineteenth century who saw an anarchic hell opening its maws under the pressure of hordes of immigrants. It is the world of Adam and Eve and the Fall, a world in which humankind lives in an Eden maintained only by the constant vigilance of managers.

Such myths, of course, abound in management texts. They are, for instance, to be found in the works of management 'gurus' and their bodies of theory (Clark and Salaman, 1998) Gurus, in Clark and Salaman's reading, 'manage' meaning in their promises of change, through 'acting as organizational myth makers or storytellers'. The myths and stories they tell are based upon the age-old myths and stories of heroes and villains, but the new heroes in the moral tales told by the gurus are the senior managers. The manager/hero is involved in a community (the organization) which faces perils (complacency leading to the death of the community/organization) unless the manager/hero can lead the organization out of peril and into the safety of profit. Senior managers, listening to these tales, know who they are and why they are important. Guru theory cannot tell any different story; it can speak only variations of this myth, for the tellers must feed senior managers what they want (recalling to mind other myths of destiny delayed through judicious storytelling). What senior managers want, it seems, is fulfilment of the promises made to them in the first management texts they may have read on the road to becoming managers.

There is one thing absent from the prefaces that is somewhat surprising: there is no reference, either implicitly or explicitly, to profit, to goods or to services. Management, this implies, is concerned not with its ostensible *raison d'être,* production and profit-making, but with ontological security.

### Thematic progression

Throughout the 40 years of publication, the prefaces have stated that the book will provide a framework for managerial knowledge. Management, throughout, is defined as both science and art, and is based upon a number of principles, i.e. 'fundamental truths applicable to a given set of circumstances'. An attempt is always made to emphasize both the scientific nature of the book's contents and its practical application. The job of the manager is explicitly stated to be essentially the same in all organizations and at all hierarchical positions of management, in that the manager is responsible for providing an environment in which the coordination of group members can be achieved. The job is made up of a number of specific functions which provide a framework into which knowledge can be fitted, and indeed the book is structured around the functions. Every edition states that the arguments within the book are based upon the discoveries and research of managers and scholars, and all later editions note the changes that have been made since the last edition, with the source of influence for the changes being given.

Changes have, however, appeared in the prefaces over the years: notably in the stated purpose of the book, as defined in the prefaces. In 1955 and 1964 it was very much the book's purpose to formulate a science of management. In 1976, with the change of title from *Principles of Management* to *Management: A Systems and Contingency Analysis of Managerial Functions*, the purpose of the book now became 'to present the basics of an operational theory and science of management' (Koontz and O'Donnell, 1976, p. ix). It seems that the authors have achieved their aim of formulating a science of management, although this appearance is somewhat belied by the statement on the following page of the wish to 'make a start toward developing a true management science', defined as 'organized knowledge, which puts new developments into a proper perspective and which makes this science useful to those who must apply it, as practitioners, to reality (ibid., p. x). Interesting, this distinction between 'science' and 'reality'. The authors therefore appear modestly to deny what they have stated they will achieve in this book, but still the advent of systems theory and its inclusion as fundamental to their analysis of management has allowed them to achieve the objective set out much earlier, in that they are now well down the road towards developing a science of management. Indeed, their modesty appears to be only a passing gesture, for in the first chapter they state that Part I in this edition is 'an introduction to the science and practice of management' (ibid., p. 2). By 1976 then, we may assume that the authors could rest comfortably in the belief that a science of management now existed.

Having achieved this original aim the authors could then move on to another aim, one that at first sight appears fundamentally different, for by 1988 the authors could open the preface by saying:

> This is an invitation to the reader of this book *to become more effective as a person and as a managerial leader* by applying the principles, concepts, and theories discussed in these pages.
> (Koontz and Weihrich, 1988, p. xxv, emphasis added)

'Effectiveness' is so important in the authors' thinking that it merits its inclusion in the glossary of terms, where it is defined as 'the achievement of objectives; the achievement of desired effects'. This opening statement is therefore stating that by reading this book and putting its recommendations into practice the reader will become the sort of person he or she wishes to be. The term 'managerial leader' too is interesting. Managers are defined in the glossary as 'those who undertake the tasks and functions of managing, at any level in any kind of enterprise', and leadership as 'influence, or the art or process of influencing people so that they strive willingly and enthusiastically toward the accomplishment of group goals'. A managerial leader is therefore someone distinct from and superior to the manager, for the leader has the capacity to inspire others and to gather a following. The leader is superior to other, ordinary mortals; the leader stands out from the crowd; the leader is a very special person. The authors are therefore saying to prospective readers:

> Read this book and put its lessons into practice and you will become the person you always wanted to be, one who stands out from the crowd and who has the capacity to inspire others so that they will follow you wherever you wish to take them.

Not all people can do this, however, for those who 'will benefit from this book' include 'all persons who work in enterprises', but this all-encompassing definition is refined by a list, i.e. 'aspiring managers, those who already possess managerial skills and want to become more effective, and other professionals who want to understand the organization in which they work'. This definition excludes the 'workers' in the enterprise, those who are neither managerial nor professional staff. The implicit message therefore is 'you have a choice: read this book and put its lessons into practice and you will become an inspirational human being; ignore it and become or remain one of the lumpen proletariat'.

The tenth edition of the book, the 'international edition', opens with the statement:

This book prepares men and women for the exciting, challenging, and rewarding career of managing in an international environment as we move toward the twenty-first century. As the title of the book indicates, this up-to-date tenth edition recognizes and responds to the global nature of managing . . . By acquiring a global outlook and applying the book's principles, concepts, and theories in their daily work, readers can surely become more effective as managers.

(Weihrich and Koontz, 1993, p. xxx)

The list of people who may benefit from the book now not only includes women, as we can see, but is further widened to include 'students in colleges and universities'. Given the 'global perspective', and the book's translation into 16 languages, the goal now becomes that of ensuring that a single model of management, delivered by a homogeneous managerial group, is put into practice around the globe. In this the authors are following a much longer pattern of argument, for in the 1960s American authors were arguing that eventually the whole world would be subject to the civilizing dynamics of American-style political and management systems. The term 'managers', as is repeatedly emphasized in the introductory chapters to the textbooks, encompasses all people in an enterprise who have responsibility for the work of others. The aim, it would seem, is to divide the world's entire population into two: the blessed who are the managers, and the lumpen proletariat who need to be governed by the managers.

## Conclusion: the narrative myth in the prefaces

The prefaces to management textbooks can be seen to contain a some-what hidden narrative that echoes the creation myth, has strong religious overtones and speaks to their readers in semi-mystical terms. What may be the effect upon readers? If we all live and understand our lives through narratives, living the stories before we tell them (MacIntyre, 1981, p. 213) can these stories be used to make sense of themselves and their lives? To be a member of a social world, narrative theory tells us, requires knowledge of that world's particular stories, or accounts of specific events, which carry the traditions, values and ways of knowing the world of that particular group, and where each story, in an intertextual world, draws on a vast stock of pre-existing stories (McLeod, 1997). The micro-narratives of the individual, indeed, cannot be separated from the macro-narratives of the culture (Skultans, 1999). This stock of stories includes *myths*, and thus it embodies or symbol-izes some of the most basic values of a society (Watt, 1996, p. xii). Myths are not just coding devices which allow actors to construct society through the codes, but discursive acts through which actors 'evoke the sentiments' out of which society is actively constructed'

(Lincoln, 1989). Lincoln, following Roland Barthes, argues that myth is 'a form of meta-language in which pre-existing signs are appropriated and stripped of their original context, history and signification only to be infused with new and mystificatory conceptual content of particular use to the bourgeoisie' (ibid., p. 5).

Myths can thus be seen as parts of the power/knowledge structures of a society. The myth that informs management texts is as shown in Box 2.2.

## Box 2.2  The founding myth of management

In the beginning there was chaos and anarchy. People, if they worked at all, operated in a muddle and a mess, lacking coordination and direction. People cried out for a messiah who would bring order to this sulphurous swamp. The messiah duly appeared but not in the form expected, for He appeared not as one man but as many, so His word was manifest through many and He became omnipotence incarnate. Each of these manifestations of the messiah was equipped with the magical twin swords of 'science' and 'art' (as we shall see below). Attempts at bringing order were halting and slow given that the sword of science was somewhat weak and the sword of art could not work until its scientific counterpart had achieved its full strength. However, the science was developed quite quickly. The word then rang out that all people could be managers, regardless of their gender or race, if only they read the good book. Having achieved mass conversions, the messiahs could set out on a pilgrimage to bring order and prosperity to the whole world. Soon everyone in the entire world could be converted into managers. Only the unworthy would fail to be converted, and they would be subjected to the benign governance of the managers.

From their very first sentences the textbooks thus speak to very deep needs within humankind, needs expressed through religion and through myths. Within psychoanalytical terms, the authors of the texts are projecting their own deep-seated fears of ontological insecurity onto the texts, fears that may be shared by readers who can then participate with the authors in grasping a promised security blanket.

The reader who has read the preface is now, with this promise echoing in her or his memory, ready to start working to develop the characteristics and skills required of the chosen ones. The reader turns the page to read 'Part I'. The narrative s/he encounters in 'Part I' is somewhat different but complementary.

## Part I: the texts

As noted above, the focus in this analysis will be upon the first part of each edition of the textbook, as these opening sections best highlight the knowledges and truth claims that have informed the writing of the textbooks over the decades.

The text's structure, from its inception, has been based on what Koontz and O'Donnell call the functions of the manager, which they identify as planning, organizing, staffing, directing and controlling. This long-standing practice can be seen to constitute the managerial role as something that has a precision and logic to which opposition would appear hollow. In 1968, for example, Koontz and O'Donnell wrote:

> How the manager does his task and what basic science underlies it is the focus of this book. As many managers in all types of enterprises and many scholars in the field have found, this analysis is approached most meaningfully by breaking down the total managerial task into its primary functions and organizing the principles, techniques, and knowledge of managing around these functions. This is what this book attempts to do.
>
> In undertaking this task, the authors have utilized the functions of the manager – planning, organizing, staffing, directing, and controlling – as a logical framework within which to classify the basic practice and knowledge of management.
>
> (Koontz and O'Donnell, 1968, p. 5)

The rhetoric used here is persuasive. The first sentence states strongly that there is one way in which managers do their 'task' and this can be identified. There *is* a 'basic science' underlying what the manager does. Their appeal to 'many managers in all types of enterprises and many scholars in the field' as a demonstration of proof of their arguments gives the impression of widespread support when in fact no proof is actually offered. This habit, of making unsubstantiated claims of support from managers and 'scholars', is adopted throughout the texts of the 1950s and 1960s. The functions of the manager are stated as absolute truths, to which there can be no objection. From the very beginning, therefore, management is identified as a specific accomplishment which comprises a range of identifiable functions. It is these functions that are used to structure the book. Here we see a double mimetic – the book is structured according to the perceived functions of the manager, and the manager is intended to develop practice according to the functions described in the book. Experience has supposedly constituted the book's structure, and the book's structure serves to constitute managerial experience.

## Part I: 1968

I am outlining Part I of the 1968 edition in some depth because in many ways this edition provides a point of departure from the earlier editions: a new world of management is heralded. The 1976 text is fundamentally different in its ostensible truth claims. This somewhat extended exposition therefore allows comparisons between editions, and also introduces the reader of this book to the style of the texts offered to students by the Koontz textbook.

In 1968 Part I had four chapters: 'Managing and Management Principles'; 'Patterns of Management Analysis'; 'The Functions of the Manager'; and 'Authority and Responsibility'.

---

**Box 2.3 Potted summary**

*Chapter 1: Managing and Management Principles – Koontz and O'Donnell (1968)*

'Introduction' – the functions of the manager.

'Why Group Activity?' Because modern civilization depends upon 'cooperative endeavour', and this can be achieved effectively only with managerial oversight. A list of contrasting organizations is given to show that, no matter what the type of organization, management is essential.

'Why Management?' Because all organized groups have managers, whether or not they acknowledge them by that name, and management is essential at all levels of the organization. Furthermore, it is a 'fact of life' that few people spend all their time managing. Lists of various types of professions and various types of managers are included, to show the statement applies to all.

'The Goal of All Managers' is defined as 'surplus' delivered through achieving group objectives with the least costs. A list of different levels of managers in different types of organizations is given to illustrate that this goal is common to all. This providing of lists is a habit, as we shall see.

'Is Managing a Science or An Art?' Management, like all other arts (a list of which is given that includes medicine, music composition, engineering, baseball and accountancy), uses 'underlying organized knowledge', i.e. science.

'Science and Management'. A science of management is just developing, and as in all other sciences scientific breakthroughs would preface improved practices. This section has three subsections, the first two of which define science, and principles and causal relationships. The final section justifies the use of a management science that is inexact, on the grounds that no science is fully achieved, and that it is necessary to use existing theories of management until 'statistical proof of principles of management' become available. It is in this section that references to published authors replace lists, signifying a change in discursive style from the list-driven to the academic referencing of authors.

'Principles and Theory'. Principles are defined as 'fundamental truths' and theory as 'a systematic grouping of interrelated principles'.

'The Need for Principles of Management'. These will 'further human progress' and will: increase efficiency; crystallize the nature of management; improve research; and attain social goals. Development has been delayed until after the Second World War because of the centuries in which business was held in low esteem, the preoccupation of economists with political economy and the non-managerial aspects of business, plus a tendency to compartmentalize academic disciplines. Additionally, the belief of managers that management is an art and not a science has caused delays, as has their discouragement of the development of a theory of management. An impetus to development grew out of the Great Depression of the 1920s and, more importantly, the Second World War, which had led to the growth in size of enterprises and a need to maximize efficiency. International competition was a later spur to a theory of management, as were 'cost-price squeezes' and accompanying pressures to maximize efficiency which were now 'of such magnitude to affect survival'.

The next section is entitled 'Early Contributions to Management Principles' and includes short discussions of 'Management in Antiquity', the Roman Catholic Church, military organizations, the Cameralists, F.W. Taylor's 'Principles of Management', and Henri Fayol's theory. The following section, 'The Emergence of Modern Thought', discusses the contributions of: public administrators, business managers, 'the Behavioralists', and, finally, 'Systems Scientists'.

The final section consists of a list of questions for discussion which are designed, it would seem, to reinforce the points made in the chapter. A list of 'selected references' concludes the chapter.

*Chapter 1 thus repeats the myth that was found in the preface, and through provision of definitions, lists, a history, claims to the power and knowledge of both science and art, presents an appearance of precision, rules, procedures and ways of being that allow the God-creature of the myth to develop an identity, but an identity to be formed through doing.*

Chapter 2, 'Patterns of Management Analysis', requires a somewhat closer reading.

This chapter argues that there are various approaches to the study of management, but states that there should be only one approach, i.e. the authors', as it is based on an 'operational model' that is of use to the manager and reflects the way 'he' sees 'his' job. Nevertheless, the authors feel that readers should understand the significant contributions made by proponents of other approaches. Commencing their arguments with their own 'school', they develop arguments that serve to demolish alternative perspectives.

The next section is entitled 'Differing Definitions of Management', a meaningful section that should provide a succinct statement of what management is. However, the authors do not provide any examples of 'differing definitions of management'. They write:

> While it is generally agreed that management involves getting things done through and with people, does it deal with all human relationships? Is a street peddler a manager? Is a leader of a disorganized mob a manager? Is a parent a manager? Does the field of management equal the fields of sociology and social psychology combined?
>
> Certainly if a field of knowledge is not to become bogged down in a quagmire of misunderstandings, the first need is for definition of the field not in sharp, detailed, and inflexible terms, but rather along lines which will give it fairly specific content. The authors suggest that the field of management be defined in the light of the able and discerning manager's frame of reference, because theoretical science unrelated to the practical art it is designed to serve is unlikely to be productive.
>
> (Koontz and O'Donnell, 1968, p. 42)

The first paragraph above at first appears so meaningless that its inclusion is problematic. The somewhat confusing rhetorical flourish of erecting a straw person that is then knocked down seems to state that management should be applied only within limited domains. However, a closer analysis shows they are making the opposite claims. They provide no answers to their list of questions, so the statement can be read as:

> The field of management encompasses all human relationships. It further equals all branches of the social sciences, so they should be devoted to achieving managerial aims. The street peddler can improve his/her sales through good management, the leader of a disorganized mob, through application of appropriate management science, can turn the mob into a disciplined army; child-rearing techniques can be improved through the application of good management practice.
>
> (ibid., p. 42)

The second paragraph again avoids any definition, but allows the 'light of the able and discerning manager's frame of reference' to illuminate and thus define the field. Again we see their recourse to practising managers for justification of their stance. If the manager has been 'able and discerning' enough to catch the message of the previous paragraph, s/he will see their territory as encompassing the whole world. The final part of the sentence, that refers to science and art, makes several swift elisions that need highlighting. First, they define 'theoretical science' as having one objective, and that is to serve the 'practical art'. This contradicts the usual distinctions between theoretical and applied science, as any engineer or physicist will be quick to point out. Second, they assume that 'theoretical science' is worthless unless it has applications in managerial practice: they do not delimit their definitions of 'theoretical science' so again we see a call to the academy to turn its attentions to the needs of management.

Later in this section they argue that the field of management 'should deal with an area of knowledge and inquiry that is manageable' (ibid., p. 43). This statement can be read in at least three ways, each of which can influence the student readers' formation of their managerial selves:

1   The field of management should be narrow enough to allow focus, so there is no need to try to know everything, for 'knowledge of the field of management must be recognized as a part of a larger universe of knowledge but need not encompass that universe' (ibid., p. 43). This reading appears to be the authors' overt intention.

2   Knowledge and enquiry should become areas that are manageable. In this reading they anticipate developments in universities whereby

management could be seen to be gaining ascendance over academics, with the potential that they could indeed define the fields of knowledge and enquiry that may be pursued by academics.

3    In leaving it to the discretion of managers to define how much of a field of knowledge and enquiry is 'manageable', they encourage managers to identify the boundaries of knowledge.

This section on 'Differing Definitions of Management' could thus be read as follows:

> The field of management encompasses all human relationships and will ensure greater effectiveness in human relationships. All branches of the physical and social sciences are to be governed by managers who will decide in which areas scientific research is to be carried out.

The reference to the managerial control of the physical and social sciences can perhaps be seen to be coming to pass, in the light of the research assessment exercise, teaching audits and the other panoply of controls that have descended upon British academics, and the longer tradition of controls upon academics in the US.

The final discussion in Chapter 2 is entitled 'Management as a System'. It states that management is a system, i.e. that it is a 'formal, systematically organized complex of relationships between people' which 'has, as a system, characteristics similar to those physical and biological systems' (ibid., p. 44). Less than two pages are devoted to a discussion of a perspective that was in later editions to alter radically the textbook's discursive continuum. However, in the light of the foregoing discussion of the territorializing imperative of the management discourse in these texts, the brief discussion presages the further urge to global control that develops in subsequent editions. Systems are seen everywhere – in industry, in society, in government and ultimately the universe. All systems are characterized by complexity, and every system 'whether physical, biological, or social – has a specific purpose to which all its parts are designed to contribute' (ibid., p. 44). Every system, having such a purpose, by definition (i.e. in the light of the authors' earlier definitions) will need management. Management now extends to the universe.

A list of questions 'for discussion' follows, and the chapter concludes with 'Selected References'.

*Chapter 2 thus establishes the need for management of everything. The grandiose claims of the myth that underpins the textbook are reinforced in this chapter.*

Chapter 3 'The Functions of the Manager', expands upon the earlier definition of management as involving a series of functions and will not be amplified here. The chapter has the effect of making something that is highly nebulous and, as numerous studies show, based largely upon talk and social interaction, appear precise, specific and orderly. The myth of the manager is thus further developed.

Chapter 4, 'Authority and Responsibility', is especially interesting for this discussion for it disappears from later editions of the textbook. In 1968, however, authority was seen as the concept on which management theory should be founded. Authority, for Koontz and O'Donnell in that year, had a 'standard definition' which was 'legal or rightful power, a right to command or to act' (1968, p. 59). In the managerial job, it is 'the power to command others, to act or not to act in a manner deemed by the possessor of the authority to further enterprise or departmental purpose' (ibid., p. 59). It was 'the key to the management job' as 'since managers must work through people to get things done, management theory is necessarily concerned with a complex of superior–subordinate relationships and is therefore founded on the concept of authority. In the manager of a company, division, department, branch, or section is vested power sufficient to force compliance, whether through persuasion, coercion, economic or social sanctions, or other means' (ibid., p. 59). The authors distinguish between two theories of the source of authority, acceptance theory wherein subordinates *accept* the manager's orders, a theory dismissed by Koontz and O'Donnell, and formal authority theory. This latter theory sees this 'legal or rightful power' having its 'ultimate source . . . principally in the institution of private property'. The 'bounds and content' of private property rights are defined by social institutions, may be traced to 'elements of basic group behavior' but '[m]ost formal authority theorists emphasize the legal aspects of private property as the source of authority, though good sociological analysis would broaden the source to include all related social institutions' (ibid., p. 61). It should be noted that their concept of 'good sociological analysis' does not include pursuing understanding of authority through an analysis of sociological writings on authority. However:

> Under our democratic form of government the right upon which managerial authority is based appears to have its primary source in the Constitution of the United States. Since the Constitution is the creature of the people, subject to amendment and modification by the will of the people, it follows that the total society, through government, is the source from which authority flows to ownership and thence to management. Indeed, the entire social institution of private property is molded not only by the Constitution, but by

many federal and state legislative and administrative regulations, and by the mores of the entire American society.

(ibid., p. 61)

The discussion of 'Authority and Responsibility' ends the first part of the 1968 edition. Its omission from subsequent editions of the textbook suggests not that the issue of authority and responsibility had been rendered unimportant but that its analysis had been rendered redundant, given that the legitimacy of the managerial position had now been achieved. In this sense, its absence from later editions speaks louder than would its continued presence, and alerts us to the need to observe how and why management had achieved this taken-for-granted status. It now appears to have been always a legitimate function, and in this position of hegemonic lassitude it is put beyond the reach of challenge or questioning. The recourse to the discourse of law did not, however, disappear from the function of management. As I shall show in Chapter 4, although now absent from the pages of the textbook it remains deeply embedded within the discursive constructions that we know as 'organizations'.

## The 1976 edition: management established

By 1976 the textbook had been renamed: it was now called *Management. A Systems and Contingency Analysis of Managerial Functions.* Part I, The Basis of Management, was extended, and most obvious among the changes is the evolution of the discursive practices of the earlier text. There are first, stylistic changes in this edition. Headings are in red, and the seeds of what are to become boxes in later editions are to be seen, as some sections such as quotations are topped and tailed by red lines. There is a change from use of the third person male singular to use of the second person singular – for example, 'It has no implication as to whether a person ought to' (Koontz and O'Donnell, 1968, p. 13) is replaced by 'It says nothing about whether you should' (Koontz and O'Donnell, 1976, p. 14) – so the text speaks directly to the reader, absorbing her/him into the world outlined in the book. Gendered pronouns are now introduced – readers are now referred to as 'he or she', or where possible the third person plural is used. The most important change in this chapter is perhaps the sentence that opens the next section, headed 'The Schools of Management' in 1968 and 'The Various Approaches to Management' in 1976 (see p. 44).

The change in the first sentence signals the move away from an insistence that there can be only one approach to management. (The sentence disappears from subsequent editions.) This is an important psychological change which allows the division of management into various 'schools', including, most importantly, the 'classical' school. In contrast

| 1968 (p. 34) | 1976 (p. 56) |
|---|---|
| It is perhaps more important that there be one approach to management than that there be a single approach to psychology or trout fishing. What is important is for students and managers to be able to classify and recognize the various patterns of management analysis. | Some may believe that it is no more important that there be one approach to management than that there be a single approach to psychology or trout fishing. But no one can doubt that it is important for students and managers to be able to classify and recognize the various patterns of management analysis. |

with this allowance for competing styles of analysis, the change in the second sentence is another example of a change in style from one of making suggestions to one of a demanded inclusiveness and dictated agreement.

One highly significant development in the 1976 text is the disappearance of the fourth chapter, on 'Authority and Responsibility'. It is never to return. The only discussion of authority in 1976 is included in the section 'Organizing', where it forms part of a discussion about line and staff relationships.

The most important of the other changes are: the use of rhetoric to give the impression that management is a science, the establishment of a 'history' of management thinking rather than, as had been the case, a disparate list of authors and publications, and the use of language in such a way as to prevent both opposition and opportunities for conceptual thought.

### Management as a science

Throughout this edition words have been omitted, changed or added to allow a cumulative impression that management is a science. For example, the chapter entitled in 1968 'Managing and Management Principles' became in 1976 'Managing, Management Science and Management Systems'. The section 'Science and Management' has a different opening section for, rather than the apology for the inadequate state of knowledge within a claimed science of management, now there is reference to several pieces of research that prove that business failures are due to poor management. Reference is made to developing countries' failure to develop, this being seen as the result of an absence of good management (no reference in support is given).

There is now a greater use of academic (scientific?) conventions, although whether the authors are using references, in the well-known academic phrase, as a drunk uses a lamp-post, i.e. less for illumination than support, is a moot point.

The section entitled 'Reasons for Delay in Development' (a sub-heading in small black print) in 1968 is now entitled 'Why the Slowness in Development of Management Thought?' (a main heading, in red capitals). A new sentence has been interposed in the introductory paragraph:

> As we shall see in the following section, this [the delay in development of management theory] does not mean that there was no concern, no theory, or no attempt to develop a science of management until this time. Indeed, many persons – mostly practitioners – attempted to bring some orderly thinking to management.
>
> (Koontz and O'Donnell, 1968, p. 26)

Deconstructing this paragraph and its title reveals the following:

1   A concern that management may not be as important as the authors claim it is, if it proved of so little concern to people in earlier decades.
2   A worry therefore that their claims to a long history of management thinking may be based on an untruth.
3   Despite this a need to assert that management has a long history in which to base a claim for status.
4   The elision of 'orderly thinking' with theory, in contradistinction to marked efforts at other points to define 'theory'.
5   The claim to legitimacy through the emergence of managerial thought arising not from scientists or academics but from practising managers.

The last point shows a tension that is present throughout the earlier editions – a tension between claiming that management theory arises from the work of practising managers, and a wish to claim the status given by having foundations within the sciences. The authors resolve the problem until 1965 by attempting to have it both ways, claiming credence both from practising managers and from the sciences. By 1988 the problem was resolved through use of the simple expediency of ignoring it. The opening sentence of the relevant section in 1988 states that 'Although modern operational management theory dates primarily from the early twentieth century, there was serious thinking and theorizing about managing many years before' (Koontz and Weihrich, 1988,

p. 25). This statement removes the issue of who was doing the 'serious thinking and theorizing'. Indeed, this edition disposes of any worry about the apparent delay in developing management thought. The impression of there being a very long heritage is thus reinforced.

The 'present' situation was called by one of the authors 'the management theory jungle' in 1968, but the word 'present' is omitted in 1976, suggesting the jungle belongs to the past – order has been achieved.

In 1976 there is a new Chapter 4, entitled 'Managers and their External Environment', which reinforces the systems model that has come to dominate the authors' thinking. A new Chapter 5, entitled 'Comparative Management', symbolizes the move to colonizing the world. Good management, the authors assert, can help ensure economic growth in all countries of the world. This chapter draws heavily not on managers' reported experience but on the findings of research, further signalling the move to 'science'. There is a tension throughout the chapter, however, in the authors' long-standing statement that management is a universal practice that applies at all levels in all organizations. To resolve this they distinguish further between the science of management, which they see as universal, and the art of management, which they see as involved in adapting the science to the local environment.

### Use of language

Language is used from 1976 in such a way as to close off any possibility of demur. For example, a new section, five and a half pages long, is entitled 'Management Practice and Analysis Require a Systems Approach', a precise statement that brooks no opposition. This chapter ends, as in 1968, with a list of questions 'for discussion'. One new question is:

> 5. Why do management analysis and practice require a systems approach? Reviewing the key elements of systems and the systems approach, how do they apply to management? Do managers operate in an open or a closed system? How?
>
> (Koontz and O'Donnell, 1976)

To 'correctly' answer this question requires the student to desist both from exploring alternatives and from being critical or analytical. The only 'correct' answer is one which adopts the arguments outlined in the text. The pedantry of this pedagogic style is not so evident in earlier editions of the textbook, in which questions had been posed which encouraged students to explore different definitions or schools.

The questions 'For Discussion' at the end of the chapter have been expanded from five to seven, and are totally new. They reinforce the idea that management as an academic discipline has a long history, with its own schools of thought, with new schools replacing the out-dated schools during the paradigm shifts familiar in the physical sciences. The changes again reinforce the student's need to regard what the authors have written as the one available truth. All that is required of the student in answering these questions is that they look back through the chapter to discover the answers. Neither thought nor ability for conceptual or critical analysis is required of or encouraged in the student.

## The construction of a history of management

A cumulative and evolutionary history of management thought is brought into existence in this edition. Authors who previously had been cited as if their works were current are now offered the place of founding fathers. The sections from 1968 entitled 'Early Contributions to Management Principles' and 'The Emergence of Modern Thought' have been moved to another chapter, a new Chapter 2 entitled 'The Emergence of Management Thought'. In 1968 it had been noted that 'scattered but significant contributions to management theory' had existed 'since early in the century' (Koontz and O'Donnell, 1968, p. 18). In 1976 this had been replaced by a note of 'the many insights, ideas, and scientific underpinnings which preceded the upsurge of management writing during recent years' (Koontz and O'Donnell, 1976, p. 25). This marked difference in the estimate of the scale of what had gone before – from 'scattered contributions' to 'many insights, ideas and scientific under-pinnings' is necessary if what is now to be called 'the history of management thought' (ibid., p. 25) is to come into being. Management, in 1976, suddenly discovers a long and prestigious history, one which had not previously existed. Management, it seems, has not emerged out of a black hole illuminated only by tiny, scattered pinpricks of light, but has been erected upon a substantial foundation whereby knowledge has been accumulating for decades.

This urge to historicize in this edition sees the authors ploughing back through the past to extend the history back as far as possible, and fore-runners for management thought are found in 'antiquity', in the worlds of the Egyptians, the early Greeks and the ancient Romans. This rhetorical flourish, this reinvention of the past, has a specific purpose. The texts, as I showed above, in each edition state that there is nothing more fundamental to humankind than the need for organizing and thus the need for management. If this is the case, then the discovery that management is a fairly new invention contradicts this statement – its shadow statement is 'we've done quite well without management in previous times and in other cultures, so surely we could do quite well without them again'. In this assertion of a long history of management thought we again see the wish to prove that management is vital to the continued existence of humankind. This claim to longevity is expanded by the introduction of a new section, signalled by a large heading, in red capital letters, 'Precursors to Taylor and Scientific Management'. There then follow brief descriptions of the work of James Watt, Jr, Mathew Robinson Boulton, Robert Owen and Henry Varnum Poor.

In the section 'Early Contributions to Management Thought', there is for the first time the grouping together of Taylor *et al.*, to whom the label of 'classicists' is now applied. We thus see the construction of a school of thought that provides the conceptual foundations and history of what can now claim to be a discipline in its own right. Just as physics can look back to Isaac Newton, and astronomy to Galileo, so management can look back to its own founding fathers who developed theories which have since been usurped. The section concludes with a discussion headed 'Criticisms and Misunderstandings of the Classicists'.

## The 1988 edition: 'dumbing down': management's own discourse?

This edition represents a further marked shift in the discursive world into which students are inculcated. Now we see the excision of any attempt to legitimize management through justifying it as a science and claiming for it a long history of sufficient span to allow paradigmatic shifts. The first two chapters contain only the vestiges of these earlier threads. The excision, I suggest, is possible because the battle had been won and management was not only successful in its striving to become acceptable but it was now rampant. Not only organizations but governments throughout the world were, by the 1980s, claiming good management as the way forward. Resting securely upon these laurels, the 1988 text instead serves to develop a 'managerial discourse', one in which language is restricted to a very narrow vocabulary that impedes nuance, reflection or analysis, where explanation is rendered redundant as statements suffice, and where the capacity for conceptual or critical thought is discouraged. I have used the ugly phrase 'dumbing down' because in its simplistic summary of a complex process of change it encapsulates neatly and descriptively that very process.

By 1988, the ninth edition, Part I had only two chapters: 'Management: Science, Theory, and Practice, and 'The Evolution of Management Thought and the Patterns of Management Analysis'. With the exception of a new section on 'Women in the Organizational Hierarchy', Chapter 1 contains arguments that are largely unchanged from the earlier editions. The style of presentation is, however, markedly different. Propositions are now stated in the form of statements of truth to which no challenge is allowed. Sentences are shortened, and the mode of writing changes from a rather 'gentlemanly' style that would not be out of place in a pre-war English novel to one that has had all embellishments and qualifications removed. The displayed material on the next page illustrates this point.

The 1988 version has expunged all reference to the authors, giving the impression that the statement has originated without intervention from human beings, so that it is a 'fact of life'. In this it is much like scientific texts' excision of the human actor from manufacture of a natural world that had existed there all along, waiting to be discovered. As Woolgar explains, 'The metaphor of scientific discovery, the idea of dis-covering, is precisely that of uncovering and revealing something which had been there all along. One removes the covers and thereby exposes the thing for what it is; one pulls back the curtains on the facts' (Woolgar, 1988, p. 55). Here, the textbook authors have pulled back the covers and revealed that management had been there waiting, all along, since its dawning in the mists of time. The above statement now becomes a command: 'this is the only view of the world that is acceptable and you will accept it'.

The lists of 'chapter objectives' which now preface each of the 25 chapters draw readers into a world in which orders are given to which they should respond unquestioningly. Chapter 1's list of 'commands' state that after completing this chapter 'you' (the reader is addressed personally throughout) should be able to understand that management applies to all kinds of organizations and to managers at all organizational levels, that all managers aim to create a surplus, that management is an art that utilizes science, that managing requires a systems approach, consists of five specific functions and finally, 'you' should be able to understand how the book is organized. From its very first page therefore the reader is instructed that there is only one view of management, and that this perspective must be absorbed. The ubiquitous statement, of management as one of the most important of human activities, prefaces the rest of the chapter. Its truncation further illustrates the change in the style of writing for where in 1968 it read:

> Perhaps there is no more important area of human activity than managing, for it is the task of the manager to establish and maintain an internal environment in which people working together in groups can perform effectively and efficiently toward the attainment of group goals.
>
> (Koontz and O'Donnell, 1968, p. 5)

In 1988, it becomes:

> One of the most important human activities is managing.
>
> (Koontz and Weihrich, 1988)

| 1968 (p. 5) | 1976 (pp. 2–3) | 1988 (p. 15) |
|---|---|---|
| In undertaking this task, the authors have utilized the functions of the manager – planning, organizing, staffing, directing and controlling – as a logical framework within which to classify the basic practice and knowledge of management. It is recognized that there are other classifications of managerial functions which differ slightly, and with most of these the authors have no quarrel. It does seem, however, that the classification used here has the advantages of being comprehensive, of being divisible into enough parts to permit logical analysis, and of being operational in the sense that it portrays functions as managers themselves see them. Moreover, these functions sharply distinguish the task of the manager from the non-managerial activities of the specialist or technician. | In undertaking this task, the authors have utilized the functions of managers – planning, organizing, staffing, directing and leading, and controlling – as a first breakdown in the classification of knowledge. While others may prefer a slightly different major classification, it does appear that this one has the advantages of being comprehensive, in that all new and pertinent knowledge can be placed within it, of being divisible into enough parts to permit logical analysis, and of being operational in the sense that it portrays functions as managers themselves see them. Moreover, as intended in this book, this classification sharply distinguishes managerial tasks from nonmanagerial ones and allows concentration on what managers do as managers. | The functions of managers provides a useful framework for organizing management knowledge. There have been no new ideas, research findings, or techniques that cannot readily be placed in the classifications of planning, organizing, staffing, leading and controlling. |

The truncation, in removing the explanation for the statement, can be seen as a rhetorical device that prevents the reader from interacting with the authors, from questioning their statements or posing alternative possibilities. No other perspective is allowed. The reader becomes a passive recipient of orders.

I will provide one further example to illustrate the change in style:

> Managing, like all other practices – whether of medicine, music composition, engineering, accountancy, or even baseball – is an art. It is know-how. It is doing things in the light of the realities of a situation.
>
> (ibid., p. 8)

replaces what in 1968 had read:

> The question is often raised whether managing is a science or an art. Actually, the practice of managing, like all other arts – whether medicine, music composition, engineering, baseball, or accountancy – makes use of underlying organized knowledge – science – and applies it in the light of realities to gain a desired, practical result. In doing so, practice must design a solution which will work, that is, get the results desired. Art, then, is the 'know-how' to accomplish a desired, concrete result.
>
> (Koontz and O'Donnell, 1968, p. 8)

The omission of the word 'question' represents a rhetorical ban against the asking of questions. In 1988 every practice is an art, thus excising totally the always-negligible question of what the authors mean by 'art'. The need to debate whether it is also a science is rendered redundant by the removal of any reference to science. The exclusion of the quotation marks from around 'know-how' renders a simple colloquialism, used knowingly to explain what the authors had presumed was a complex point, into a statement that needs no explanation. The phrase 'doing things' is used in 1988 to replace 'the practice of managing', mak[ing] use of, 'appl[ying], design[ing] a solution; get[ting] desired results, and accomplish[ing]. Activities that had been delineated in 1968 now become the very vague doing of 'things'. This is a poverty of language and of ideas – it is a 'dumbing down', via writing, of concepts and conceptual abilities.

The result is a marked reduction in text, and reliance upon diagrams and illustrations. Topics which in 1988 require 15 pages, including 3.6 pages of diagrams and boxes, in 1968 had deserved at least 24 pages of closely typed script, and in 1976 about 20 pages.

The academic style of 1976 is replaced by a pedagogic mode in 1988. The questions for discussion placed at the end of each chapter are accompanied by brief case studies and 'Exercises/Action Steps'. This last phrase uses three words all with very similar meaning to make its point – exercises are actions and steps are actions – an act of repetition repeated throughout the book. This is further illustrative of the 'dumbing down', of a mode of addressing readers assumed unable to handle concepts until they have been repeated in ever more simplistic terms. Readers who have watched BBC TV's *Teletubbies* programme, designed to mimic the throught processes and conceptual abilities of babies and toddlers, will be familiar with this technique.

References, which in 1976 had taken up much of the space on each page, are now found again at the end of the chapter, and take up only one page.

Chapter 2 in 1988 is called 'The Evolution of Management Thought and the Patterns of Management Analysis'. It subsumes within one chapter the second and third chapters from 1976. Stylistically, it differs even more from previous editions than did the first chapter. Its 26 pages of text replace the 48 pages of 1976. The 26 pages include three 'figures' which take up about three pages and which provide highly simplistic summaries of the points made in the text. There are two tables, one of which suffices as a summary of all the 'major contributions to management'. The figures and tables represent a scale of increasing simplistication:

1   Authors regarded as influential in the field write texts.
2   These are summarized very briefly and often simplistically in textbooks, with little attempt to look outside the field of management for further understanding or explanation.
3   The simple summaries are further summarized until little but the author's name, title of *his* text, year of its publication, and a miniscule overview of his arguments are given.

F.W. Taylor's work and its treatment within the Koontz textbook is especially illustrative, given not only the alternative reading offered to it by Harry Braverman's (1973) *Labor and Monopoly Capital*, but also the warm reception given it by Lenin and by many early Japanese industrialists. The management student who comes to Taylor through the pages of Koontz and O'Donnell will remain totally ignorant not only of the worldwide phenomenon that was Taylorism, and of major critiques of Taylor's work, but of *any* criticism. The only hint that Taylor's work was not received universally with rapture is in a reference to Taylor's testimony to a committee of the House of Representatives. Taylor 'was forced to defend his ideas before a group of congressmen, most of whom were hostile because they believed, along with labor leaders, that Taylor's ideas would lead to overworking and displacing workers'. It seems that only those degenerate enough to ally themselves with trade unions would criticize Taylor, who, in the land of the free, was 'forced' by them to defend himself.

Students will read a potted biography that borders on the hagiographic in that it emphasizes his success and gives the impression that he was a philanthropist devoted to improving harmony between workers, managers and owners. They will read of the importance he gave to a scientific approach to management, and their attention will be drawn to a blue box that summarizes Taylor's 'Principles', implying that they were the work of a humane philanthropist for the summaries read:

1   Replacing rules of thumb with science.
2   Obtaining harmony in group action, rather than discord.
3   Achieving cooperation rather than 'chaotic individualism'.
4   Working for maximum rather than restricted output.
5   Developing all workers to the fullest extent possible 'for their own and their company's highest prosperity'.
(Koontz and Weihrich, 1988, p. 28)

This already partial and attenuated account of Taylor's work is summarized further in 47 words in Table 2.1 in this edition of the textbook.

Taylor is thus treated much like Moses, although Moses was allowed to have certain shortcomings. Given the accolade of founding father of modern management, Taylor is sanctified and put above critique, and thus management thinking is elevated with him, into the realm of the sacred.

Further stylistic changes include, for the first time, the use of photographs. These five photographs, the only ones in the book, are of early management thinkers. I will explore them in Chapter 3, Management as science.

For the rest, the chapter differs little from earlier editions, save for the removal of several paragraphs and sections. The major exception is the removal of all reference to the ancient Greeks and Egyptians, and the erasure of any attempt to provide management with any history extending backwards from the twentieth century.

Few major changes to this section had been made for the 1993 edition, and so I will not explore that later text.

## Summary and conclusion: from modernism to post-modernism

The above close reading reveals that management texts are based on a foundational myth that 'proves' the need for management. This myth states that without management the world will descend into chaos and anarchy. This myth remains a constant throughout the 40 years of the textbooks, but otherwise there are major changes in the texts. They can be seen to have three distinct periodizations: to the mid-1970s when they sought to establish the status of management; the period of the mid-1970s when they assured themselves that they had established this status through proving that management was a science; and from the mid-1980s when the emergence of a discourse specific to management emerges, one that is based on a poverty of language, argumentation and aspiration that can only be labelled 'dumbed-down'.

To return to my earlier borrowing of Derrida's theorizing of the archive, the knowledges *con*signed in the museum of the textbook through the institution, within management, of the archontic, are those knowledges which in twentieth century Anglo-Saxon Western culture are seen to have most power: i.e. art, science and justification in law. The fourth, the repressed knowledge that informs the other, that informs the archontic, is located in the subtext: that management is the materialized metaphysics of modernity. The next section of this book, 'Deconstruction', explores in turn each of these four claims to truth, but the reference to modernity ushers in a reminder that periodization cannot be a simple, descriptive term, but requires explanation.

The three periods I have identified in the textbook I will here reduce to two, for I suggest the first two, the attempt to achieve status and satisfaction with that status, are reflections of the same historical epoch, i.e. that of modernity. The last though, is different, and its difference is to be located in the period in which the texts were written, during which there was an ushering into prominence of a new historical epoch, post-modernity. Such a statement implies very strict boundaries between rigidly defined epochs, an implication I wish to abjure immediately. The papers and books attempting to delineate the modern from the post-modern are too numerous to list, and there is no room here, and if there were it would not be fruitful, to argue the distinction. However, there is a need for a sense of what I am implying about the textbooks' reflection of the broader societal and cultural changes occurring over the half century in which they have been influential. I will start first by outlining the distinction between the modern and the post-modern which has arguably had most influence in management studies: Cooper and Burrell's (1988) discussion.

For Cooper and Burrell (1988) modernism, or at least that dominant form of modernism they call 'systemic modernism' or 'instrumental rationality', is an epoch whose primary concern is with the rational and efficient organization of large institutions, where functional rationality is brought to the ordering of social relations. There is an emphasis upon reducing complexity through mechanizing social order, for the world is seen as 'intrinsically logical and meaningful', and constituted by Reason. Here *performativity*, or the capacity to produce goods effectively, is a 'principle of realization and objectification' which has precedence over 'thought itself' (Cooper and Burrell, 1988, p. 96).

Post-modernism, on the other hand, is beset not by Reason but by 'irreducible indeterminacy'. Meaning and understanding are not naturally intrinsic to the world but have to be constructed, and the 'omniscient, rational subject' of modernism is denied. Organizations, rather than being seen as structures having their own, objective existence, are interpreted as *representations* for subjects who/which attempt to 'appropriate and master the system as a field of knowledge' (ibid., p. 105). Rather than modernism's normative-rational individual subject, post-modernism's subject is understood as a material flow which produces itself. Organizations thus are not structures but *processes*. *Performativity*, as I outlined in the opening sections of this chapter, in this post-modernist perspective refers not to the efficient and profitable production of goods, i.e. to the organization of production, but to its reverse, in Cooper and Burrell's much-cited phrase, that is, to the production of organization. Performativity in this perspective is 'the reiterative and citational practice by which discourse produces the effects that it names' (Butler, 1993, p. 2), whereby the materiality of matter is achieved through the effect of power, thus granting viability within the domain of cultural intelligibility.

These two systems of thought, for Cooper and Burrell, are so radically different that they may be fundamentally irreconcilable.

The difference is not so great for Fredric Jameson, who explores how the modern intrudes into the post-modern. His delineation of the distinctiveness of the modern from the post-modern appeals due to his attempt to retain a Marxist formulation throughout his analysis. His attempts to remain overly loyal to Marx weaken his work (see the essays in Kellner, 1989) but do not ultimately detract from his insightful rendering of a post-modern capitalism. Jameson's work is a skilful blend of the theories of Marx, Marxist writers such as, notably, Ernst Mandel and Guy Debord, and post-modernist theorists, notably Jean Baudrillard. In this perspective, post-modernism is the reflex and the concomitant of yet another systemic modification of capitalism itself (Jameson, 1991, p. xii), in which there is an immense dilation of the sphere of commodities, a quantum leap in the aestheticization of reality, and a 'commodity rush' stimulated by the consumption of sheer commodification.

Capitalism penetrates the psyche and enters into the very molecules of material society. 'Post-modern people', who possess a new 'structure of feeling' are produced. There are 'new forms of practice and social and mental habits' (Jameson, 1991, p. xv) formed out of a continuous reciprocal interaction and feedback loops between the cultural and the economic (ibid., p. xiv/xv). A depthlessness brought about by the culture of the image or simulacrum, exists alongside a weakening of historicity, post-modernist mutations in the lived experience of space, and the economic world system of globalization. Rather than the alienation of the subject there is the subject's fragmentation. Categories of space dominate over categories of time, and everything is pastiche, involving 'random cannibalization of all the styles of the past' (ibid., p. 18). The world is thus transformed into sheer images of itself. In this epoch, the dominant sense is the visual, so that were 'an ontology of this artificial, person-produced universe still possible, it would have to be an ontology of the visual, of being as the visible first and foremost, with the other senses draining off it' (ibid., p. 1). The key to understanding this stage of capitalism, for Jameson, lies in understanding culture. Culture has become material (ibid., p. 67), and is no longer autonomous but has expanded prodigiously throughout the social realm, to the point at which everything in our social life – from economic value and state power to practices and to the very structure of the psyche itself – can be said to have become cultural (ibid., p. 48). The 'real' is transformed into so many pseudoevents.

The contrast with the securities of the modern era are profound. There is an end to truth and an end to 'reality'.

Such a sharp distinction between two eras, albeit that it acknowledges the continuing intrusion of the relics of the old into the new, is of course open to critique. Best and Kellner (2001), for instance, prefer to see the opening decades of the twenty-first century as a period in between the modern and the post-modern. Indeed, Jameson himself in his most recent work, an *Essay on the Ontology of the Present* (2002), states that the assumption that modernism is superseded is naïve, for it has, like the Freudian repressed, returned. I would suggest that it has not so much returned as never gone away, and that post-modernist concepts have grown to fill voids of understanding that exist in the modern world, displacing some but only some. That, however, is another argument and this is not the place to start it. Suffice it to say, for the purposes of this work, that the epoch of the management textbook can be divided into two: a modernist epoch in which the texts attempted to reflect a pre-existing reality and to seek ways of improving the functioning of that reality, and the post-modernist, in which the texts attempt to create the object of which they speak – the personally addressed, aspiring manager occupying the subject position of management.

And so I return to the competing definitions of 'performative', as these two epochs, if such they be, reflect those distinctions. The first reflects the managerialist definition of a search for knowledge about how to maximize output for minimum input, and the second a post-modernist understanding whereby the performative act brings into being that of which it speaks. The first epoch attempted to inculcate managers in how to *do* management, the second in how to *be* managers. These are distinctions I will explore throughout the text.

# Part II

# Deconstruction

In Part I, I showed how management textbooks had constructed the manager and the managed organization, using in this act of construction four claims to truth: that management is an art, a science and Enlightenment Rationality, or modernity, based in law. Part II analyses each of these claims, devoting one chapter to each claim. In each chapter I venture outside the disciplinary barriers of management, for the self-referentiality of the management textbooks may, in part, account for the narrowness of their focus. So, when exploring the textbook's claim that management is a science I draw upon arguments from the sociology of scientific knowledge; when exploring law I venture into critical legal studies, art into art history, and enlightenment rationality or modernity into gender theories.

The aim of this deconstruction is therefore to offer a profoundly different reading of management textbooks and the management and managers that they constitute.

# 3 Management as science

One of the four dominant claims to truth in the management textbook is that of the truth of management being a science. Tracing this claim through the various chapters of the more recent editions reveals a somewhat confusing anomaly: the claim is accompanied by both an abjuring and denigration of science, in favour of anecdote, homily, personal experience, hypothetical examples and unreferenced quotes from 'real' managers. With the authors' acceptance that management now has scientific status there therefore comes a rejection of the tenets by which that status is upheld. Importantly, this occurs at the same time as the 'dumbing down' of the texts. Where the semblance of academic credibility appears, the publications referred to are those of the famous names in management writing – for example, Argyris, McGregor, Drucker – that are untested in practice, and these too are often referred to in the format of an extended anecdote. Weber, for example, is known in management texts only as a management consultant who recommended the value of bureaucracies and got it wrong, an error the textbooks forgive on the grounds that he was writing so long ago, before management knowledge had really developed (see especially Daft, 1997, for a highly illustrative example). It would be too easy to argue that this is another example of the classical Freudian oedipal conflict, whereby the son first desires the love of the father but then overthrows the father and takes his place, but that argument would lack explanatory power, unless we were to argue further about the increasing managerial domination over academia, and thus over the physical and social sciences, and that is an analysis that belongs elsewhere. Rather, my search for understanding of this contradictory relationship of the management textbook to science will draw upon early work within the sociology of scientific knowledge (SSK), intertwined with Foucauldian perspectives. This allows me to show that management textbooks mimic the scientific world in that they first, like science, make a claim to being scientific, second, use a rhetoric similar to that of scientists to propound their claims, and third, where the 'soft' school of SSK shows science constructs socially the physical world of which it speaks, management textbooks can be seen to be constructing a managerial identity that is compliant, pliant and no threat to the capitalist enterprise. It is an identity that is assured of its scientific, and thus superior, status, while at the same time it is an identity which is discouraged from thought, experiment and imagination, and which is thus discouraged from ever questioning its own practices, for with questioning could come threats to the capitalist order. Management degrees, through the management textbooks they use, can thus be seen as a form of disciplinary practice which produces quiescent managerial subjects.

## The science in the textbooks

In Chapter 2, I showed that the Koontz textbook's claim to a scientific status for management has proved foundational to the textbook's reflection of the discipline's self-understanding. Indeed, the need for and definition of science found in the textbook has remained unchanged over the years, in marked contrast to its understanding of the state of development of a science of management. In 1993, for example, in its tenth edition, science is defined much as it has been throughout its ten editions as 'organized knowledge underlying the practice [of management]' (Weihrich and Koontz, 1993, p. 12), and, three paragraphs below, 'science is organized knowledge'. Without science underpinning their practice, executives must manage guided by nothing more than 'luck, intuition, or what they did in the past', something it seems that must be avoided. Science is established as the opposite of trial and error in statements such as 'In managing, as in any other field, unless practitioners are to learn by trial and error ... , there is no place they can turn to for meaningful guidance other than the accumulated knowledge underlying their practice' (ibid., p. 12).

Science is defined in the Koontz textbook as having the essential feature that it is 'the application of scientific method to the development of knowledge' (ibid., p. 12). It thus 'comprises clear concepts, theory, and other accumulated knowledge developed from hypotheses (assumptions that something is true), experimentation, and analysis' (ibid., p. 12). Concepts are 'mental images of anything formed by generalization from particulars', using words and terms that are 'exact, relevant to the things being analyzed, and informative to the scientist and practitioner alike' (ibid., p. 12). This is the base for the scientific method, which involves 'the determination of facts through observation' (ibid., p. 12). These 'facts' are classified and analysed, and causal relationships between them are sought. The causal relationships are 'generalizations or hypotheses' which should be tested for accuracy, and if they are true, in that they 'reflect or explain reality', then they are called 'principles' and have predictive value (ibid., p. 14) and are 'fundamental truths ... explaining relationships between two or more sets of variables' (ibid., p. 15). They may be predictive or descriptive, but not prescriptive, and must be blended with 'reality' by the manager. A systematic grouping of interdependent concepts and principles together form a theory which gives a framework to a 'significant area of knowledge'. In management, theory's role is the provision of a means of 'classifying significant and pertinent management knowledge' (ibid., p. 14).

Other management textbooks share this definition. It is a very restricted definition even within conventional perspectives of science. Compare it with that of Chalmers (1990), who states that the aim of the physical sciences is 'to establish highly general laws and theories applicable to the world. The extent to which those laws and theories are indeed applicable to the world is to be established by pitching them against the world in the most demanding way possible given existing practical techniques. Further, it is understood that the generality and degree of applicability of laws and theories is subject to continual improvement' (Chalmers, 1990, p. 7). The sciences call upon such characteristics as replicability in order to persuade the audience that some fact or field lies beyond matters of persuasion (Myers, 1990). Science, in its own terms, is or should be: neutral, value-free, rational, cumulative, of a privileged status, universally valid, ahistorical, and hold absolute, objective standards. In short, it must, in Wolpert's (1992) somewhat intemperate and unobjective perspective, be positivist, for scientific truth depends upon hypotheses being testable. But this line of argument, heralded by reference to Wolpert, holds the danger of being lured into the infertile battlegrounds of 'science wars' and the debates over what can or cannot be classified as science. To state that the Koontz textbook's claim to management as a science is a false claim would be both simplistic and untenable. SSK, like Foucault, warns against such easy assumptions, for scientific knowledge should be seen as but one knowledge system among many. In this perspective, rather than accusing the textbook of making a claim to a status it cannot justify, the truth claims that it does make, in the name of science, must be explored.

## Deconstructing the textbook: the 'science' of management by objectives

The Koontz textbook, in defining the science upon which management is based, should, one would assume, offer a model that develops throughout the texts its truth claim. The reader should expect to see evidence of how the results of scientific research have improved the management of organizations, showing causal relations between 'facts' that have been discovered to have predictive value, or that are descriptive, but which never are prescriptive. The theories offered should classify significant and pertinent management knowledge derived from research. Such expectations are misplaced, for the texts offer prescriptions for managerial practice that are largely supported by anecdotes and hypothetical examples, the former based usually on examples from well-known companies or from unnamed managers. There is a paucity of research-based references and little recourse to findings arrived at scientifically. To illustrate this, I have selected at random (i.e. I closed my eyes and opened the book at whichever place it chose, and analysed the chapter thus discovered) one of the 24 chapters of the 1993 edition to analyse how it uses 'science' and to trace the ways in which it develops its arguments. The chapter is Chapter 6, 'Objectives'.

The chapter opens with a scene-setting quotation. Highlighted in a blue strip, reminiscent perhaps of the sky, is the quote from Odiorne that 'Management by objectives is viewed in a larger context than that of a mere appraisal procedure. It regards appraisal as only one of several sub-systems operating within a larger system of goal-oriented management.' This quotation is set just below a stylized drawing of a globe (this edition offers a 'global perspective' on management and this drawing appears at the opening of all chapters) in which America features prominently but the other shapes that supposedly represent other continents are unrecognizable. The 'larger context' in which management by objectives (MBO) is viewed is clearly delineated in the pictorial discourse of the page – it is that of the entire world (albeit a world dominated by America outside whose shores, the vagueness of the image suggests, there be dragons). Six objectives are set for the reader which, if achieved, seem to qualify her/him to implement a successful system of MBO. None of them require the reader to argue against the concept or to rigorously critique it. Indeed, they are to be acquired as a result only of *reading the chapter*, such a passive form of encountering a text that suggests the reader is asked to let the words wash over them until they absorb them, osmosis-like, through their skins. The first page thus constructs the reader as a passive absorber of 'facts' which, when integrated into the self, will equip them to face the entire world.

The value of objectives in allowing managers to achieve their goal of creating a surplus (this is adamantly stated – there can be no other goal, and indeed the thing of which there shall be a surplus is left to the imagination – in my imagination it is a surplus of control) opens the discussion. Objectives are shown to form a hierarchy, from those of a society through those of the organization and its various parts, down to those of the individual manager[1] – the diagram which illustrates this stops at the level of 'lower-level managers', showing by their absence that only managers can have objectives. No evidence is adduced for the existence of such a hierarchy; instead there is a taken-for-granted assumption that everyone in an organization in a management position will have objectives and that these will become more important the higher up an organization is the manager located. The notion of a 'controversy' over which is the better, a bottom-up or top-down approach, is introduced and immediately resolved by an observation from 'personal experience' that a combination is necessary. The discussion is peppered with hypothetical examples.

The next section not so much explores how goals and objectives form a network but states adamantly that they do. This is illustrated by a full-page diagram. One study is cited to show that 'companies too often set goals that are unrealistic without recognizing the many constraining factors such as the economic condition or the moves by competitors' (Weihrich and Koontz, 1993, p. 146). Now there comes an observation that conflicting priorities 'must be balanced', so that managers do not pursue their own, individual objectives unless they conform to the total network of aims. Unfortunately they may not understand the overall aims, a potentially 'catastrophic' eventuality. An unnamed executive is quoted in support of the stated need for a 'matrix of mutually supportive goals'. Two 'perspectives', i.e. blue boxes containing a heading and a bullet-pointed list, illustrate how organizations *might* have a 'multiplicity of objectives'. In these we have the only major reference to science in this chapter, but it is to be found in one of the hypothetical examples, where it is suggested that an anonymous university *might* have, as one of its objectives, 'discovering and organizing new knowledge through research' (ibid., p. 148). Every level of the hierarchy will have multiple objectives, the reader is told, for managers may all be pursuing 'as many as ten or fifteen significant objectives'. Recommendations are made that appear to be 'common sense' and against which no argument could be broached.

The discussion now shifts to MBO. But look at the story that is evolving. The organization is presented as a structure that is extraordinarily complex, consisting of a hierarchy of individuals determinedly involved in goal seeking, and who each have multiple objectives. The metaphor here is of a gigantic nervous system. The potential for chaos is evident, for without clear control from a central nervous system each 'receptor' in the system may fire off in all directions.

MBO, the textbook now states, is practised around the world. However, there is confusion about what it actually is. This confusion is resolved by a clearly stated definition, i.e. MBO is 'a comprehensive managerial system that integrates many key managerial activities in a systematic manner and that is consciously directed toward the effective and efficient achievement of organizational and individual objectives' (ibid., p. 149). It is a 'system of managing'. Here the authors may be seen in the act of constructing themselves as omnipotent, all-knowing beings who can resolve at a stroke a worldwide lack of knowledge by the simple statement of a definition – the reader is thus persuaded to put more and more trust in these almighty intellects. The origins of MBO are then traced – it has no specific founder but is based (not on science but) on centuries-old common sense. Some people are mentioned who have 'speeded its development as a systematic process' (ibid., p. 149). These are Peter Drucker, who in 1954 'acted as a catalyst by emphasising that objectives must be set in all areas where performance affects the health of the enterprise' (ibid., p. 150). The General Electric Company was meanwhile using MBO. Douglas McGregor took forward Drucker's ideas in 1957, developing a 'new approach' that involved the manager as a 'coach' who 'elicits the active involvement of sub-ordinates' and thus motivates them. Several studies, almost 30 years old at the time this edition was published, are cited in support of this 'new approach'. The claim to scientific credibility becomes ever more distant. A form of 'common sense' which seems to have always existed, and is practised worldwide, has to be identified and labelled by managers who will gather it under their disciplined wing and henceforth train people in how to use this form of common-sense-now-labelled-management.

This, first, is remarkably similar to the rhetoric of science, which tells of a 'nature' that exists but remains hidden until scientists come upon *her* and expose her to the public gaze. The conclusion, it follows, is that employees can no longer be relied upon to use common sense unless they are motivated to do so by superior, managerial others. The employee constructed in these texts is truly awesome in his/her absence of any of the human graces: devoid of brain power (Braverman, 1973), subject to the lures of the flesh (see Chapter 2) and incapable even of using the most basic forms of intelligence unless organized by managers: this employee is a zombie (and are managers thus voodoo priests?), or the stereotype of the lumpen proletariat (and managers are the ones who will prevent their leading themselves to the chaos that would follow upon rule by such an empty-headed behemoth). Second, the justification of using 'common sense' rather than science betrays the earlier arguments that management is a science and uses scientific methods. Indeed, in elevating 'common sense' over science, the authors cast science into contempt.

Consider now the statement 'Researchers, consultants, and practitioners have long recognized the importance of individual goal setting' (Weihrich and Koontz, p. 150). There can be no brooking the sentiment of this statement, for opposition would require that the lowly student challenge the authoritiy of this esteemed, if anonymous, crowd. This 'importance', the succeeding sentences make clear, is in the way motivation is improved and thus productivity is raised (the two are assumed to go hand in hand). Citations from four early studies are given to support this view, but these are secondary in the task of justification, the prime role being afforded to the sweeping claim to universality. Imagine its suppressed opposite – those who are not sufficiently academic or in management posts and whom no one would bother for advice remain wandering ignorantly and aimlessly, like headless chickens. Anyone with any sense (the readers are invited to join this exclusive group) will recognize the importance of individual goal setting.

Objectives, however, the textbook warns, may be vague and focus only on the 'short term'. That this is 'undesirable management behaviour' is illustrated by three hypothetical examples, of machinery breaking down, customers turning away and failure to develop new products. The rhetorical persuasiveness of the nightmare images thus conjured must be admired. The manager's gaze should thus be to the future and also to the whole organization, for in the next paragraph the authors assert that MBO is a comprehensive system of managing.

What appears to be a practical guide to implementing MBO now follows. The prescriptions (i.e. neither based on scientific research nor on description and thus contradicting the textbook's definition of science) are summarized in the ubiquitous full-page diagram and two anecdotal examples are given in support. 'Superiors' now, rather than being trainers, must be 'patient counselors' (Weihrich and Koontz, 1993, p. 154), who help their subordinates overcome 'human nature', take responsibility for the decisions arrived at and ensure they explain that MBO 'emphasizes self-control and self-direction' (ibid., p. 162). The manager is thus equipped to recognize unreasonable demands made by employees, and there is a checklist for their use in ensuring that the objectives set are thorough, a checklist that claims to be universally applicable.

The detailed discussion ends with an exploration of the strengths and weaknesses of MBO. The reader is facilitated in understanding the perspective by learning 'from experience and research' and thus 'taking a realistic view' (ibid., p. 159), a statement that implies that research is unrealistic and must be tempered by personal experience. Further, they are encouraged in their use of MBO by anecdotal statements apparently made by unnamed executives of famous companies, all supporting MBO. The advantages are given in the form of honest-seeming platitudes, and the weaknesses are shown to be due to poor management: the weaknesses thus form part of the guidelines to implementing a programme of MBO. A series of questions for discussion and two case studies, one hypothetical and one based on the history of a large airline company, complete the story. Finally, the chapter ends with a list of references, one-quarter of which are to works by the authors of the textbook.

The rhetorical subtext of the prefaces, of chaos and disorder in a world without management, thus continues as the subtext of this chapter. This is a story of an organization that is in fact its opposite: chaos. Here there is, rather than organization, an organism whose cells are firing off in all directions and becoming cancerous. There is a pre-existing cure, but only managers have the wherewithal, in terms of knowledge and authority, to use it. Through calm and measured steps they can control the chaotic cells and ensure they all fire in the same direction, ensuring the organism becomes organization, and perpetuates itself into the future. This will be a difficult task – the text emphasizes regularly the complications involved in developing and maintaining an MBO system – but the good manager, who acts as trainer and counsellor, will not be defeated and will work his/her way through to a successful conclusion, so long as s/he recognizes the wisdom of the textbooks. The reader is reinforced in her/his understanding of a world without management. However, there is a subtle change, for scientific knowledge is not needed to achieve these delightful ends; rather common sense and the support of the textbook authors, replete with folk wisdom, gossip and common sense, are preferred.

## Patterns of analysis in the textbook

The chapter on MBO is representative of most chapters in the textbook, but some do draw more heavily on theorists and claims to research. When this happens, as in chapters devoted to motivation and leadership, there is a common structure of thesis/anti-thesis/ synthesis that serves to negate science and to promote managerial 'common sense'. This is achieved as follows.

### Thesis

The claim is put that the topic discussed is important. This claim is in the format of 'common sense' arguments given a veneer of sophistication, with generous use of anecdotes, irresistible hypothetical examples such as 'who has not felt a conflict between the time demands of a job and the desire to play golf or go to a movie?' (Weihrich and Koontz, 1993, p. 464), and references to examples from major organizations. At the end of this long discussion the student knows how important is the topic.

## Anti-thesis

This section summarizes the more ubiquitous theories in the field. Every manager, it seems, has to know about Maslow, Herzberg, Vroom and McClellan. The format for discussing each theory is a brief overview of the theory and its strengths, which is followed by a short discussion of its weaknesses or criticisms, designed ostensibly to give balance. However, the cumulative weight of this analysis is such as to render the research as either discredited or too complex to be applied by 'the manager' (and hence not much use in the 'real' world). The discussion then moves, without notice, into the synthesis, and back into the 'common sense' approach to the topic. The message of the anti-thesis is that 'scientific' research provides little assistance to the manager.

## Synthesis

Techniques that are supposedly easily available to the manager are discussed here. They include, in the chapter on motivation, money, quality of working life and job enrichment, all of which have no doubt been stimulated by the reader's assessing what motivates them after undertaking an earlier exercise to discover their 'motivators'. There is little recourse, if any, to research in this section, but much to anecdotes, hypothetical and real-life examples, appeals to 'common sense' and taken-for-granted knowledge. The manager, it is concluded, must use a 'contingency approach'. The implications are that the manager should use his/her own 'common sense', given that the scientific evidence is so contradictory, vague or impractical.

What is going on here? We have seen a powerful claim to developing management as a science, one that has shaped the development of the discipline, but when we examine the textbook in any depth we find folk wisdom, gossip and 'common sense' elevated in importance over science, so that science disappears from the discussion save in the vestigial form of recourse to a limited number of rather elderly references. Can it be that, having stated that management is a science, the rest of the textbook is suffused by a scientific glow that allows readers to think they are reading scientifically supported information? I suggest that this is so, for unless the student has studied science s/he will be unaware of the deviation from the norms of scientific analysis. Even those with scientific knowledge can be so overwhelmed by both the *credibility* of management and the seeming sheer 'common sense' of what they are reading that they are lulled into accepting the rhetoric of the management texts (Bacharova, 1999). Further, can it be that something akin to science, or more accurately what scientists do, as defined by the sociology of scientific knowledge (SSK), is taking place, in that the text is, first, constituting an orderly managerial world out of the chaotic, and second, sedimenting this supposedly orderly world under layers of rhetoric that allow the manager to carve a meaningful life world? Models from within SSK reveal that this hypothesis is, indeed, workable.

## Constitution of worlds through sedimentations in writings

Latour (1987) shows that even the 'dullest, most mechanical, most systematic and most straightforward' of laboratory processes is 'chaotic, illogical, opportunistic, contextual and constantly reconstructed' (p. 69), and so far removed is it from the world of order, logic and rationality that disorder is the very substance of science. It is the task of scientific writing to transform this disorder by giving it the appearance of order, of scientific logic. Furthermore, the existence of scientific writings allow 'facts', however arrived at, to take on a life of their own, distinct from the circumstances of their production. Every time the phenomenon is referred to as a fact its factuality becomes more firmly established, its 'out-there-ness' becomes more concrete (Woolgar, 1980). This is mirrored in the Koontz textbook, which, however, starts one stage further back in that *it brings the chaos into being* and then discursively controls it through elevating managers as the bringers of order and rationality to this now jumbled organizational world. Management theory is thus founded in a chaos of the authors' own discovery, and the manager is similarly constituted. Just like scientific writings, the textbook (1) uses rhetorical devices to construct a world that is apparently based solely on logic, and (2) sediments previous findings of a world of chaos out of which managers have wrought order.

Science, Myers (1990) has observed, is like other discourses in relying on rhetoric, although the rhetoric it uses is of a different kind. This rhetoric is highly impersonal and imbued at its essence with *logic*. In its written form, all pronouns are deleted and the passive voice is used, so that something was done, rather than somebody doing something. This 'empiricist repertoire' (Mulkay *et al.*, 1983) seems to allow the natural world to speak and act for itself, for fallible human beings are excised from the scene and science, in the guise of what Harré (1990) calls an 'impersonal engine of methodology and logic', achieves its findings. The rhetorical devices of the management textbook are largely similar – pronouns are not used and the passive voice operates – but there are some important differences, notably in that human beings do appear throughout, in the guise of the managers of the anecdotes and quotations. This can be illustrated through examining a model given on pp. 151–3 of the 1993 edition, shown on the facing page.[2]

The managers who illustrate the arguments, whether named or totally anonymous, always appear in the guise of successful implementers of

| | |
|---|---|
| For example, in one company the system was first started in a division where it was carried down to the lowest level of supervision with an inter-locking network of goals. | *Anecdotal example using passive voice* |
| Under the personal leadership and tutelage of the division general manager, it succeeded in the areas of profitability, cost reduction and improved operations. Soon, some other division managers and the chief executive became interested in, and attempted to implement, similar programs. | *Continuation of anecdote, but intrusion of managers* |

the recommended managerial practice. No hint is given of any limita-tions to their success, or problems encountered along the way. They are established, specifically so in this case, as ideal exemplars whom everyone should admire and follow. They are not fallible human beings but heroes and gods who through their success will earn adulation, recognition and disciples. Readers of the textbook are incited to follow their example.

Further, even in this adamantly non-scientific text, the rules of scien-tific writings are followed. To show this I will use a model arising out of the works of Woolgar (1980, 1988) and Gilbert and Mulkay (1980).

Scientific papers, first, incorporate a claim to be taken seriously through their very position, in a 'serious' journal. In contrast, the text-book's legitimating claims are found in the preface's suggestion, implicit throughout, that management is the most important task in the world. Scientific papers, further, guide the reader through the arguments in the way desired by the author, through the careful use of openings and headings, as, of course, does the Koontz textbook. Both scientific papers and management textbook presume an isomorphism between text and presumed reality, and use social accounting devices which claim a collec-tive belief among the scientific community on the one hand and the management community on the other.

Scientific papers use externalizing devices, such as use of the passive or semi-passive voice (it could be seen, I was able to) to suggest that the phenomena described have an existence of their own, beyond the realm of human agency, so they appear as something which is come across, perhaps almost by accident. So too in management textbooks which, as I have shown above, introduce human agents only in the form of all-powerful, aspirational managers. Scientific papers also use pathing devices which establish relationships between current and past work so that experiments appear as the latest stage of an extended process of linear-cumulative development to present a picture of a sequentially connected series of events. The very development, between 1955 and 1993, of Koontz' claim that management is a science follows this apparently linear path, as do the major and minor lessons in the textbook. In the beginning there was Taylor who was eventually overthrown by a more humanistic approach which was eventually overthrown/absorbed into a more scientific approach which was revealed as having problems so was replaced by a more encompassing scientific approach, etc. Most importantly perhaps, just as any opposing scientific perspectives are excluded from or maligned in scientific papers, so too is any perspective excised from the textbook that organizations be run in any way than under the tutellage of managers. Indeed, only one way of managing is allowed, and only one way of viewing management. There is no room for alternative perspectives, for any challenge to the view of the manager as highly rational, devoted to the organization and superior to the worker. Where an opposing view is allowed entry, it is passed over or immediately dismissed. Take, for example, the reference on p. 159 (Weihrich and Koontz, 1993) to 'A review of 185 studies [which] showed that it is rather difficult to evaluate the true effectiveness of MBO.' This contradicts the whole tenor of the discussion of MBO, it would seem, and indeed of the scientific basis of the arguments. Four sentences follow this statement, each adumbrating reasons why it is difficult to evaluate MBO. These are followed, without let, hindrance, interruption, pause or introduction, by the statement 'As pointed out several years ago – and it is still true today – if a goal-oriented management approach is to produce results, it has to be adapted to the specific situation' (ibid., p. 159). Readers are then told they must take a 'realistic' view. 'Realistic' is juxtaposed to 'science', and science is deemed the loser in this war of rhetorical devices. The authors thus slide over any possible flaws in their arguments, evading discussion, refusing argument, imposing upon the reader one world-view which, by implication, is seen as beyond challenge.

Scientific papers contain systematic and meaningful differences between the informal and formal accounts of the process of experimentation. The unique, specific actions of each individual experiment is rendered so as to appear as if it is a highly routinized activity which does not differ from invariant and legitimate scientific procedures. The laboratory is, so to speak, writ large in the management textbook in the form of 'the organization' which now appears as orderly, systematic, untouched by human emotions or failings, except those that may be threatened to erupt from those who are managed and which managers will thus control. Further, scientific texts use sequencing devices to connect described events and activities, constructing the objectivity of the fact while eliminating any other potential paths, and giving the appearance of an uninterrupted linear process (e.g. by citing evidence accruing over a number of years, in date order). Management textbooks mimic this process. In the chapter on MBO studied here, for example, Drucker's work in 1954 is referred to, followed by McGregor's work in 1959, and the chapter ends with a case study of Scandinavian Airlines that takes the reader from problems in the airline experienced in the 1970s, its turn to MBO in the 1980s and the objectives it wishes to achieve 'after 1995'. Similarly, just as science claims logic as the basis for valid inference, the management texts assert loudly that what the manager does is based on logic and any challenge to that logic is, by definition, illogical. Neither scientific papers nor management textbooks, by this device, allow alternative ways of reading the text.

In sum, readers of both scientific papers and management textbooks are engaged within a traditional version of rationality in which personal or social factors are deemed to be separable from and irrelevant to the depersonalized propositions and practices of both disciplines. Readers, whether of management textbooks or scientific papers, are prevented from exploring the possibility of alternative ways of proceeding.

In management textbooks therefore we have a claim to scientific status followed by arguments framed within rhetorical devices that mimic those of scientific papers. Management textbooks, it seems, achieve a sleight of hand, claiming the status of science without actually using science. Moreover, as I will now show, they construct a world in which to locate the manager.

## The constructivism of science and management

Science is a constructivist activity that constitutes its objects through discursively oriented social practices, in a process which can be identified as having five stages (Woolgar, 1980):

Stage 1: scientists have documents, including publications, papers, previous results, research apparatus, received opinion, etc. These documents follow the strictures of scientific writing.

Stage 2: some of these are used to project the existence of a particular object.

Stage 3: splitting occurs – the object is now perceived as an entity separate and distinct from the documents used in Stage 2.

Stage 4: inversion. The relationship between documents and objects is inverted, and the documents are used to explain the existence of the object.

Step 5: the crucial phase of the rewriting of history so as to give the discovered object its ontological foundations, i.e. the first three steps are pushed into the background, forgotten or denied.

This model, informed through a Foucauldian reading of power/ knowledge (1980), allows us to see how difficult it has become, in the space of half a century, to be able to conceive of any world other than the managed one. However, using Foucault requires an additional stage, the post-modernist stage where the discourses that speak through texts serve in the construction of identities.

### Stage 1: scientific documents which follow the strictures of scientific writing

By the late 1920s large organizations in the US were run by professional managers (Chandler, 1977), but by 1955 there was, if we take the arguments of the Koontz textbook at face value, no coherent science of management although there were so many studies, opinions and writings about management that its authors could claim the existence of a 'management theory jungle'. Although many of the papers available at that time probably would not pass muster as 'scientific', some, such as the works of F.W. Taylor, certainly laid claim to that name. There were it seems, on the one hand, writers about organizations and, on the other, organizations in which, in Foucault's analysis of power/ knowledge, capitalism had physically entrusted wealth, in the form of raw materials and means of production, directly in the hands of workers. This wealth, Foucault argued (1980, p. 41) needs to be protected, and the means of protection is a 'rigorous morality'.

The elevation of management to its present status seems at first sight to deny this statement, for management since Taylor has applied direct, external controls rather than 'rigorous morality'. However, the managerial impetus arising from the human relations school of thought, and more recently the management of quality (Willmott, 1993) and culture (Anthony, 1994), among other potential forms of control, speak of an attempt to impose such a 'rigorous morality' through disciplinary practices found in the micro-techniques of power, and through surveillance techniques ranging from cultural practices of moral endorsement, enablement and suasion to more formalized technical knowledge (Clegg, 1998). These, in Clegg's analysis, allow calculation of an organizational rationality from 'distinct auspices of power and knowledge. From such potentially discursive babel any formally efficient organization will normally attempt to construct the architectonic of some overall strategic practices of discipline. A storehouse of disciplinary techniques is available for organizations to achieve this aim' (ibid., p. 39). Here, I am suggesting, the textbook is a disciplinary technique over management.

But at the time that management textbooks started to appear, the 'discursive babel' of numerous documents, all advising ways in which organizations could be run more effectively, could be seen as a 'jungle', in Harold Koontz' terms. Managers, too, remained an unknown quantity, yet they were responsible for ensuring that the wealth physically entrusted in the hands of workers was transformed into the necessary outputs. Who could guarantee that managers would be good, compliant employees?

## Stage 2: use of documents to project the existence of a particular object

The first Koontz textbook of 1955 gathered together numerous documents that purported to describe the role of the manager within the organization. Books of readings followed shortly after the first edition. The textbooks, with their supporting readings, projected the existence of two particular objects: organizations deemed to be always already chaotic, and managers chosen to be rational and destined to be the bringers of order out of chaos. In 1955 therefore we see the bringing together in one textbook, from the vast number of papers available, a collection of arguments based on only those documents which project the desired view of organization and manager.

Here we see the start of what Foucault (1980) calls a 'rhythm of transformation' of knowledge, such as has occurred in other forms of knowledge such as biology, political economy, psychiatry and medicine. Such transformations lead to a break with previous ways of speaking and seeing which served as supports for previous regimes of knowing. These, Foucault argued, are not simply new discoveries, but a whole new regime in discourse and forms of knowledge. This led him to pose the question 'How is it that at certain moments and in certain orders of knowledge, there are these sudden take-offs, these hastenings of evolution, these transformations which fail to conform to the calm, continuist image that is normally accredited?' It is not, he suggests, a result of a change of content, such as refutation of old errors, nor a change of theoretical form, but 'a question of what *governs* statements, and the way in which they govern each other so as to constitute a set of propositions which are scientifically acceptable, and hence capable of being verified or falsified by scientific procedures' (Foucault, 1980, pp. 112–13). The problem then is one of 'the politics of the scientific statement', where knowing what external power imposes itself on science is not the main question, but rather the effects of power which circulate among scientific statements and which constitute their internal regime of power, and how and why these undergo global modifications.

In Foucauldian terms, therefore, we must ask: What politics surround a scientific statement that is not scientific? What effects of power circulate among statements that claim the status of science but then reject it in their construction of ideal practice? I suggest two processes are at work.

First, the term 'science' in Western culture is value-loaded, in that the labelling of an activity as 'scientific' or 'unscientific' has social and political ramifications which go well beyond mere taxonomy. To label a body of knowledge or a belief system as 'scientific' in Western culture is to accord it the high status and the cognitive authority of the sciences. The according of scientific status to a system of thinking about the world thus renders it not as a subjugated knowledge but rather a regime of truth, through which 'management empowers the manager and objectifies and subjects the managed, allows knowledge, power, and the body to be interrelated in the achievement of subjugation' (Ball, 1990, p. 165). Although management is, through its claim to scientific status, couched in an ideology of neutrality, it is rather a political technology which advances by taking what is essentially a political problem, removing it from the realm of politics and recasting it in the neutral language of science. The result is that what was politics becomes instead the technical problems of specialists (Dreyfus and Rabinow, 1982). Thus is power won for management (although perhaps not for the manager).

Second, the manager who is constituted through the texts, the rational, emotionless, totally loyal, automaton-like manager, is a manager who can be entrusted with the protection of the wealth that has had to be put in the hands of workers. Managers could otherwise be dangerous. They are by definition highly skilled, intelligent, the 'best for the job', potential leaders of men (and women). When Lenin called upon the bourgeoisie to lead the Communist revolution, he did so on the presumption that only the bourgeoisie would have the necessary knowledge and skills of leadership. Would the manager be the person who took good care for the profit-making ability of the organization, or could s/he not perhaps be the Pied Piper of Hamelin, entrusted with the most precious wealth and willing, if not mollified or controlled, to turn treacherous?

The manager, I suggest, has to be controlled just as much as does the worker, and the management textbook, through its 'dumbing down', its limiting of managerial knowledge within certain, unquestioning, uncritical, non-analytical bounds, its capacity to prevent the manager from learning to think (Anthony, 1986), is a controlling technique. Butler's (1997) analysis of Foucault suggests how this may be done, through the aegis of the power/knowledge nexus of the business school or university system which demands of its students that they read the management textbooks and absorb their messages.

'As a form of power, subjection is paradoxical', she commences. 'To be dominated by a power external to oneself is a familiar and agonizing form power takes. To find, however, that what "one" is, one's very formation as a subject, is in some sense dependent upon that very power is quite another' (Butler, 1997, p. 1). Butler thus allows us the prospect of exploring how the power/knowledge nexus of management and business school produce, or discursively constitute, the 'self' of the manager, the student, the academic, indeed of anyone who has an involvement with organizations. We are used to thinking of power as what presses on the subject from the outside, she states, as if it is something that subordinates, sets underneath, and relegates to a lower order. That is, however, a fair description of only part of what power does, for she follows Foucault in understanding power as *forming* the subject as well as providing the very condition of its existence and the trajectory of its desire. We therefore depend on power for our existence and what we harbour and preserve in the beings that we are. Management discourses produced in texts therefore provide the discursive conditions for the articulation of any 'we'. Subjection, Butler argues, consists 'precisely in this fundamental dependency on a discourse we never chose but that, paradoxically, initiates and sustains our agency' (ibid., pp. 1–2).

The objects projected by the documents are thus first a claimed scientific status that renders managers' position as non-political and hence closed to challenge. The second object is that of the manager her/himself, who is both a subject of the texts and subjectified by them. The potential manager reading about her/himself in the pages of the textbook, and projecting themselves forward to when they are managers enacting the world of the text, are simultaneously offered power while being subjected to that very power. Managers who might represent a challenge to the social order are constituted, through the texts, as safe, controlled, unquestioning, loyal servants, and thus they suggest the guards too can be trusted. Furthermore, with the 'dumbing down' of the texts comes the inability to think critically or to ask questions. The managerial student is, in a sense, brainwashed into acquiescence.

### Stage 3: splitting occurs – the object is now perceived as an entity separate and distinct from the documents used in Stage 2

This stage in the development of management occurred in the UK, I suggest, in the 1960s. The development of management education in Britain has been a very long and very slow process (Armstrong, 1996). The Franks Report of 1963 recommended the establishment of university-level management education modelled on American lines. The history of this Report is interesting, for it arose in part, in Armstrong's analysis, as a result of the work of the Foundation for Management Education which had been established by three people, prominent among whom was Keith Joseph. Joseph was an early apostle of what was to come to be known as the New Right philosophy that proved to be highly influential upon Margaret Thatcher's political philosophy. The introduction of management principles into the British public sector in the 1980s, in which Keith Joseph played a major part, both in his role as Education Secretary in the first Conservative administration and as *eminence gris* to Mrs Thatcher, is thus linked to the establishment of business schools in Britain, for in 1964 industry contributed £5 million and the first British business schools were established at London and Manchester. A second appeal in 1969 led to the establishment of further schools at Aston, Warwick and Bradford. Here we have the overt powers of capitalism and politics, powers that differ from Foucault's concept of micro-powers, but powers that perhaps act as catalysts that allow micro-powers to become available for activation and lead to effects not dreamed of by the catalysts.

Indeed, the power/knowledge nexus afforded by the business schools and university departments of management constituted a world of their own, distinct from that of industry, for the history of management education by this date was such, Armstrong argues, to ensure that syllabi were based on Fayolian notions that depended upon a process of abstraction in which management was defined so as to exclude much of the actual work of real life managers. Originating in the work of Henri Fayol, what Armstrong calls a 'latter-day version of the Platonic doctrine of forms' (Armstrong, 1996, p. 279) is reproduced in the vast majority of management writing since Fayol's day, resulting in discussions of management divorced from any acknowledgement of the world of the managerial worker. The result was complaints from employers about the relevance of the new degree programmes, with rebuttals from what Armstrong derides as a management education movement which appeared to develop a sense of itself as an 'apostolic elite with a mission to convert the atheistic mass of British industry' (ibid., p. 289). But at the simplest level of analysis one may ask why, if 'employers' are so averse to the products of business schools, has the MBA become one of the guarantors of 'fast-track' careers and high salaries, and why do students flock to study management degrees? Armstrong's analysis oversimplifies by setting against each other the opposites of bluff employer and supercilious academic, but more fundamentally errs in ignoring the shift in discourse that occurred with the establishment of business schools and university departments of management.

For, I suggest, the ostensible purpose of management education, i.e. to produce managers who can ensure an organization works efficiently and effectively in the achievement of its goals, is far from the actual purpose. We see, with the founding of the business schools and the development of university-level management education, a manager and an organization constituted by the textbook yet deemed to exist in their own right. It becomes the function of higher education institutions to educate raw recruits into the simulacra of the 'ideal-type' manager who will work in the 'ideal-type' organization. This is assisted by Stage 4.

## Stage 4: inversion – the relationship between documents and objects is inverted, and the documents are used to explain the existence of the object

The time is now ripe for research *in* 'organizations' to be undertaken by academics informed by the concepts contained in the canonical texts. Dale and Burrell (2000) suggest that organizational theorists require their own 'theoretical object' to help maintain and perpetuate disciplinary boundaries, provide a structured place of theorizing, mobilize resources and give the writer meaning. The organization becomes privileged as a fixed object with ontological status that is bounded from the non-organization, and real operations of power are obscured. There is now a seemingly ontologically secure object to which researchers can turn their attention through the standard process of undertaking research in the social sciences which is, of course, to begin with a literature search and review that ensures the researcher is aware of current theories and descriptions, and alert to gaps in knowledge. The literature search that reveals that 'organizational structure' is an issue allows Burns and Stalker, Joan Woodward, the Aston school and others to examine organizations and identify 'structures'. Their new theories of organizational structure become the fodder for later literature searches that inform later generations of researchers of the supposed reality of the concept, until 'structure' becomes so reified as to be carved in stone. Popular management theorists, such as Peters and Waterman (1982), may set such a train in motion by identifying the somewhat elusive factors that, they claimed, ensured organization success. In a process identified in pre-war Austria by Ludwik Fleck (Arksey, 1994), the popular may be taken up by the scientist and turned into 'real science'. Intangible elements such as 'quality', 'culture' and 'change' can thus be given the aura of tangibility; they can be taught to managers in business schools and on training programmes; they become 'real' although no one can quite define what they are (Alvesson, 1993). The 'science' of management can thus now race ahead. 'Organizations' can now exist, not in the form of the 'real' world, but in a management text that is constituting a new 'reality' of organization. Moreover, I am arguing here, managers are also now constituted through the documents of the textbook.

But it is the documents which are deemed to be 'real' and to explain organizations and their management.

### *Stage 5: the crucial phase – here occurs the rewriting of history so as to give the discovered object its ontological foundations, i.e. the first three steps are pushed into the background, forgotten or denied*

Rational management and structured organization now exist in their own right, it seems, independent of the textbook or the documents that contribute to the textbook. The result is that studies which reveal that managers do not conform to the patterns dictated by the textbook, such as the series of behavioural studies of the 1960s and 1970s that showed managers did not calmly plan, organize, staff, control and coordinate, suggest it is the manager and not the textbook that is in error, for any managers who fail to live up to the strictures of the texts are deemed to be so little in charge of themselves and their work routines that they fail to act as the textbooks dictate. Another example is found in the management of 'quality', for where its introduction proves ineffective, it is its application by management that is deemed to be at fault rather than the assumptions and prescriptions upon which quality management is based (Wilkinson and Willmott, 1995). Yet 'a great deal of management education', Roberts (1996, p. 73) writes, 'still seems to play on the insecurities and greed that wish to believe in the possibility of such managerial omnipotence, and enormous amounts of energy and suffering are generated in the attempt to make an organizational reality of such illusion'. Students meanwhile flock to study management degrees, graduation from which, they expect, will equip them to undertake well the job of manager. But the subjects they are taught, the new objects of power, are based upon the concepts of management and organizations constituted by the management sciences, worlds markedly different from the lived worlds of organizations.

### *Stage 6: the post-modern stage*

By the 1990s, the textbooks were being read by millions of students in many countries. This is the era when it is recognized that texts are used in the constituting of identities, when 'identity' is something that is manufactured by the individual, when, in Baudrillardian terms, there is no such thing as a manager but the simulacrum of a manager, an identity to which those who wish to *be* managers will aspire.

## Conclusion: the conundrum of management as science

Let me first summarize the story so far.

Readers who come new to the management textbook will find themselves assailed by a rhetoric which leads them into assuming that without management all will be chaos. Assaulted surreptitiously by this message, they will then be told that they are engaged in the study of a scientific discipline. Science, perhaps, may assuage the fears of chaos that have been awakened and make her/him determined to be one of those who will work to stave off the threatened anarchy. Lulled into the sensibility of reading works from within a body of scientific thought, they will then be rehearsed in a denigration and abjuring of that very concept. The text they read will form part of a history of development from a situation where:

- First, there were numerous organizations being managed and administered by vast numbers of people, many of whom do not have the title of 'manager'. A vast number of documents exist which discuss some of these organizations and the ways they are run.
- The authors of the first management textbooks draw selectively from the range of documents available, choosing works that represent a certain view of the world, based upon positivism and the assurances of one particular way of thinking. These authors aspire to represent a discipline that will have the status of a science of management. In their texts they project the existence of two particular objects, i.e. 'an organization' and its 'management'. The organization should be managed in one specific way. Management students in the US have access to such textbooks and, from the mid-1960s, so do students in the UK.
- By the mid-1970s the textbook authors are satisfied that they can now claim the status of science for management thinking. The existence of those objects they had earlier projected, the organization and its management, is now widely studied and the results of such research is fed into management textbooks.
- Where managers had once been the ostensible objects of study and thinking, and what they did had formed the recommendations of good practice found in textbooks, now those who do not conform to the tenets of the management textbooks are regarded by the textbooks as poor managers – the textbooks dictate what is the good manager. The popularity of management degrees starts to surge.
- The reader of the textbook uses the text to construct his/her identity as manager. This is the post-modernist era, where identities are not given but actively constructed.

This, of course, does not explain why the textbooks should make the claim that management is a science and then denigrate the very thing to which they aspire, i.e. scientific status. This is the conundrum at the heart of this chapter.

If I were writing as a modernist, I could simply argue that there is a need for a new textbook, one which removes the discrepant conundrum. Many authors have indeed done this. Armstrong's (1996) critique of the distancing of academic management from the lived world of managers is located in the modernist era, when it could be assumed that there was a 'real' organizational world which existed separate and distinct from the imagined organizational world of textbooks. Today we can assume no distinction – the realm of the book and the realm of the social are inextricably intertwined, each informing the other. We must therefore seek ways in which the distorted claim to scientific status serves to provide the conditions of existence of certain managerial identities. Similarly, when' Mintzberg (1989, quoted by Thomas and Anthony, 1996) was worried by the lack of evidence to show that management theory achieves its aims in organizations, his worries were similarly modernist, as were the arguments of Thomas and Anthony (1996) that the academic market in professional management had acquired sufficient size and synergy to 'secure its safe separation from managers' although it 'preserve[s] some indirect relationship with them in order to demarcate its academic stakeholding' (Thomas and Anthony, 1996). Thomas and Anthony saw academicians as having removed themselves to a safe distance from the world of managers, just as, Anthony has argued in an earlier work (1986), managers have removed themselves from direct contact with workers. Today, the separation of academic texts and the managerial world cannot be maintained: each is imbricated in the other. That, indeed, is the thesis of this book.

Let me return to the definition of post-modernism I used earlier (pp. 55–6), that given by Fredric Jameson. Jameson's concern is elucidating what he regards as the most advanced stage yet in the development of capitalism, post-modern capitalism. In the Marxist perspective, we should be looking at systems of control over workers, but Jameson's concern is with the cultural and so he offers little directly applicable to this argument. Foucault's work, of course, is concerned with a discovery of mechanisms of control which not only subject but subjectivize the individual. In a late interview he forecast the eventual reappearance of Marx and acknowledged that Marx was at work in his own theories (Foucault, 1994, p. 458). Could there therefore be a reconciliation of Foucault and Marx? I will, drawing upon Fredric Jameson's example, hazard such a reconciliation and argue that we are encouraged, in post-modern capitalism, to make of ourselves worker identities that are more or less attuned to the demands of capitalism.

The manager is a category of worker that is more attuned than most, I would suggest, to the subordination of identity to the requirements of work. Thus, an explanation for what I am calling the conundrum of the textbooks' claim is to be found in exploring how they work to constitute managerial identities that will subordinate themselves to the needs of the capitalist enterprise. This is important, for managers are workers who could perhaps form the most successful vanguard in a revolt against the organizational malfeasance *vis-à-vis* workers.

Thus I would suggest that the conundrum informs the psychic world of the manager in the form of constituting an always-present uncertainty. The manager is told that s/he must be a scientist, but then is told that s/he must act according to rules that oppose that identity, through using anecdote, homily, even perhaps that elusive thing called 'common sense'. The ubiquitous famous chief executives, always held up as the paragons of homespun wisdom, are the models to which the ambitious, and even the not-so-ambitious, manager must aspire. The manager must therefore, the textbooks inform her, aspire to two incompatible, even mutually exclusive, identities, and in aspiring to the one the other must fail. The manager is always therefore destined to failure. This, I suggest, produces a state in managers of an always-present uncertainty, for no matter what they do they cannot be doing it right and these are people, let us remind ourselves, whose *raison d'être* is 'doing it right'. The internal world of the manager is therefore one of an ever-threatening sense of failure, of chaos, which contradicts the demands to be successful and to control chaos.

These tensions will render the manager pliable, for the manager will forever be trying to attain one or other status and, in always being doomed to failure, must try harder and harder to roll the rock of control up the slippery hill of chaos. In psychoanalytical terms, the manager will project this inner chaos and turmoil onto the organization and seek firmer control of the organization, and thus of the inner self (Gabriel, 1999). The more uncertain the manager feels in her identity *qua* manager, the more s/he will try to conform to the ideal of 'the manager' and the more s/he is opened to control by the organization. Rebellion is out of the question: the manager in seeking to become the perfect manager becomes utterly controllable.

Thus the seeming conundrum behind the textbooks' claim that management is a science is resolved within the managerial psyche which, penetrated by post-modern capitalism (Jameson, 1991), becomes the ultimate locus of organizational control.

# 4 Management as legal authority

## Introduction

Koontz and O'Donnell petitioned for management's overarching role on the basis of four claims to truth: that management is art, science, heteronormative rationality and founded in legal authority. For this last, until 1976 when the issue started to disappear from their discussions, they claimed that managerial authority is embedded within a 'right to manage' given by delegated authority from shareholders and thus the law of property in particular, and the legal system more generally. They devoted a chapter in their textbook to 'proving' this assertion. By the sixth edition of the textbook this argument had disappeared. Koontz and O'Donnell were not alone in this nonchalant treatment of their recourse to law, and indeed there is a pattern in many textbooks of the period. It seems management's right to manage was by the late 1970s so entrenched, so taken for granted, that the case no longer needed arguing. That at least is one reading of the cause of the disappearance of the chapter. However, I have suggested that the changes which took place in the textbook in the 1970s heralded the start of a shift from the modern to the post-modern. In this chapter I will show how the changes in the articulation of claims to legal status were part and parcel of the inauguration of the textbook as *producer* of the objects of which it speaks – managers and management.

With regard to law, the developments I am exploring involve the lingering trace of the claim to legal authority, and the transmutation of that claim from textual into material practices. I have in front of me as I write copies of three disciplinary procedures drawn from very different organizations. These, I will show, reveal that law operates at the workplace, a law in which managers form the law-makers, judiciary, police officers and investigators. However, the overarching law, the law of the state, has not disappeared but leaves its trace, transmogrified into the law of the phallus, for the law serves not only as a means of managerial control over the enterprise, but also as a means of control of the manager.

This chapter will begin by exploring Koontz and O'Donnell's arguments in more depth, including comparisons with other textbooks to show that the changes in references to the law was a shift that occurred in management textbooks more generally. My aim in the discussion that follows, which explores disciplinary procedures, is not a discovery of the putative reasons for the change from external to internal models of law, but the unravelling of the material practices that have become available in organizations through the claim to law, whereby the manager's body is seen as inscribed as law. The discussion will then move on to an analysis of jurisprudence, which similarly shows a shift from the modernist to post-modernist understandings of law. Arguments from within critical legal studies will allow the development of the second part of the arguments in this chapter, that management is not only law in practice, but is itself subjected to law, but now to phallic law. I will show that the discourse of law within the organization is one that brings into being the patriarchal and phallocentric manager who is at the same time subjectified and impotent.

## The disappearing chapter

Authority, for Koontz and O'Donnell in 1968, had a 'standard definition' which was 'legal or rightful power, a right to command or to act' (p. 59). In the managerial job, it is 'the power to command others, to act or not to act in a manner deemed by the possessor of the authority to further enterprise or departmental purpose' (ibid., p. 59). It was 'the key to the management job' as 'since managers must work through people to get things done, management theory is necessarily concerned with a complex of superior–subordinate relationships and is therefore founded on the concept of authority. In the manager of a company, division, department, branch, or section is vested power sufficient to force compliance, whether through persuasion, coercion, economic or social sanctions, or other means' (ibid., p. 59). The authors distinguish between two theories of the source of authority: acceptance theory wherein subordinates *accept* the manager's orders, a theory dismissed by Koontz and O'Donnell, and formal authority theory. This latter theory sees this 'legal or rightful power' as having its 'ultimate source . . . principally in the institution of private property'. The 'bounds and content' of private property rights are defined by social institutions, may be traced to 'elements of basic group behavior' but '[m]ost formal authority theorists emphasize the legal aspects of private property as the source of authority, though good sociological analysis would broaden the source to include all related social institutions' (ibid., p. 61). It should be noted that their concept of 'good sociological analysis' does not include pursuing understanding of authority through an analysis of sociological writings on authority. They conclude:

Under our democratic form of government the right upon which managerial authority is based appears to have its primary source in the Constitution of the United States. Since the Constitution is the creature of the people, subject to amendment and modification by the will of the people, it follows that the total society, through government, is the source from which authority flows to ownership and thence to management. Indeed, the entire social institution of private property is molded not only by the Constitution, but by many federal and state legislative and administrative regulations, and by the mores of the entire American society.

(ibid., p. 61)

They were not alone in this claim. Many textbooks published before the 1980s deemed it so necessary to argue the case for managerial legitimacy that they devoted entire chapters to its exploration. Haimann and Scott (1970), for example, allotted a chapter to authority. They defined it as 'a difficult concept and one which we should lead into gently' but *interpreted* it as 'an attribute of a managerial position in an organization' (Haimann and Scott, 1970, p. 189). It is an 'impersonal feature of the organizing activity'; its source, they hint, is lost in the mists of time, for 'early students of management took authority for granted and had little doubt about its nature, purpose, and origin. To them it was a necessary building stone in the formation of an organization' (ibid., p. 189). As in Koontz and O'Donnell's case, they find the 'ultimate source of managerial authority in America' in the Constitutional guarantee of the institution of private property. The Constitution is, they write, quoting an earlier textbook on management, 'the creature of the people, subject to amendment and modification by the will of the people' (ibid., p. 190). Further, without authority there can be no organizations for 'without the delegation of authority, there are no subordinates and hence no organization exists' (ibid., p. 194). However, authority is delegated to positions rather than people. Haimann and Scott make no reference to Weber's theories of bureaucracy and rational–legal authority, although their text is impregnated with them. In an early demonstration of incestuous reflexivity, their references and their recommended 'supplementary readings' are all to other management writers, and they and their readers remain ignorant of the theorists from the social sciences who have influenced their analysis.

The texts used by students in the first two decades of management degree courses therefore pondered upon the legitimacy of managerial authority, and indeed went to some lengths to prove it. By 1983 Burack and Mathys, writing an introductory text to management focusing upon 'a career perspective', like Koontz and O'Donnell by that date did not feel the necessity of including a chapter on authority. Single paragraphs now appear that summarize the earlier, chapter-length arguments. More recently Daft (1997), writing from an American perspective, midway through his book devotes a paragraph to the issue. He defines managerial authority as 'the formal and legitimate right of a manager to make decisions, issue orders, and allocate resources to achieve organizationally desired outcomes' (p. 320). This authority has, for Daft, three characteristics: (1) it is vested in organizational positions rather than people; (2) it flows down through the vertical hierarchy; and (3) it is accepted by subordinates. Acceptancy theory, criticized by writers in the 1970s, is here used by Daft to justify and explain his last characteristic. The British rendering of this argument is given by Cole (1995) who defines authority as 'the legitimate power to act in certain ways' (p. 152). The use of the word 'legitimate' features strongly in Cole's as in other writers' texts, but definitions and exploration of it as a concept are not to be found. A generation of British personnel managers will have read Thomason's (1988, p. 113) professorially legitimated and sombrely intoned injunction that 'Many of society's main cultural values and imperatives for action are embodied in law. . . . Because society places a high value on both the generation of wealth and its distribution through the employment relationship, the law closely structures the relationship by defining rights in or ownership of real personal property and in labour.'

This thing called 'law' is left unquestioned, unchallenged, as something standing above and beyond both society and critique.

The topic is ignored even in management texts aimed at the narrow group of managers whose status is not automatically regarded as legitimate, such as those working in the NHS. When management replaced administration in the NHS in the 1980s its authority was, as it continues to be, challenged by the medical and other health professions, the media and the public (Learmonth, 1998). Of the texts devoted to health management, one of the more weighty, in terms of pounds and ounces rather than intellectual content, is La Monica's *Management in Health Care. A Theoretical and Experiential Approach* (1990), an American text adapted for the British market by Philip Morgan. Dr La Monica adopts a somewhat cavalier approach to the history of management thinking: readers are told, in a reading of management history which one can only admire for its insouciant approach to accuracy, that classical theorists developed their principles at 'the turn of the century'. With the exception of a passing reference to authority as legitimate power (La Monica, 1990, p. 202), she expunges all analysis of authority from her text, although the concept of power is given a chapter to itself. Power is treated as a resource available to 'managers and leaders' who should be 'astutely able and willing to put its forces to work effectively in accomplishing specified goals. A manager without such ability and willingness is relatively impotent' (ibid., p. 199).[1] The climate in which British health service managers work requires a somewhat more rigorous analysis of sources of authority, yet instead they are treated to a discussion, devoid of analytical content, of how to 'structure' an organization using a choice of 'several design options'.

Managerial authority was therefore claimed until two decades ago to rest in legal authority, but the whole debate regarding their authority has now disappeared from management texts. In a short period of time the legitimacy of their position appeared to move beyond need for proof. Yet the law continues to resonate through management, as I will now show, for the examples of organizational disciplinary procedures I am analysing here signal the continued relationship between management and law, albeit in a context in which managers now act as the entire judicial system – law-makers, police officers, investigators, judges and juries – of the organizations in which they work. Where the textbooks looked outside the organization to the overarching law of the state, managers today work with a law that has been internalized within the organization.

## Law in action: the organizational juridical system

In Britain, since the Industrial Relations Act of 1971, employees have had the right to appeal to a tribunal against unfair dismissal. The Advisory, Conciliation and Arbitration Service (ACAS) provides guidelines for organizations establishing a disciplinary procedure which, if followed, allows organizations facing a claim of unfair dismissal to prove in their defence that they have fair and proper procedures. Organizations, in following these guidelines, will typically encapsulate their disciplinary procedures in policy documents which contain: details of the types of offence that will merit disciplinary action; a list of actions that will be undertaken in exploring the accusation of breach of the disciplinary code; details of the persons who will participate in the procedures; and penalties that will follow a finding of transgression.

The three examples of disciplinary procedures I am examining are drawn from various organizations and are typical of the many dozens I have seen previously in a role as assessor of students studying human resource management by distance learning, one mechanism through which knowledge of disciplinary procedures is disseminated.

Typically, the policies commence with a statement of the purpose of disciplinary procedures, i.e. the purpose is not to punish but to assist employees to reach 'high standards of performance and behaviour'. Activities that will lead to a charge of indiscipline tend to be categorized according to the severity of the punishment that will be inflicted upon transgressors. 'Gross misconduct', which can lead to summary dismissal, includes the following actions:

- theft, fraud and deliberate falsification of records;
- fighting, assault on another person;
- deliberate damage to company property;
- horseplay and practical jokes;
- serious incapacity caused by the effects of alcohol or being under the influence of illegal drugs;
- serious negligence that causes unacceptable loss, damage or injury;
- a serious act of insubordination;
- sexual or racial harassment;
- unauthorized absence;
- wilful breach of confidential information.

Less serious offences include:

- insubordination (refusal to carry out a reasonable and lawful instruction);
- obstructive or disruptive behaviour (physical or verbal);
- unauthorized use of official vehicles;
- lateness;
- loss of or damage to property;
- poor performance of duties;
- failure to wear uniform;
- poor appearance;
- disregard of no smoking policy;
- use of company stationery for private purposes.

Even a cursory perusal of this list demonstrates that many actions that are perfectly acceptable in the home or in most places outside the workplace, and which would not be punishable in a court of law, now become rules which must be followed on pain of discipline. Moreover, the loose definitions allow degrees of latitude in interpretation that seem to contradict law's stated aims of equity and fairness.

Actions to be taken following the occurrence of an incidence of misconduct are then listed. These tend to follow strictly ACAS guidelines, i.e. the procedure is divided into distinct stages:

- informal stage involving 'counselling' and verbal discussion, with a note to be kept on the employee's file and an agreement reached as to what improvement the employee should make in his/her behaviour;
- a verbal warning which follows if improvement has not been achieved, with a note of the warning kept on the employee's file for six months;
- a written warning, again with a note kept on file for six months;

- a final written warning, a copy of which is to be kept on file for one year; and, finally,
- dismissal.

Disciplinary interviews will be held at each stage, although that held at the 'counselling' stage is informal. The term 'counselling' is rarely defined. Triggers for the next stage are activated if an employee fails to improve his/her performance. Employees are entitled to be accompanied by another employee or a trade union representative at these interviews. Managers will previously have carried out an investigation of the alleged incident(s), and witnesses may be called. The 'interview' takes place, followed by an adjournment during which the manager arrives at a decision as to whether or not misconduct has been proved, any mitigating circumstances will be weighed, and appropriate penalties, if any, determined. Managers are warned to call a break in proceedings if any intrusion of emotion, such as crying or anger, on the part of the defendant/worker, is seen, again reinforcing the seemingly rational and non-emotional nature of the procedure. However, note that this advice constructs the manager as rational, logical, in control, and the worker as a hotbed of seething emotions that are only loosely controlled under a veneer of civilization. Employees have the right to appeal against the decision of any disciplinary interview. The manager hearing the appeal should not have been involved previously in this disciplinary procedure. Details of who has power to issue penalties are included: the more senior the manager the more severe is the penalty that s/he may impose.

It can immediately be seen how closely these procedures mimic our common-sense notions of how the law proceeds – a violation of acceptable norms is perceived; an investigation undertaken; the miscreant, assisted by a third party, tried by a judge; a decision as to innocence or guilt arrived at after due deliberation; and punishment, after appeals procedures have been exhausted, meted out. They too follow Weber's sociological definition of law:

> An order will be called law if it is externally guaranteed by the probability that coercion (physical or psychological), to bring about conformity or avenge violation, will be applied by a staff of people holding themselves specially ready for that purpose.
>
> (Weber, 1954, quoted in Hunt and Wickham, 1994, p. 99)

The major differences between these procedures and those that take place in a court of law are in the qualifications of the people who enact the procedures. In the national legal system an officially state-sanctioned body undertakes the investigation and another such body the hearing, each served by people who are highly trained and experienced in the duties of, respectively, investigation and judicial judgement or, in other words, constructing the life-world of the law. The organizational legal and judicial system meanwhile involves the undertaking of investigation and hearing by line managers who are next in superiority to the accused. However, the state sanctions managers to avenge violation of organizational rules, so long as the managers themselves follow rules claimed to ensure equity and fairness. The state thus delegates its authority for the maintenance of the law, and indeed allows a broadening of the definition of what is and is not legally acceptable conduct, for behaviours which would hardly trouble a court of law can result in the loss of job if they take place within the workplace.

But there is more taking place here than analogies. Legal interpretation always involves 'discovery' and 'invention', and always involves the justification, and not merely the perpetuation, of the norms embodied in past decisions (Cornell, 1995). In the courtroom/disciplinary interview the judge/manager is involved in the process of compiling a narrative of the events which led the defendant/worker to be summoned before this hearing. Scattered events are gathered together and constructed into a narrative. Ricoeur (1981, cited in Douzinas *et al.* 1991) argued that events become story through the process of emplotment, where a story is made out of events, and an event is therefore more than a single occurrence but something that contributes to the development of a plot. A story is more than an enumeration of events – it makes an intelligible whole of the incidents and provides it with its 'theme'. In these courts of law the narrative constructed out of episodes is then judged against the narrative of what the society/workplace should be like. The court hearing/disciplinary procedure becomes a story set within the context of a wider story, that of society. Derrida, Cornell (1995) argues, 'wants us to see that what masks itself as simple discovery is in fact discovery through a projection of *the ought to be*' (p. 253, emphasis added). This is because we 'project forward the truth of the past of the never has been as the "ought to be"'(ibid., p. 254). Derrida argued that:

> The memory we are considering here is not essentially oriented toward the past, toward a past present deemed to have really and previously existed. Memory stays with traces, in order to "preserve" them, but traces of a past that has never been present, traces which themselves never occupy the form of presence and always remain, as it were, to come – come from the future, from the *to come*.
>
> (1986, quoted in Cornell, 1995, p. 254)

In Cornell's words, 'when we remember the past we do so through the "ought to be" implicit in the not yet of the never has been' (ibid.,

p. 261), an 'ought to be' to which we cannot avoid appealing (ibid., p. 262). Jameson (2002) similarly argues that the present requires for its own understanding that we look to the future as a 'Utopian space of projection and desire, of anticipation and the project' (p. 26) and our anticipation of how that future will judge us when we are its past. We thus draw upon an idealized past or an idealized elsewhere which we project onto the future and which we strive to see created and recreated. Applied to disciplinary procedures the normative, idealized narrative is of the 'ought to be' workplace where emotion and nature are eliminated and the manager is in total, rational control. Employees who introduce emotions, the physical world of the body and irrationality into the workplace can be tried for indiscipline and judged against this ideal. Where they bring their emotions and their indiscipline into the courtroom of the disciplinary hearing they must be silenced (the hearing suspended) until they have learned to deport themselves in the acceptable, controlled manner. Here, 'the law' of the workplace is homologous with laws of modern societies, for Hart, one of jurisprudence's foremost modernist thinkers, saw the emergence of a legal system out of pre-existing laws as the move from pre-modernity into modernity. This transition is a strategic device of some significance, argue Douzinas *et al.* (1991), for whom Hart needed to create a fictional 'pre-modern' world to establish the modern's specificity and demonstrate its progressive character. The pre-modern is thus the creation of the modern, a trick of reversals they see as characteristic of much modernist jurisprudence. We see similarly in the management text of disciplinary procedures this attempt to eradicate the 'pre-modern', the irrational, the uncontrolled, from the workplace. It is part neither of the misremembered past nor the future 'ought to be'.

There is therefore a judicial system at the level of the organization mimetic of that of the state system, a legal system in which laws are passed which establish standards of self-discipline required under modernity. That is, this form of law lays down rules which require behaviour inside the enterprise to be serious, disciplined and unlike that which could be acceptable or forgivable in other fora: fighting, horseplay and practical jokes, negligence, insubordination, wilful breach of confidential information, obstructive or disruptive behaviour (physical or verbal), loss of or damage to property, poor performance of duties, failure to wear uniform, poor appearance, disregard of no smoking policy and use of company stationery for private purposes. Further, behaviour outside the workplace must not be allowed to affect behaviour within it. Employees must not incapacitate themselves through drinking too much or taking drugs before arriving at work, oversleep, live lives that affect the way they perform their duties, dress badly or, indeed, take command of the way they spend their time without reference to others. They should conform to an exemplar of the 'ought to be' worker – an automaton totally committed to rational organization. This is not, of course, to imply that they do such a thing, only that they are required to do it.

Organizations, through the law of the enterprise, thus reach out their tentacles into their workers' private lives, seeking to ensure employees discipline themselves in their personal lives. Workers must keep themselves sober, undrugged, living a lifestyle that allows them to be in work by the due time, which does not involve transgressions of the criminal law, etc. It does not matter that disciplinary procedures are rarely used, nor that managers dread the time-consuming and costly process and seek to avoid it if they can:[2] the very fact that the procedures exist is sufficient to act as a warning and to constitute the discursive practices of the workplace.

The disciplinary procedure is but one of a range of tools available to managers, either directly or via personnel management, to discipline the interior of the organization through governance of time, space and movement within it (Townley, 1998). Townley has subjected to the Foucauldian gaze several of personnel management's micro-technologies that enable the exploring, knowing and regulating of the worker. We can add disciplinary procedures to Townley's array of micro-technologies. They are management's recourse when other technologies of the self have seemingly failed in producing the disciplined individual, when what appears to be pre-modernity breaks through and challenges the rationality of modernity. Further, as I have shown, they reach out beyond the workplace and into a person's private life.

Why do managers arrogate to themselves this right to become the judicial system within an enterprise? Why does it appear so natural, so acceptable, that they should? The answer to these questions is to be found, I suggest, in law's status as a regime of truth. As such, law lays down seemingly implacably binary opposites: what is legal and what is not, what is to be punished and what pardoned, what can or cannot be subject to redress; it is a discourse that claims not only to reveal the truth but to authorize and consecrate it (Hunt and Wickham, 1994). Law, as enacted in the enterprise, is a discursive practice arising out of a form of power/knowledge that has achieved a power far greater than many others, but a power that is neither an effect of a human subject and its volition nor of some overarching structure (Clegg, 1998). It is a discourse spoken through the managerial subject. Although Foucault devoted little attention to law, it is inescapable that it is a form of knowledge, like medicine, from whose gaze and rulings no one can subsequently escape (Foucault, 1973). Further, Foucault presented discipline and law as dual but opposing processes operating within modernity, with discipline operating independently of law. Seeing law as located in the pre-modern period where law was part of the might of the sovereign, he wished to abandon it to history. In this he ignored law's claim to truth and its implications as a practice available in constructions of power/knowledge, its potential as an internalized mechanism of control, and the way in which it can become inscribed upon the bodies of those who practise it.

## Modernist and post-modernist law

### Law as Enlightenment project

The discourse of law available to the manager on the Clapham omnibus is one that accedes to law the power to right wrongs – law is a force for good, so legitimate is its place in the order of things that it has the power to legitimize others' place in the order of things (Smart, 1989). This pervasive perspective, shared by citizen and practitioner alike, comes from a tradition of law that was until recently dominated by legal positivism. Legal positivism stakes its truth claims by arguing that law is a human creation which can be studied and understood by adopting the objectivity-seeking methodologies of the 'natural' or 'physical' sciences. Hart, widely regarded as the foremost legal positivist of modern times, summarized possible tenets of legal positivism as follows: laws are commands of human beings; there is no necessary connection between law and morals, i.e. law is as it is and ought to be; a legal system is a closed logical system in which correct legal decisions can be arrived at through logical analysis of predetermined legal rules, and moral judgements are inferior to law, being incapable of being established or defended through rational argument, evidence or proof (Morrison, 1997, p. 5). In this perspective, law becomes a mutable human instrument, a tool, an instrument of the modern state, a force for the good.

This is, of course, the modernist perspective of law: law is seen primarily as a system of rules organized within a pluralist framework comprising a set of stacked legal systems or spheres (Benton, 1994) which will ensure the Enlightenment project achieves its ends in the social world. This perspective claims for itself a long pedigree, indeed Sabine (1951), writing just before Koontz and O'Donnell started work on their first edition, made the irresistible claim that law stretched back to the Middle Ages where it was 'rather like a circumambient atmosphere which extended from the sky to the earth and penetrated every nook and cranny of human relationships ... Literally all law was felt to be eternally valid and in some degree sacred' (Sabine, 1951, p. 194). Pospisil's (1971) anthropological approach saw law as a system of social control consisting of two overarching types: customary or that law internalized by the members of a social group and thus considered by them to be binding; and authoritarian, which is a law elevated as an ideal by a strong minority. Societies, he argued, are made up of many social groups or subgroups and as a consequence in a given society there will be as many legal systems as there are functioning social units, and law is one of the organizing principles of all societies. Immediately the resonance can be seen of this standpoint of law for early writers of management textbooks, ignorant though they may have been of the finer details of jurisprudence. The law is omnipotent, omnipresent, eternally valid, endlessly benevolent.

The belief propounded in this purview is that law should be the law of the people, an assumption whose roots date back to ancient Greece and stretch forward to Thomason's (1988) above-mentioned injunction to personnel managers that 'Many of society's main cultural values and imperatives for action are embodied in law.' Being the law of the people (a definition that in ancient Greece excluded women and slaves, an inconvenience that had long been brushed under the carpet until feminism lifted the rug to expose the hidden embarrassment), it was in effect the beliefs and wishes of the male citizens of the city states that defined how society should be ordered (as continues to be the case, as we shall see). Hence the law was, *ab initio*, the will of the (male) people incarnate. It remained so, so this narrative of law continues, even in the 'Dark Ages' following the fall of Rome, when the Germanic tribes who spread over Europe carried with them their own laws. The law was then conceived of as 'belonging to the folk, or the people, or the tribe, almost as if it were an attribute of the group or a common possession by which the group was held together ... Germanic law in this early state was never written but consisted of customs perpetuated by word of mouth and constituting, as it were, the wisdom by which the peaceful life of the tribe was carried on' (Sabine, 1951, p. 194). In the Middle Ages, all law was still felt to be eternally valid and in some degree sacred. So too with the common law of England, literally the law of the 'common man' as it is seemingly, in the eyes of the judges charged with its interpretation, a systematic representation of what the citizen feels should be the law in *his* society. Grounded in the will of the people, the law simultaneously can claim for itself a status equivalent to that of the sciences.

How apposite this narrative appears for textbook writers building the foundations upon which the edifice of management can rise. That a legal system should operate within the workplace as but one part of the whole, benevolent legal system seems to promise the stability, the justness, the justice, of our common heritage. It is, of course, although traditional experts of jurisprudence would have it otherwise, an edifice built upon myths, involving, like all myths, a birth story, a tale of genesis, of origins and identity (Fitzpatrick, 1992).

The 'real' that is created by the myth of the law is a world where all things can be reduced to the statements of the law, for nothing can exist outside the law. This is a law that claims that its aspirations are to be benign, equal, judicial; it seeks to become discursively and administratively more sophisticated day by day (ibid., p. xiii). These claims conceal the profound inequalities and powers of negation upon which it is built. Myths so powerfully influence the ways in which we perceive, articulate and act in our worlds that critique is rendered difficult so limited are the discourses available to us. In law, indeed, the modernist perspective remains so embedded that critical assessment is made difficult for it makes 'an awkward scaffold for observed behavior, so that we begin to feel like early astronomers mapping heliocentric orbits on a geocentric universe' (Benton, 1994, p. 224). Writers within critical legal studies (CLS), however, seek to develop an understanding of law informed with a post-modernist inflection. They ask 'What if law is not like this? Or rather, what if we can think its hold on us differently? Trying to think our relationship to a legislative concept differently may be a necessary step in transforming lived 'reality'.

## Law as discourse

One of the earliest critiques of the established perspective of law that I have come across is Grace and Wilkinson's (1978) argument in favour of the law as social construction. Law, they argued, attains a social character and exists as a resource for social action only as a result of the intersubjectivity of the social world. Here, the apparent objectivity of law is an achieved status that has no existence independent of individual states of consciousness, its apparent factual existence is established and sustained in social action.

Grace and Wilkinson's work ushered in an era of critique which has dented a jurisprudential imagination that has sought to reinforce the desire for rational mastery of the social world. Morrison (1997), for example, wishes to explore the types of (non-)knowledge excluded from the rules of the 'mainstream jurisprudential game'. Law's claim to an 'objective scientific method' has been challenged, legal positivism's dominance over interpretative understanding or hermeneutics disputed, underlying fissures, contradictions and tensions revealed, the inescapably political nature of law exposed, and scepticism developed towards any claim for the purity of law. All these add up to an explanation of how law as a field of action maintains its hold over the social world and thus becomes a significant constituent in the production and reproduction of human subordination and domination (Hunt, 1993). Law is seen in this perspective as one among many systems of meaning which appear to prove that hierarchical relations within society are natural and necessary. It becomes regarded as a political process in which social relations are continually being negotiated, and human hopes and ideas distorted and truncated. Ideological, in the Althusserian sense of ideology as a constituent of the unconscious of social individuals, it is not an external mechanism of regulation but is internalized by individuals for whom it becomes a guide to social relations (Hunt, 1993).

Within the context of Foucault's intertwining of power/knowledge, Leonard (1995) suggests that the law should be understood as a discourse of power/knowledge, i.e. a complex apparatus or mechanism of power which produces and is produced by the hegemonizing knowledge and truth necessary for the existing order. The law, furthermore and importantly, is positioned so that it may produce the discourse of its own legitimacy, and in doing this it also produces and circulates a discourse of discipline. The law is thus a system of knowledge, or a 'truth machine'. Rules of law, in this interpretation, should be seen as cultural signifiers of power struggles, as a form of domination. Law is therefore 'a massive field of discursive productions – involved in producing, namely, the truths of legitimacy' (Leonard, 1995, p. 144). Where opposition arises it is challenged by further systems of rules which are developed to reinscribe but another form of hegemony. Here we have that concept of 'legitimacy' again, and we are dragged back to Koontz and O'Donnell's original claim to the use of law. Just by using the law at the level of the enterprise managers make a claim to the legitimacy of their status. That this claim is rarely refuted testifies to the power of managerial discourse to, in Foucault's words, invert the meaning of the original claim to law. For law masks domination and is a vehicle of legitimization (Hunt and Wickham, 1994).

Hunt and Wickham (1994) discern a hint in Foucault's writings that law is *constitutive* of the forms of modern power that began emerging in the eighteenth century, in that where disciplinary powers arise that are external to law, law responds by seeking to control or recode them as law. Such processes, they point out, have been aptly described as 'juridification', for non-legal forms of discipline acquire legalistic characteristics. Importantly for this present analysis, they use the law of the workplace as an example. Institutional rules such as those to be found at the workplace, they write, 'not only come to be couched in legal language but evoke legalistic procedures, such as the right of representation and rights of appeal' (ibid., p. 48). Labour discipline furthermore has, in the twentieth century

> seen the growth of juridification through the proceduralisation of work discipline that operates alongside the Taylorist economic devices, such as the piece-work system, regulating the intensity and quality of work-activity. At every stage in the complex history of the regulation of labour, legal mechanisms and devices have operated alongside the disciplinary 'counter-law' or 'underside of law' that Foucault highlights.
>
> (ibid., pp. 65–6)

In sum, the post-modernist interpretation sees law as constitutive of modern forms of power, and one of these forms of power is a managerial discourse which has resulted in the juridification of the workplace. Law, as a regime which is able to produce the discourse of its own legitimacy, bestows this mantle upon other practices that call upon law, and this is where the relationship between Koontz and O'Donnell's call to law and managerial enactment of law at the workplace is reconciled. In making the claim that the legitimacy of managerial authority rested in law, the textbooks first made the connection between law and management, one which heralded the leap from text to materiality, i.e. the juridification of the workplace. The law of the workplace is a system of meaning that has become an internalized mechanism of control, operative whenever someone says 'I won't have another drink – I'm working tomorrow' or 'That TV programme is on too late – I have to get up for work in the morning'. It is a form of power available to managers. It is unimportant that it is rarely called upon in practice, and that managers dislike the process of disciplinary procedures. Just like the panopticon it does not always have to be occupied: the possibility of its use is good enough. But it is not only the existence of the mechanism as an external form of control and its subsequent internalization that are important: its construction of the manager and the worker, the one as law-maker and keeper, the other its opposite, marked as always potentially a law breaker, cannot be ignored.

And thus we see the construction of the manager as legal authority within the workplace. But there is more to this *trace* of the legitimacy sought in law, for not only is the manager law in action, so to speak, s/he is also subjected to the law but a more subtle, more all controlling law, the law of the Father.

## Managerial subordination to the phallic law

It is feminist jurisprudence that has revealed the gendered nature of law, but feminist jurisprudence tends to presume the existence of one all-encompassing model of the male that is deemed applicable to all those who wear their genitalia externally. In this section I wish to use feminist jurisprudence to show the gendered nature of law as hegemonic masculinity, but then read that through a queer theory lens to argue that the male law castrates those over whom it has domain, reducing them all, effectively, to the status of the abject Other. Where this Other is for feminist theoreticians female, and for queer theorists homosexual, here I will argue that the Other is the Other of 'the organization', i.e. the human actors. (In queer theory, the very terms 'male' and 'female' are opened to question, and they are therefore used here carefully, as overly familiar signifiers that need to be separated in some degree from their signifieds.) Queer theory allows an exploration of how the manager is subordinated to the phallic and phallocentric law.

Let us begin with Carol Gilligan's (1997) influential research which suggests that the ethics of the law are gendered as male. She found that women have an ethic of care (i.e. no one should be hurt) and men an ethic of rights (that everyone should be treated equally). There will therefore be differences in the ways the two sexes judge legal and moral dilemmas, leading to inequality at the base of a range of types of law, from tort to taxation. Look again at the list of transgressions that can lead a worker to be summonsed before the organizational court of law. Actions that are categorized as 'gross misconduct' and thus lead to summary dismissal include theft, fraud and deliberate falsification of records; fighting and assault; deliberate damage to company property; horseplay and practical jokes; serious incapacity caused by the effects of alcohol or being under the influence of illegal drugs; serious negligence that causes unacceptable loss, damage or injury; a serious act of insubordination; sexual or racial harassment; unauthorized absence; and wilful breach of confidential information. Less serious offences include: insubordination (refusal to carry out a reasonable and lawful instruction); obstructive or disruptive behaviour (physical or verbal); unauthorized use of official vehicles; lateness; loss of or damage to property; poor performance of duties; failure to wear uniform; poor appearance; disregard of no smoking policy; and use of company stationery for private purposes. The 'masculine voice of moral judgement' (Smart, 1989) permeates through and through this list of transgressions. There is no sanction for failing to respect one's colleagues, for failing to provide care, to treat people with respect and dignity, unless of course they happen to be managers, and thus one's 'superiors'. Those things valued by those who elevate care above rationality can be transgressed without fear of punishment. Indeed, many actions of managers could result in their being hauled before an organizational court of law if a more femininized list of 'crimes' were listed. Where then would be the managers who have participated so actively in 'downsizing', restructuring and organizational mergers that result in profound distress even to those who have retained their jobs, who exhibit symptoms of 'survivor syndrome' and extreme emotional disturbance (Ford and Harding, 2004). Surely these are transgressions against humanity that in a world not built upon such a restricted model would be regarded as criminal?

However, to continue the argument that it is some metaphysical masculinity which is to blame for this state of affairs is to avoid findings ways of reducing the inequalities. Before challenging this perspective of masculinity and its enactment within law, let me first outline some further feminist critiques of the law, for they are important to this argument, albeit as stepping stones to the conclusion.

As its most extreme, and most open to critique, is Catherine MacKinnon's (1989) argument which sees law as the sexual relationship writ large. She writes 'Man fucks women; subject verb object' (p. 124). It is the role of woman (the 'fuckee') to be the one who gets fucked and the role of man (the 'fuckor') to be the one who does the fucking. Out of this difference, out of the structure of interaction in the mode of activity of sexuality, comes domination. The domination of the law is thus one where male experience and the force of violence (and Foucault cautions us never to forget the violence at the root of the law) downgrade the experiences and perspectives of women, thus losing many things of value to humanity. The law is inherently unjust in its treatment of women.

More pertinent for the present argument is Kerruish's (1991) development of an argument which shows how the individual constructed by jurisprudence is remarkably similar to the 'rational man' upon which the discipline of economics (and, we could add, of management) has built its theories. Jurisprudence identifies legal 'persons' who are bearers of fetishized rights and duties. The individuals so imagined are constructed, Kerruish points out, without recourse to any theory of the individual or society other than one drawn within law's own limited boundaries. This individual, being a category of thought, can be invested with whatever characteristics are desired. This individual is disembodied, decontextualized and alien to real people. Importantly, the individual so imagined is interested only in the pursuit of its own interests, to the point where it cannot live harmoniously with others. This fundamental philosophy at the core of law, of conflict as inherent within social life, leads inexorably to the belief that only the law can prevent endemic conflict from destroying society. Law thus sees itself as a 'foundational necessity'. Social life, within this perspective, is 'a dualism or interaction of "persons" presided over by the state' (Kerruish, 1991, p. 116).

Kerruish's analysis of the rationality of law and the legal person so constructed suggests the imposition of a very male view upon the world, a 'male' forged in the heat of Enlightenment rationality, where emotional or physical impulses are subordinated to the dominance of the mind. Ahmed (1995) has similarly shown that the person imagined as the legal subject is male; the body of the law, as Ahmed (1995) shows, is a male body. But there is a mimetic interaction here, a mutual construction of law and lawyer, for the law is not, Smart (1989) shows, 'rational because men *are* rational, but law is constituted as rational as are men [or as men are assumed to be], and men as the subjects of the discourse of masculinity come to experience themselves as rational – hence suited to a career in law' (p. 87). Here, the law is built upon a model that echoes the model of the male, and for Smart their opposites, their 'other', are the women whose subjectivity and consciousness are defined in law's terms so that resistance becomes difficult against the power of the phallocentric law.

If, as discourse theories tell us, it is discourses which constitute identities, then I must disagree with Kerruish's argument that this way of looking at society as an amalgamation of self-interested individuals who are kept together by the Law is the 'rationality of empowered white men who see themselves as superior to others and who like to explain that superiority in terms of the power of their intellects' (Kerruish, 1991, p. 122). Kerruish here recentres the subject, so to speak, threatening an *ad hominem* argument which reduces the power of her analysis. Rather, I would suggest that it is (to use an overused term) the discourse of law, built upon this desiccated individual and speaking through the individuals who embody the law, that serves to maintain both patriarchy and capitalism, which, as she argues, in justifying the legal maintenance of the existing order of things justifies that order. Such an argument applies similarly to Smart's analysis, for she envisages the living male as the pattern upon which the law is modelled, rather than the identity of the lawyer being constituted through the law.

However, what cannot be denied is that the law is gendered as male, a male order which the above research has shown imposes itself upon women, rendering them undefended within a patriarchal system, supine under its mighty weight. What I wish to do now is show that men too are subjected and subjectified within a patriarchal order, so that both managers and workers are subordinated within it. Thus I will argue that managers are subjected and subjectified by 'the law'. This raises something of a problem, for many managers are women and my arguments run perilously close to being phallocentric. In a later chapter I will return to this issue, when I will argue that managers in the postmodern are constituted as degendered, and that all are subjected to the phallic law of the organization. Ultimately, women are inescapably and visibly gendered, and this 'failure' to be degendered makes it inordinately difficult for there to be equality within organizations. For now, I am concerned with exploring how managers are not only law-in-action but are also themselves subjected to the Law.

Stratton's (1996) analysis of the phallic state facilitates entry to this analysis of the gendered, phallicized law of the enterprise. He uses Freudian and Lacanian theory which observes that the expression of male power lies in a penis which is also an expression of male powerlessness, through its transmogrification into the phallus. The phallus is always beyond the masculine reach, for even in maturity there is always something that has phallic power over him and which renders him symbolically impotent under its huge sway. Stratton argues that the growth of the overmighty state in the nineteenth century represented the appearance of what appeared to men as the Freudian Father whose phallic power was so qualitatively greater than the individual male's penis that it became nought but a tiny child's in comparison. The phallus represents the social and psychic edifice of the authority of a patriarchy which contains the abstracted and elevated ideal of a sovereign masculinity, against which the 'less than heroic status of the penis' measures itself (Solomon-Godeau, 1997, p. 177). No man's penis is ever as big as the mythic phallus of the State and so the male is rendered powerless in comparison. The all-powerful State became able, through the Foucauldian gaze, to reach into and regulate the daily lives of all its citizens, much as could the patriarch in the family. There is, however, within this male order of surveillance and phallicization a hierarchy, for the modern State surveys and dominates all men; bourgeois men survey and dominate working class men; and all survey and dominate women. In this phallic order therefore the Body of the Law is not the entire male body, as perceived by Ahmed (1995), and her surprise at the seeming metaphorization of the Law as Body when the body is so antithetical to male rationality is explained in Stratton's thesis: the Law instead is the Phallus, i.e. the body of the (male) law need be represented only in its one, all-powerful representational member, the penis as transmogrified into the powerful phallus.

Stratton, importantly, allows us to see the law as one form of (phallicized) rationality that dominates all women and all men, although the degree of domination experienced by men will vary according to their position of power. Where some men dominate other men the manner of domination may differ from that achieved over women. This possibility is supported by Ashe's (1995) interpretation of Julie Kristeva's work. Kristeva's 'Other' appears peculiarly feminine, Ashe argues, but Kristeva does not restrict herself to defining as 'Other' only those who are biologically female – she includes in the term 'Other' all those defined by the dominant Western, white male culture as 'Other'. This, in Ashe's (1995) terms, 'implies recognition that whatever has been silenced as "Other" has been taken to be in some sense "feminine"' (p. 109). The feminine, in Freudian theory, lacks a penis, and is, by definition, castrated. Can it then be that the phallicized law, in subordinating men, symbolically castrates them – reduces them to the status of the feminine? In this interpretation managers, in their endeavours to impose law upon workers, seek to capture the phallus for themselves, and in so doing seek to castrate symbolically any who may compete with them in this pursuit. What can be seen as 'masculine' behaviours (horseplay, etc.) are seen as chargeable offences – only a specifically defined male behaviour, that of the manager, is allowed at the workplace, so one form of masculinity attempts to subordinate another. Further, managers, we have seen, are told to expect that men summoned before the managerial court may break into tears or express anger, and the manager is warned to be ready for such outbursts of emotion, to stay calm and to call a halt until dignity has been restored.

The 'accused' is thus constructed as having supposed female properties of emotions that may tend to go beyond easy control, having previously demonstrated masculine behaviours – the change from masculine to feminine, the symbolic castration of the male. This is, of course, a denial of the female within the male, as termed by Freud, a projection onto the other of that which one cannot acknowledge within one's self and thus the reinforcement of an always equivocal sexual identity (Campbell, 2000). What Fitzpatrick (1992, p. 37) called the 'instrumentally ordered reality' of law can thus be read, ironically, as a reality ordered by the instrument of the phallus.

In this reading juridification results in an organizational hierarchy that, rather than being an ascending hierarchy of legitimacy, is as a patriarchal hierarchy of decreasing masculinity. At the top is 'the organization' or the big 'Other', beneath are heterosexual managers required to subordinate themselves to a particular model of masculinity, and necessitating, in this maintenance of a fragile ideal, the symbolic castration of other males working in the enterprise, with those blessed with the particularly unattractive attributes, in this world, of female characteristics (including gay men), at the depths of the ranks of subordination. Managers, charged with upholding the dominance of patriarchal law, are inheritors of the symbolic power of the phallus but yet (at least for those who are male) are possessors only of the puny power of the penis, for the phallus is always unobtainable.

## Conclusion: management as law, the manager as law, the manager subordinated to the law

In this chapter I have shown that management texts originally turned to the law to claim for managers the justification for their superordinate position in organizations. This claim was epistemologically located in a functionalist perspective that, as a claim to truth, disguised the power of legal discourse to dominate and to attempt to make the world in its own image. That required a similar theory of the law, one that held it as above everything else in its powers of rational authority. Management's relationship to law is thus that of a succubus, feeding off it and dependent upon it. When law comes to be retheorized, as a dominant discourse (albeit a discourse that has, if not an army and a navy, then at least a judiciary and a police force in its support), then the reliance of management upon that law, albeit that it is only now there in the form of a trace, must be seen also as altered.

There are thus now two theories of law within the enterprise: the juridical law and the law of the Father as evoked through the symbolic power of the phallus. The textbook's claim of management's right to manage and the claim of the law in support of this assertion has given way to the juridification of the workplace which has a legal system homologous to that of the wider legal system. Now the organization, through its legal practices, can spread its controls over workers' lives out of the workplace and into their homes and leisure pursuits. This is juridical law.

Further, Stratton's analysis of the phallic state opens the possibility of a space for a reading of management that takes us beyond the perspective of management either as neutral law-giver or as the agents or tools of capitalism or patriarchy. The law of the Father, where the law which is no longer discussed, towers above the manager and controls him, provides a hierarchy of gendered subordination within the workplace. It allows us to ask such questions as: what 'manager' is constituted through the discourse of law? What 'subject position', or multiple, dynamically ongoing and discursively constituted (Hughes, 1999) subject occupies the site of 'the manager'? I have suggested that managers, who enact the discursive practices of the juridified enterprise, are not so much involved in having their position legitimized by law but in being themselves, as managers, constituted by law. Managers here become the corporeal enactment of phallic law. In Foucauldian terms the law is inscribed upon their bodies and it renders them docile, just as they in turn render workers docile. Rather than the law being a resource for managers, the subject position that is the managerial self is constituted, at least in part, by the law. Managers are made docile for, just as the prisoner in the Panopticon is formulated through a discursively constituted identity as prisoner, is *made* through her/his subjection to the organization within which s/he is incarcerated, so too is the manager activated or formed as a subject by the juridified organization. The organization, like the prison, forces the subject to 'approximate an ideal, a norm of behavior, a model of obedience. This is how the prisoner's individuality is rendered coherent, totalized, made into the discursive and conceptual possession of the prison' (Butler, 1997, p. 85). The individual, here the manager, becomes the principle of his/her own subjection.

# 5 Management as art

In a paper given at the First Critical Management Conference held in Manchester in 1999, Christopher Grey presented the thesis that, given the falling into disrepute of Marxism and the offering of only a relativist cul-de-sac by post-modernism, the way forward for meaningful critique could be found in a turn to aesthetics. The succeeding conference included a stream devoted to aesthetics, and several books have now been published exploring the development of an aesthetically informed method of understanding management and organizations (Strati, 1999; Linstead and Höpfl, 2000; Carr and Hancock, 2003). This I find somewhat ironic for, as I have shown in Chapter 2, one of the foundations on which management's discursive house is built is its claim to be an art. While aesthetics is not reducible merely to art, there is a certain irony in turning management's claim to art back on itself and challenging it with the judgemental tools offered by the arts. This, Koontz and O'Donnell might chide me, is an elision, for I am here defining 'art' not in the way they had meant but narrowly, as the production of (beautiful?) objects for appreciation, and indeed I will in this chapter be narrowing the definition even further as I will be borrowing for my analysis arguments from within only that branch of art devoted to painting (hereinafter referred to as 'art'). My riposte to Koontz and O'Donnell is that in choosing one aspect of the arts I am not transgressing the managerial domain by critiquing it with something from an incommensurable domain for, in its wilful refusal to define what it means by itself as an 'art', management opens itself to a critique from the arts, however defined.

Indeed, management, in declaring itself to be an art, is petitioning for something to which, when we ask what might be this thing it is claiming, it offers in answer only nebulous incursions into its reticence. In pursuit of their territorializing imperative Koontz and O'Donnell claim managing to be 'the most important of all arts' yet their definition of 'art', this thing in which they have elevated management to the prime position, is no more than 'the "know-how" to accomplish a desired concrete result'. Compare this with the definitions of Griselda

Pollock, Professor of Fine Art, who writes that art is, 'of course, arti-fice' (1999, p. 55); it is 'where the meeting of the social and the subjective is rhetorically presented to us. It happens in ways which mystify that relation, giving canonical authority to a particular kind of experience of subjectivity and social power' (ibid., p. 103).

This definition of Pollock's allows us to state that in management 'art' can be defined as the meeting in the social worlds of organiza-tions of the subjective worlds of managers, the managed and teachers and students of management, meetings which are presented to us, through rhetoric, in such a way as to mystify the relationship between management and organization, giving canonical authority to manage-ment as possessors of a social power that informs the subjectivity of managers, employees, and teachers and students of management. This is the 'art' to which management lays claim when, in claiming for itself the status of an art, it seeks to paint itself a self-portrait that serves to privilege a reflection of the world in its own image.

The intention of this chapter is therefore to deconstruct the claim that management is an art, and no better way offers itself than in the application of the tools offered by art critique, for the painterly arts offer much in the way of analysis and debate, and so it is to them that I will make my call for investigative assistance. I will do this both tentatively, for the field of art history is immense and its arguments complex, and selectively, for I need to draw from the discipline only sufficient to allow this exploration of the managerial claim to the status of art. My recourse to art history is, however, no sheer happenstance for Koontz and O'Donnell were writing their first edition at a time when dominance in art had, for the first time, travelled over the Atlantic from Europe to America, and in the same era America had become the manufacturing powerhouse of the world. It is therefore apposite to commence our exploration with the work of Jackson Pollock, one of the leading lights of the American abstract expressionist movement whose star was not to be eclipsed until after Koontz and O'Donnell had first put pen to the paper of their managerial *oeuvre*. Analysis of his work offers us the opportunity to gain an understanding of the context in which Koontz and O'Donnell could first claim management as an art, for debates in the world of art both foreshadowed and echoed debates in the wider society; and indeed artists claim to explore and explain wider society. This temporal coincidence of debates – one concerning the meaning of art and the other the establishment of management – provides us with a means of understanding manage-ment's claim to be an art.

Having explored Jackson Pollock and Abstract Expressionism, I will then turn to the work of Griselda Pollock, whose text, *Differencing the Canon* (1999), illustrates how the production of art is 'historically specific and politically loaded, deeply contradictory and troubled – a product of its historical conditions and moment, bourgeois, racist, individualistic' (Pollock, 1999, p. 139). I will read her interpretation over into management's claim to 'art'. This facilitates an analysis of Koontz and O'Donnell as artists and their management textbooks as works of art. In Chapter 2 I showed how the decline into the simplistic discourse of the more recent texts closes off possibilities of critical and conceptual analysis. In this chapter I will show how the replacement of wording with photographs sends powerful messages that reinforce symbolically the debased messages of the texts.

## Jackson Pollock, Abstract Expressionism and 'art'

I saw the exhibition of Jackson Pollock's work at the Tate Gallery in London in the spring of 1999, as I was pondering how to approach management's claim to be an art (this book has been a long time in the writing). I was unprepared for the welling of emotion that such abstractions can rouse in the viewer. The first impression is their size: they are enormous and they overwhelm with it; their power is perhaps phallic – other artists' work appears in comparison miniscule, suffering an inarticulate lack. I do not remember such an emotional response to my first reading of Koontz and O'Donnell, when I was an undergraduate in the early 1980s, yet they are products of the same national culture and of the same era.

Jackson Pollock (1912–56), famously if not notoriously, constructed his most celebrated paintings by dripping paint onto canvases laid upon the floor. His canvases, large and very wide in proportion to their height, tended to the unusual in shape. The leading figure of Abstract Expressionism, which became the dominant international art movement of the two decades or so following the end of the Second World War, he symbolized in his rivalry with Picasso the rivalry between the artists of Europe and the artists of America. It was indeed through Abstract Expressionism that the centre of gravity of art was to move from Europe to America. Jackson Pollock's 'keynote' period was brief, from about 1947 to 1950, but impressive, as he left not only ideas that influenced the subsequent history of art, but also contributed in a major way to the idea that 'art' is remote from 'real' life, as seen in 1950 when *Life* magazine asked its 12 million readers 'Is He the Greatest Living Painter in the United States?', its intention being both a sarcastic exploration of what art had come to mean as well as a lauding of one of America's leading sons (Lewison, 1999).

This is the cultural milieu in which Koontz and O'Donnell were gathering together the ideas that were to lead to their textbook on management.

Jackson Pollock's leadership in the development of abstract expressionism built on an artistic process which had begun in the nineteenth century. Where the classical tradition of art sought to represent the objects it painted, the modern art movement sought something else. It was born out of the radical changes in subjective experience occasioned by nineteenth-century capitalism, when modernity was more a condition than a range of physical objects, so the task of art, the more experimental painters of the time argued, became not that of an apparently straightforward depiction of real things in the world, but an expression of ideas which represented the condition of modernity. The task of the artist became also that of reminding viewers that they were looking not at the subject that was represented in the painting, but at *a* painting, i.e. a decorated flat surface. The form of art itself, conceived as 'the bearer of the modern experience', thus became a major preoccupation of avant-garde, largely French, artists. In sum, 'what had come to be at issue was the kind of truth that needed to be told, how it could be told, and no less importantly, whose truth it was' (Meecham and Wood, 1996, p. 14).

This development of a self-conscious interest in the power of the work of art itself, in its role as producer of modern effects and sensations, led, in the twentieth century, to the development of abstract art. The painting as a thing, as a decorated surface, was now no more important than what the painter did in the process of painting. This led to a change from providing *im*pressions of the modern world (cf. the impressionists) to *ex*pressions of the artists' responses to the world (in the work of the expressionists). Now the artist became a producer of original expressions of what was being felt or emotionally experienced, in a move to the self-expression of an authorial self. In modern art then 'the visual experience of a work of art matches the density of experience *per se*' (Meecham and Wood, 1996, p. 18), and the artist searches for more direct and hence more powerful ways of expressing responses to the world.

It is a small step, according to Wood (1996), from expressionism to abstract art, from replacing the visual fidelity to the shape of objects with their expression in colour and shape, to allowing the colours and forms alone to carry the 'weight of expressive meaning'. The emphasis upon colour and form in paintings which were to continue to offer 'the possibility of imaginative, critical reflection upon lived experience' (Wood, 1996, p. 115), despite the removal of story or imitation, was to leave a pure art of intensified expression. In Foucault's later terms, the object was decentred, and the discourses of colour and form were what were available to the artist seeking to relate to a world of human experience and emotions. This move, from expressionism to abstract art, occurred in the interwar years in Europe, a move that laid the foundations for the transformation of abstraction by American artists in the early post-war decades. After the Second World War and the shift of the centre of gravity of the world of modern art from Paris to

New York, the valorization of independence and autonomy which had always been only one strand in avant-garde debate now became the dominant strand in the critical explorations of art. European influences remained profound – the development of psychoanalysis by Freud and other psychoanalysts such as Jung, with its new understanding of the unconscious, was also to inform art throughout these years. Still, the 'structure of rivalry' (Krauss, 1996) between American and European artists was resolved in the ascendancy of the Americans.

The American art heritage of the interwar years, however, was one of more orthodox forms of art, inspired both by conservative and radical social ideologies. The latter influence produced socially conscious art. The context in which Pollock and his contemporaries thus worked was complex: 'Social responsibility, self expression, originality, art as a weapon in the wider struggle for emancipation, art as a utopian model, all claimed the attention of Pollock's generation' (Wood, 1996, p. 123). Koontz and O'Donnell too were of Pollock's generation, and they too were claiming to establish an art, they too were enmeshed in this complex array of influences. What I wish to argue is that abstract expressionism was one way in which Americans responded to these influences; that managerialism as espoused by Koontz and O'Donnell is another – both claiming the status of art. I can use Jackson Pollock's own words to support the first part of this assertion for in an interview he asserted that modern art is 'nothing more than the expression of contemporary aims of the age that we're living in' (quoted by Wood, 1996, p. 123). Koontz and O'Donnell meanwhile, as I showed in Chapter 2, saw the contemporary aims of the age as control over chaos and the achievement of supposedly joint goals through good management. However, where abstract expressionism ostensibly sought to reveal the emotions engendered by that epoch, managerialism in its focus upon rationality, logic and order through the seemingly precise functions of planning, organizing, staffing, directing/leading and controlling, sought to control and suppress them. My use of the word 'ostensibly' signals the need to pause and to anticipate arguments I will present below, lest the impression be given that an unproblematic comparison of these arts is possible, for both 'arts' are inherently conservative in their support of a white, male, bourgeois society. In this they are but different artistic reflections of, and upholders of, a narrowly defined status quo.

But this is to jump too far ahead.

There are many interpretations of Jackson Pollock's work. For the abstract expressionists the unconscious is displayed upon the canvas: Jackson Pollock, analysand at different times to both Freudian and Jungian therapists, sought in his work access to the unconscious while other abstract impressionists, such as Cy Twombly, too saw the canvas as a vehicle of 'self-revelation', a mirror composed of 'the same metaphysical substance as the artist's existence' (quoted by

Krauss, 1996, pp. 263–5). Critics of Jackson Pollock's works admitted that in their first sight of his paintings they saw only 'wild heedlessness' but later they came to see order. One important critic, Greenberg, thought Jackson Pollock's work allowed viewers to gaze subjectively on their own consciousness; another, Michael Fried, that the work was evacuated altogether from the domain of the object and installed within the consciousness of the subject (Krauss, 1996). Those art historians of the 1950s and 1960s who abjured formalist criticism initially saw Abstract Expressionism as linked to contemporary existentialist themes of individualism and alienation. Other interpretations included: formal configurations appealing to nothing other than eyesight; traces of anxiety at the onset of the nuclear age; a sense of both achieved aesthetic unity and its irrevocable loss; traces of hedonistic physical joy; metaphysical meditations on being; attempts to explore and understand and thus live with urban life; an elevation of the process of manufacturing the product over the finished product itself (Wood, 1996, p. 124).

Whatever one's interpretation, Wood suggests, Pollock's work demands that the spectator develops an attitude, or 'an aptitude for exercising the imagination: an attitude at once trusting that there is something worthwhile going on yet also sceptical of the mystification which abounds in talk of art' (Wood, 1996, p. 127). To the committed spectator the works offer 'a form of consummation', putting at issue 'your imagination, your perspicacity, your attention. The painting offers . . . a form of imaginative meditation on self-consciousness' (ibid., p. 127). Koontz and O'Donnell, meanwhile, offered works they defined as 'art' that were ultimately to close down the imagination, to corral it within tight compounds of impoverished language and compressed confines of the thinkable. Where abstract expressionists sought to express the world as they saw it and their emotional response to that world through the medium of paint, Koontz and O'Donnell, in their claim to management as an art, offered an alternative expression of the world. Where artists sought to express subjectivity, they saw management's task as controlling it and turning it towards the needs of the enterprise. Koontz and O'Donnell use writing to express their art, and writing orients itself to the horizontal surface of the table but painting to the vertical field of vision: thus representing, in Krauss's (1996) interpetation, the opposition of culture to nature. Koontz and O'Donnell, in this perspective, offered up management as culture in opposition to the *nature* of the worker, but what a restrictive, denuded culture they offered.

Let us return to the America of the 1950s in order to place these arguments within a temporal location. This was a culture and an epoch imbued with the virulent political propaganda of the Cold War and the terror of the atomic age. It was an age of unparalleled prosperity, and suddenly it was shown that the age of the mass market meant the age of kitsch. In this period, '[d]escriptions of nuclear destruction had become an obscenity, for to describe it was to accept it, to make a show of it, to represent it' and so the artistic community, always politicized even when it attempted to abjure politics, 'had to avoid two dangers: assimilation of the message by political propaganda, and the terrible representation of a world that was beyond reach, unrepresentable. Abstraction, individualism, and originality seemed to be the best weapons against society's voracious assimilative appetite' (Guilbaut, 1999, p. 246). In this context the work of many avant-garde artists, including the most prominent such as Pollock, seemed to become 'a kind of un-writing, an art of effacement, of erasure, a discourse which in its articulation tried to negate itself, to be re-absorbed. There was a morbid fear of the expressive image that threatened to regiment, to petrify painting once again' (ibid., p. 246). The America of this period, Guilbaut shows, was one in which the threat of a Third World War was openly discussed in the press, and Europe was thought to be about to topple into the Soviet camp. Americans represented themselves to themselves as living in the last bastion of freedom, of democracy and of plenty, and now they could claim for themselves cultural supremacy. Expressionism 'became the expression of the difference between a free society and totalitarianism' (ibid., p. 249).

We thus now have a picture of a culture and an epoch in which two seemingly contradictory ways of coping with the world were concurrently expressed, and what differences there seem to be in the modes of expression. Where the arts are involved with opening up the world to allow the spectator to meditate upon their own self-consciousness, on their own interpretations of the world, Koontz and O'Donnell's art closes down abilities to meditate, to contemplate, to ponder the meaning of life. The former explores subjectivity, the latter attempts to define it out of existence. Where artists in their required freedom of expression are moving metaphors of revolt against totalitarian societies, Koontz and O'Donnell offered a guide to making the totalitarian organization where employees bow to managerial will. Thus Koontz and O'Donnell's definition of 'art' as the managerial 'know-how' to accomplish a desired concrete result is such a highly impoverished denotation that the concept appears reduced to meaninglessness.

Perhaps, however, the differences are not so great. Critiques of the art history that elevates Jackson Pollock and the abstract expressionists to the position described above suggest that this conclusion can be only an interim one. The critique from politics is but the first step along this next path of our investigation of management's claim to be an art. The decades prior to the Second World War had seen much debate about the political potential of art as a way towards the securing of a socialist economy, and avant-garde art was seen by many people in the post-war years as an expression of freedom. Yet the abstract expressionists, according to Guilbaut (1999), suffered the bitter defeat of being unable to prevent their art from being assimilated into right-of-centre politics. Rather, it became integrated into the 'imperialist machine' of the Museum of Modern Art and so aligned itself with the majority of the population which, after 1948, moved to the political right. Indeed Cockcroft (1999) argues that the CIA funded artistic enterprise in a propagandizing exercise in which the image of a 'free' US was projected; 'dissenting intellectuals' such as Pollock could not evade the enmeshing powers of this propaganda machine, for 'The artist creates freely. But his [sic] work is promoted and used by others for their own purposes' (Cockcroft, 1999, p. 90). Abstract Expressionism, in this reading, although stated by its producers to be a symbol of political freedom, was used for political ends. So too can Koontz and O'Donnell's work be seen as serving political ends, and more specifically the ends of capitalism, as the many texts within the labour process debate, beginning with the work of Harry Braverman, testify.

The critique of management to be found in the labour process debate is echoed in the critique of abstract expressionism that arose with the advent of post-modernism. Amid suspicions that his genius had burned out, Jackson Pollock died, in a drunken car crash, in August 1956. Post-modernist ideas, which penetrated the interlinked fields of art practice, art criticism and art history, subsequently brought a fundamentally different reading of both his work and that of his fellow abstract expressionists. Where art history had claimed art's role in 'self-expression', this now came to be seen as the expression of a self that was appropriate only to middle-class European men. Modern art was accused of racism and exploitation, with Expressionist artwork capable of being interpreted as a form of cultural exploitation. Art could not escape, in this reading, from a constellation of social injustice and psychic imprisonment. Whether art is embedded in a set of wider social relations or has relative independence from them is a question at the heart of controversy over modern art's meaning and value (Meecham and Wood, 1999), for the new art history which dominates contemporary debates is sceptical about the suppositions of freedom, purity and originality which were granted prominence within modern art. Art thus cannot be seen purely as an aesthetic effect, but as implicated in and imbricated with politics, cultural imperialism, racism and sexism. This is a theme I will return to at the end of this chapter.

How far have we come then in this application of art history to an understanding of Koontz and O'Donnell's claim that management is an art? It seems already a long way.

Point 1: the art of artists and the managerial arts can be seen both as expressions of the age in which the centre of gravity of the art and the manufacturing worlds swung to the US.

Point 2: but where one sought to express the sense of one's (the artist's and the spectator's) humanity in a hugely complex world, the other sought to control all expression, to stifle the emotions and ensure conformity and compliance. Management's claim to be an art therefore seems to defile the concept, to abuse and demean it so much that a charge of linguistic violation must be levelled at those who so loosely and cavalierly use and misuse the language to their own rhetorical ends.

Point 3: yet artists' work too has been used and misused for the political ends of American capitalism, and abstract expressionists have been charged with removing artists from what had been for much of the twentieth century a politically informed stance. Art has, in addition, been charged with becoming a mode of consumption in a consumer-oriented society, wherein the middle classes (including, it would seem, many from the burgeoning ranks of managers) consume art and therein recognize themselves as middle class. Further, the economy of the symbolic goods produced by artists is based on belief (Bourdieu, 1998), just as the economy of the managerial function is based, as this book argues, on our beliefs in the need for management and, hence, the social construction of management and managers.

Point 4: perhaps, therefore, managers and artists both are caught up in a paradox of existence, wherein they construct themselves according to the labels they apply to themselves, the label produces the meaning, and meanwhile capitalism, in selling products that in a dialectically reflexive irony produce these constructions of the artistic and managerial selves, benefits. It is only around the expression of emotions that difference can be found: the artist expresses; the manager suppresses.

We thus have two readings of management's claim to be an art: one that it traduces the very concept; the other that both managers and artists are caught up in a constructionist bind whose defining difference is the relationship to the emotional life. This is but the starting point of this analysis of management as art. Griselda Pollock's work takes us into the second stage.

## Griselda Pollock: critiquing the 'canon' and aiming it at management

Griselda Pollock, in offering a feminist reading of art history, allows us to explore art historical criticism in more depth and thus to develop a more insightful interpretation of management's claim to be an art. The power offered to us by her explication can be demonstrated by a simple paraphrasing of some of her introductory statements in *Differencing the Canon. Feminist Desire and the Writing of Art's Histories*

(1999). Her intention, she writes, is to deconstruct 'the question of a single standard of absolute, transhistorical artistic value embodied in the outstanding, exemplary, representative yet universalistic artist' that contains 'the idealised Story of Great Men' (Pollock, 1999, p. xiii). The canon of great artists, she argues, should be understood 'both as a discursive structure and a structure of masculine narcissism within the exercise of cultural hegemony' (ibid., p. xiv). Having read 40 years of management textbooks, how apposite it seems to write that the purpose of this present book is to deconstruct 'the question of a single standard of absolute, transhistorical *management theory* embodied in the outstanding, exemplary, representative yet universalistic *manager* that contains the idealised story of how Great Men should act'. The profundity of the next phrase of this paraphrase, 'the canon of great management writers should thus be understand both as a discursive structure and a structure of masculine narcissism within the exercise of cultural hegemony', will become clear only as the rest of the story of this deconstruction of management texts unfolds. Where Griselda Pollock seeks, through re-reading of canonical texts, to reconfigure them so as to allow other readings, I too am seeking to re-read management textbooks so as to allow different readings. Where she applies her theoretical arguments to understanding the works of van Gogh, Toulouse-Lautrec, Artemisia Gentileschi, Mary Cassatt and other artists, I borrow her theoretical arguments and apply them to achieve greater understanding of the writings of Koontz and O'Donnell/Weihrich and through them of management textbooks in general, and thus their role in constructing the managerialized world. The canon, she argues, is both a myth and a fabricator of myths. It is a myth of creativity and gender, class and racial privilege, and it fabricates myths that naturalize meanings. We need to 'pierce' this 'naturalising carapace of myth', she writes, so as to understand how the canon maintains the hegemony of dominant social groups and interests. In this section I will attempt such a piercing.

I do, however, stray from using some of her theoretical devices, for where she uses Freud to inform her readings, my recourse to the understandings offered by psychoanalytical theories will draw largely upon Freud's successors or interpreters. Where her arguments contribute directly and in a major way to feminist theory, I am drawing on feminist theory in my exploration of the social construction of management. In light of these similarities and differences, I will adopt and adapt Griselda Pollock's theoretical purview to assist a re-reading of the Koontz textbook and thus of management textbooks in general. The aspects of her arguments upon which I am placing a major focus in this chapter are her exploration of how a canon is established (which allows me to develop the argument that management has its own canon), and the selectivity of the canon (which, of course, assists in a tracing of the selectivity of the managerial canon). The borrowing of these two aspects of her work leads, I suggest, to a profound re-reading of management textbooks.

### Defining the canon in the textbook

Canons are 'benchmarks of greatness'. However, rather than being an objectively situated measure a canon is 'a discursive formation which constitutes the objects/texts it selects as the products of artistic mastery and, thereby, contributes to the legitimation of white masculinity's exclusive identification with creativity and with Culture' (Pollock, 1999, p. 9). It is a 'retrospectively legitimating backbone of a cultural and political identity, a consolidated narrative of origin, conferring authority on the texts selected to naturalize this function. Canonicity refers to both the assumed quality of an included text and to the status a text acquires because it belongs within an authoritative collection' (ibid., p. 3). With the rise of academies and universities, canons become the signifiers of the most significant texts in literature, art history or music. The canon sets 'the single standard of the greatest and the best for all times', but, '[a]lways associated with canonicity as a structure ... is the idea of naturally revealed, universal value and individual achievement that serves to justify the highly select and privileged membership of the canon that denies any selectivity' (ibid., p. 4). It thus includes legitimating or enabling predecessors, 'versions of the past [that] ratify a present order', but erase the fact of their selectivity.

In sum, canons constitute the objects they speak of through retrospectively conferring authority on a number of texts which thus become the most significant in the field. The choice appears so natural that the inclusion of some and exclusion of others is rendered as beyond question.

In this perspective, the management textbook can be seen as having produced a managerial canon consisting of the works of a small number of the many thousands of writers on management. No matter which textbook of the 1980s and 1990s one chooses, the choice of 'great names' included varies little. Koontz and O'Donnell differ slightly from the majority in that they make only passing reference to Max Weber and they elevate the work of Munsterberg and one or two other little-known names, but with this exception both the 'early thinkers' and those deemed as contributing to later theories appear again and again in many management textbooks. This is in a field where the outpouring of books on management is phenomenal, where the number of writers is legion. Why, out of all these, are some selected and others dropped? The speed with which new texts appear, and the way the majority of them disappear into the dustier recesses of the library, never more to be referenced by later authors, can be seen by contrasting two books of readings edited by Koontz and O'Donnell, published in 1959 and 1964, designed to support their textbook and each following the functional layout of the textbooks. The second edition was substantially revised, allowing us a glimpse of the changes taking place in a very short period. The number of papers included rose from 56 to 81. The readings that support 'The Basis of a Theory of Management' altered substantially between the two editions, with only three of the six readings, texts by Fayol, Talcott Parsons and James D. Mooney, going forward to 1964. Gone are the works of Leon C. Megginson, Catheryn Seckler-Hudson and an anonymous piece entitled 'The Source of Managerial Authority'.[1] The ten readings on 'organization' were expanded to 15 in the second edition, only one of the original ten (one of Lyndall Urwick's three original contributions) having been excluded. 'Staffing', however, received a thorough re-reading, with only one of the original seven papers, by Booz, Allen and Hamilton, joining the 11 papers of the 1964 edition. Five of the original seven papers on 'direction' were deemed worthy of being included in both editions, with the works of Auren Uris seemingly unsuited to be included in the 13 readings of 1964. 'Planning', meanwhile, saw its supportive readings rise from 14 to 17, but five of the original contributions had disappeared. The support for 'control' had risen by 66 per cent, from 12 to 20 readings, with only the writings of T.S. McGinnis and Earl J. Wipfler being consigned to the dustbin of history.

This rather repetitious list illustrates the potential numbers of people eligible to join the 'canon'. So many of these names have now been forgotten. Of the 81 included in 1964, only the works of perhaps nine – Fayol, Mooney, Urwick, Ernest Dale, Rensis Likert, F.J. Roethlisberger (but in association here not with Elton Mayo with whom he is customarily accorded the role of amanuensis, but Carl Rogers, who was to attain fame in another field), Peter Drucker, Chester I. Barnard and Herbert A. Simon – stand out from the crowd because of their continuing appearance within the annals of management. Even among these, of the list of contributors to the canon, only works by Fayol and Barnard appear in these books of readings. Neither of these are accorded the significance they were to be given in the 1976 and later editions. There are no illustrations from Taylor's work, nor from the Gilbreths, Gantt or the European social scientists. Only Talcott Parsons, America's leading social scientist of the period, represents the social sciences in this book of readings, and he disappears from the list of those who support the 'basis of a theory of management' when these are elevated into a canon. It remains an imponderable as to why so many were rejected and so few live on, immortalized not only by Koontz and O'Donnell but also by the numerous other writers of management textbooks. There has been a plethora of writers, both supportive of management as we now know it and critical of it; sometimes offering,

in the manner of management texts, ways of 'improving' the management function, but often offering alternatives, sometimes radical, to
the disposition by managers of the large gatherings of people that
we now label 'organizations'. The simple response to this is that the
authors chosen for canonicity must be the best, the leaders of the
field who offered new ways of seeing management that others had
not recognized. That this is a simplistic untruth can be seen by reading Jacques' (1997) review of D.A. Wren's (1997) selection of texts of
'Early Management Thought'. Jacques shows what the list of major
writers *omitted* from Wren's selection of contributors reveals: the reinforcement of 'the dominant managerialist ideology that the coalescence
of today's industrial order was an inevitability, that all responsible
authorities agree today (and agreed then) on the problems and solu-
tions, and that the present order, as it developed, was in the unified
interests of all' (Jacques, 1997, p. 4). This explains why the majority
of writers have been written out of history, it does not explain
why, when there are so many managerialist writers to choose from,
the same few are repeated, tediously and *ad nauseum*, throughout all
management textbooks.

I suggest that neither the writers themselves nor indeed what they
wrote are today important. What defines them as important and merits
their inclusion in the managerial canon is what they signify, i.e. conven-
tionality, continuity, the conservative way, or, in one word, patriarchy.
They have become a mantra taught to generation upon generation of
management students, Taylor, Fayol, Mayo and others, an incantation
of names and dogmas that inculcate the student into, and keep the teacher
entrenched within, a patriarchal, American and capitalist world.

By 1988, management 'thought' is divided by Koontz and Weihrich
into two: classical and modern. There is a table on p. 26 of that edition
which reproduces the lineage, as shown on the next page. The classicists' line ends in this table with Chester Barnard. The most obvious
point of note is that, with the exception of Lillian Gilbreth (of whom
more later) the list contains only white males. The group of 'scientific
management' thinkers are wholly American, while the psychologists
and sociologists who dominate the remainder of the list are largely
European. The only Americans in the latter group are Walter Dill
Scott, and Elton Mayo and F.J. Roethlisberger. Scott, although deemed
to be an American of such a high status as to merit inclusion, is worthy
of only two sentences outlining his life and work, and Roethlisberger
is mentioned only as part of an inextricably entwined parcel with
Elton Mayo. With the exception of Mayo, one of the first and most
influential of the translators of Weber's work into English, the major
social scientists drawn in to provide support to the all-American scientific management school are European. In this it can be said that they
mirror in management (even though they were not to know themselves

---

**Scientific Management**
F.W. Taylor
Henry L. Gantt
Frank and Lillian Gilbreth

**Modern Operational-Management Theory**
Henri Fayol

**Behavioural Sciences**
Hugo Munsterberg
Walter Dill Scott
Max Weber
Vilfredo Pareto
Elton Mayo and F.J. Roethlisberger

**Systems Theory**
Chester Barnard

**Emergence of Modern Management
Thought and Recent Contributions to
Management**
Long list, highlighting:
Peter Laurence
William Ouchi
Thomas Peters and Robert Waterman

---

that their theories would be put to these ends) what the schools of painters prior to the Second World War had meant to the abstract expressionists.

The Europeans called upon had formed ideas, established traditions, forged paths that the inheritors (or purloiners) of their mantles could use when carving their own names in the list of the canonized. When Weber and Pareto are referred to, it is not what they said that was important or which deemed them worthy of merit; it was rather the fame and status that accrued to their names and the legitimacy that use of their names offers those seeking to develop credence in management as a science. Thus Weber, deemed so important as to be included in this table of merit, has less than four lines of text devoted to his work, and Pareto earns a comparatively generous ten lines. Durkheim earns three lines of text, but no place in the table. Talcott Parsons, a sample of whose work as a leading American social scientist merited his inclusion in the earlier books of readings, is, significantly, noticeable in his absence from this list.

Taylor, Gantt and the Gilbreths, who top the table and thus suggest a mimetic relation between the first three columns of this table and an organizational chart that is topped by the senior members of the managerial hierarchy, are American. They represent powerfully for the US the legitimation of their right to wrest the centre of gravity of manufacturing from Europe to the US and to place themselves in a ruling position. Again it is not their writings that are important, but their citizenship and the dates of their publications. Any other American writers on management from the same generation, whose works support the dominant managerialist hierarchy as seen from the early twenty-first century would, I suggest, have done equal service.

In the continued rehearsal throughout management textbooks of the same stories, the same theories, the same names, we thus have a 'consolidated narrative of origin' which serves to confer authority onlater management writers. In the modern school of management writers the numbers of contributors are still expanding. Peter Drucker, W. Edwards Deming, Laurence Peter, William Ouchi, and Thomas Peters and Robert Waterman are included in the 1993 edition, the first two of these appearing there for the first time. The list of classicists remains unchanged. The classical 'canon' is now firmly established and as set in stone as the canon of great painters.

However, the restructuring of this table in the 1993 edition is instructive. Now it covers 1.5 pages, even though its content is exactly the same as in the earlier edition and no advantage in clarity or legibility is gained by this spatial expansion. Now the first three columns (scientific management, modern operational-management theory and behavioural sciences) are placed on one page, and are separated from systems theory, the domicile of Chester Barnard, by the intrusion of the first part of the discussion of Taylorism at the bottom of page 32. Systems theory now hovers uncertainly above modern management thought. This signifies, it seems to me, the liminal space of systems theory in this series of textbooks. As I showed in Chapter 2, the 1976 edition of the textbook elevated systems and contingency theory to be *the* science of management, its status heralded by the new title of the textbook: *Management. A Systems and Contingency Analysis of Managerial Functions*. Where previously the authors had included Taylor *et al.* in a rehearsal of major, albeit early, thinkers in management, we see their corralling in that year into the Classical School of Management Thought, or the 'classicists'. Later editions are markedly different from their earlier progenitors: where the early editions had sought legitimacy and status these later editions ooze with the sense of status achieved. This is the difference between adolescence and maturity, of promise and achievement. The 1976 text is thus the liminal space which heralds the transition between adolescence and maturity, the process Arnold van Gennep (1906; 1960) had observed in the rites of passage of the cultures that were the objects at the turn of the century of his anthropological gaze.

Management, it seems, achieved its maturity when it satisfied itself that it was a science. It was thus able to relegate the earlier theorists to the halls of the canonized, and again this can be explained by reference to Griselda Pollock's example and her use of Freudian analysis to show how the Oedipus complex has influenced the work of the artists who form the canon. In patriarchal societies, Freudian theory tells us, men always have to overthrow the father in order to win what they want and need, i.e. in a heteronormative world a woman. The patriarch/father denies the dual nature of his sexuality, part male and part female, and enacts the role of a man both feared and loved. In a society where the patriarch rules, where the feminine side is denied, there is constant conflict, requiring endless negotiation if social order is to be maintained, but conflict must ensue for the sons, to win their own place as father, must kill the father (Easthope, 1990). In this sense, the 1976 text of Koontz and O'Donnell represents the coming of age of the sons and with this their ability to overthrow the patriarchal father (Taylor *et al.*). Freed of his tyranny (and not yet challenged by their own successors) the writers on management can throw off the shackles that kept them tied to the home, and now they can roam free around the world. They have won the 'woman', i.e. the organization that represents for them the female that they wish to control and to dominate.

Griselda Pollock's analysis of the artistic canon, read over into management texts, thus allows us a markedly different reading, one that allows us to interpret the corralling of certain writers into a specific school as the elevation of a management canon. These versions of the past that ratify the present have been chosen not because of what they wrote but because of what they signified: American capitalist patriarchy. They make it appear inevitable that this is the way management should be. Furthermore, this elevation of the canon has another function for the discipline of management, a psychological function, for it enables, through a symbolic enactment of the Oedipal complex, the reaching of maturity of management. The members of the classical management school are the deposed fathers: the sons are free now to pursue their own paths.

### Selectivity and exclusion

The canon serves, however, as Griselda Pollock shows in great depth, to exclude, to stereotype, to discriminate and to oppress. It is part of a hegemonic discourse that has so profoundly saturated society that its citizens live it as 'common sense'. But it relies upon those it negates to secure its supremacy, and in a phallocentric culture this means it negates women and gay men so as to secure the supremacy of heterosexual masculinity within the sphere of creativity. Where *Differencing the Canon* can analyse the works of van Gogh and Toulouse-Lautrec in arriving at these conclusions, the photographs included for the first time in the 1988 edition of the Koontz textbook must suffice for this analysis, and indeed they serve us proud. Management textbooks are now so replete with photographs, diagrams and graphs that it is something of a shock to realize that this has not always been the case, that indeed the substitution of text with pictures is a recent phenomenon. I will here, drawing on Griselda Pollock's guidance, analyse the significance of this gallery that has now been intruded into the textbooks.

In the 1988 textbook there are only five photographs: a head and shoulders photograph of Taylor, his handsome, moustachioed face captured slightly in profile, above a wing collar and impeccably knotted tie; a similar photograph of Henry Gantt, his heavily moustachioed face turning away from the camera in the opposite direction to that of Taylor's. Gantt is shown as balding, and he is wearing a suit with a shirt with a rounded collar. The generously moustachioed Hugo Munsterberg is shown seated at a desk, his bald head atop glasses through which his eyes are seen to be cast downwards at the book his right hand is touching. The desk at which he sits holds a candle-style telephone and a number of other objects. George E. Mayo is shown from an angle slightly above, as if the photographer is standing while he is sitting. His face is mobile: he has been captured in the act of laughing or of arguing. He has no moustache but is bald and obviously of a venerable age. His hand holds what could be a pen or a cigarette in a holder, and he is wearing a suit with a bow tie. Chester Barnard is shown in a painted rather than photographed portrait: he is visible to mid-chest although his hands and arms are not to be seen. Wearing glasses and a generously cut suit that could date from the 1930s or 1940s, he has no moustache but a balding head. The 1993 edition includes two additonal photographs. One is of Henri Fayol, wearing a wing collar, a generous head of white hair, and the sort of moustache and chin beard worn by Edward VII. The other is of the Gilbreths, Lillian and Frank. They are shown with her standing to his right. She is a few inches shorter than he, and wears her hair in a bun. Her dark dress reveals her neck and some of her shoulders and chest. He is dressed in a severe suit with a shirt and tie that extends almost to his chin. Balding, clean shaven and bespectacled, he gazes directly at the camera, almost smiling, while she peers into the distance, mouth pursed as if she is trying to suppress a smile. Other textbooks contain similar photographs, although some also include Mary Parker Follett and, in

British texts, Joan Woodward, in their gallery. I have in front of me Daft's recent textbook which, in being far more generously endowed with photographs than the Koontz and Weihrich text, is perhaps more typical of current texts. In this an impressive, impervious, hirsute Max Weber, boasting a full head of hair, moustache and beard, glances at the camera from under hooded eyes.

That then is the 'gallery' of portraits of members of the canon.

Importantly and inescapably, these photographs are all of men, with the sole intrusion of Lillian Gilbreth, to whom I will return. Where painters have tended, in the modern era, to paint women, often in the nude or semi-nude, here women are made visible by their absence.

There is absolutely no room for doubting the sex of the men portrayed, for this is symbolized by the very masculine absence of hair on the head, and/or of generous growths of facial hair. Of the eight men portrayed in the textbook, only three have full heads of hair but their masculinity is in each case enhanced by a moustache (Taylor), or both moustache and beard (Weber and Fayol). These photographs therefore immediately tell the reader that management is a masculine function. This may have been important to Koontz and Weihrich when they first introduced the photographs, for at that time they were also acknowledging the presence of women in management, albeit some-what reluctantly. In the ninth edition (Koontz and Weihrich, 1988, p. 6) they noted that 'In the last decade or so, women have made significant progress in obtaining responsible positions in organizations. Among the reasons for this development are laws governing fair employ-ment practices, changing societal attitudes toward women in the workplace, and the desire of companies to project a favorable image by placing qualified women in managerial positions.' Women, it seems, were appearing in management not because of their abilities but because society demanded that these implicitly second-rate people be seen in the managerial ranks. The immediate response of the authors was to reassert the masculinity of management by introducing portraits that demonstrated that management had been, *ab initio*, a reserve of very masculine men.

But hair is not only a symbol of sex, it is an ideological symbol (Synott, 1993). Rosabeth Kanter noted in 1977 that:

> Managers at Indsco had to look the part. They were not exactly cut out of the same mold like paper dolls, but the similarities in appearance were striking. Even this relatively trivial matter revealed the extent of conformity pressures on managers ... The norms were unmistakable, after a visitor saw enough managers, invari-ably white and male, with a certain shiny, clean-cut look. The only beards, even after beards became merely rather daring rather than radical, were the results of vacation-time experiments on camping

trips, except (it was said), for a few in R & D – "but we know that scientists do strange things", a sales manager commented.

(Quoted in Synnott, 1993, p. 112)

Significantly, only two of the eight men whose images are portrayed in this managerial gallery, Fayol and Weber, have beards, and these are both Europeans. (Munsterberg was German, but he appears to have emigrated to the US at the age of 29 to take up a post at Harvard. He is prominent in Koontz and O'Donnell/Weihrich's canon, but does not figure in many other textbooks.) In Daft's textbook, more replete with photographs than the Koontz text, very few men can be seen wearing beards. Those seen participating in meetings, reaching agreements, celebrating success, planning what their business is about, etc., have taken the time to shave every morning. They echo the managers of Indsco. In the latter half of the twentieth century beards have come to signify either hippydom and rebellion or the foreign other. In these later texts a clean shaven appearance therefore signifies the opposite, i.e. conformity and the conservative. Beards represent too a masculine nature that can be untamed and uncontrolled: the male is revealed as close to nature by the evidence of bodily hair that threatens to become uncontrolled if not rigidly removed at regular periods.[2] A clean shaven chin demonstrates the suppression of nature and its elision from the controlled managerial world. Beards thus represent an otherness – they belong to a different time, to, literally, another country. In showing only Fayol and Weber as bearded they signify that European men are somehow closer to nature, less civilized, their animal characteristics more evident, than those of the American male who thus is seen as superior.

In this introduction of these imprints of past times into the modern textbook we see the visual imposition of what Jacques terms a 'hierarchy of ethnocentrism' in American management writing, i.e. 'Moderns appear to be superior to other people because we see clearly what has hitherto been seen through the eyes of bias and superstition; English are superior among Moderns because they are the ones who produced the entire body of early work; Americans are superior to British because they have superior character' (Jacques, 1997, p. 3). Fayol was of course French, and Weber German, but their work was unavailable until it was translated into English, rendering all Europeans discursively 'English'.

The portraits are therefore projecting a pictorial discourse of masculinity, American ethnocentricity and the domination of culture over nature. But they say more to the management student than 'to be a successful manager you have to aspire to be white, North American and male'. They offer students a patriarchal heredity and invite them in as adopted sons. These are the symbolic progenitors of the new generation of managers and management writers. Management is not a fashion or a fad, they say, the production of the young, fashionable or feckless. It is a product of the wise, the venerable; of the male who, throughout the ages, has been head of the family and who has thus kept law, order, security and freedom from want. The student, through them, enters a long line of descent, from the father to the son who becomes in turn a father who passes on his (managerial) heritage to his successor. As Griselda Pollock writes, the 'canon is fundamentally a mode for the worship of the artist, which is in turn a form of masculine narcissism' (Pollock, 1999, p. 13), a statement which has resonance for this work if the word 'artist' is replaced by the word 'manager'. Using a Freudian interpretation, she suggests that the artist functions as a heroic object of narcissistic fantasy, for he inherits the adoration previously accorded to the (male) spectator's father. This, she argues, may explain the strong interest in psychologically informed biographies that function to tell a story of the artist's life, one which is always imbued by heroic journeys through struggles and ordeals and battles with professional fathers for the final winning of a place in the father's canon. In this, the 'artist is thus a symbolic figure, through which public fantasies are given representational form' and they 'function to sustain a patriarchal legend' (ibid., p. 14).

The biographer (and into this slot we must place Koontz and O'Donnell/Weihrich and other writers of management textbooks as begetters but also biographers of the growth of management thinking) not only displaces onto the admired hero fantasies about the father but through this hero-worship reveals 'a narcissistic identification with an idealised hero' (ibid., p. 15), a hero who has to appear different from the norm. Canons, it follows, 'actively create a patrilineal genealogy of father–son succession and replicate patriarchal mythologies of exclusively masculine creativity' (ibid., p. 5). This returns us to the Oedipal complex, outlined above, for the gallery of photographs in the management textbooks provide reinforcement for that conclusion.

Yet the offspring who will eventually overthrow the fathers are born, it seems, through acts of immaculate conception, for not only are women largely absent, the body is noticeable in its absence in these head and shoulder portraits, with only a minority having visible any body below the chest, and none possessing anything below the waist. The photograph of Frank and Lillian Gilbreth is shown more fully in a British textbook (Buchanan and Huczynski, 1997), where they, or at least their clothes, are visible down to their knees, something again to be noted when Lillian Gilbreth's inclusion is discussed. Contrast this with any visit to an art gallery, where women are shown resplendent in nudity. These portraits therefore symbolize the body-less manager, the non-biological and thus non-emotional manager. The tightly restricting collars literally cut off the managerial head from the biological body – the manager is all head, all brain, all mind.

### Interpreting the woman: Lillian Gilbreth and her husband, Frank

Now it is time to return to the photograph of Frank and Lillian Gilbreth. At first sight, this photograph appears to pay homage to the importance of this woman pioneer of management history; it seems she belongs there in the canon because of the sterling work she carried out. Griselda Pollock warns us against such easy assumptions. The canvases of these textbooks contain not only photographs but also accompanying biographical details, so I will first look at what the textbooks tell us about this anomaly, this female intrusion into the male canon.

It needs only a little feminist imagination to retort that, but yes, Lillian Gilbreth is included only because of her work with her husband. Indeed, it needs only an introductory tutorial in feminist reading to note the demeaning tones in the 30-line biography of the Gilbreths given by Koontz and O'Donnell/Weihrich (1988, pp. 29–30). It starts: 'The ideas of Taylor were also strongly supported and developed by the famous husband-and-wife team of Frank and Lillian Gilbreth', and continues as shown here on page 126.

But this is a very crude reading. We can add a layer of sophistication if we look at the way pronouns, and first and third person singular pronouns are used in the text.

Frank Gilbreth is referred to by his full name (first and family name) three times, Lillian Gilbreth only once. They are introduced in full (his name first, of course), and referred to as 'the Gilbreths' once. She is referred to once by her first name only, he never, allowing a familiarity with the woman that is at once patronizing and demeaning.

'He' and 'his' are used nine times: in four cases the pronouns are followed by verbs (he rose, he made possible), in four they are used to denote possession of work-related items (ideas, work or firm), and in only one case, a reference to 'his wife', do they relate to the private aspects of his life. This constructs him as an active man who undertakes and who possesses. 'She' and 'her' are used ten times. In only two instances do these relate to her own achievements as a woman rather than as a wife or mother. There are four cases when they refer to her husband or his work, and three where they refer to their marriage or children. The final reference is to her long life, again a reference to a biological phenomenon. Only once is 'she' followed by an active verb, and in this case it refers to her carrying on her husband's work. She is thus constructed as passive and concerned largely with supporting her husband and with raising their family.

Thus the very structure of the text is such as to make him an active achiever, while she is the passive receiver (of his ideas, his sperm). Their 12 children are referred to as 'her' dozen children, and in this a curious rhetorical double-play is achieved, for his virility can be claimed (he is

| Koontz and O'Donnell/ Weihrich | Re-reading |
|---|---|
| Frank Gilbreth's history (nine lines) | A self-made man, no university education. |
| In undertaking his work, Frank Gilbreth was greatly aided and supported by his wife, Lillian. | He was the leader of this team, she nothing more than his assistant. |
| One of the earliest industrial psychologists who combined earning her doctoral degree with having 12 children. | So she was not able to devote too much of her time to her work, was she? (*But note the reference to the 12 children and pursue this.*) |
| He died in 1924, and she carried on his work until her death in 1972. | He had started his work with Taylor in 1907, so spent 17 years establishing his theories. She had 57 years after receiving her doctorate in which to develop her ideas. This figure is not stated – the calculations have to be made by the reader. The sum of years implies Lillian Gilbreth was not bright enough to develop her own ideas, and in this lack had to continue to propagate those of the inspirational member of the team long after his death. |
| The two had a rare combination of talents. | Unfortunately, they had only nine years in which to work as a team, if we assume her contribution started largely upon her achieving her doctorate. Did she continue to rely on his ideas in the 48 years left to her after his death, or should she be credited with her own? |
| The section concludes by returning to his work. | She disappears from the discussion at this point. He therefore has the last word: his work is elevated to the dominant position. |

the father of 12 children) but it appears he has had no active part in their creation (they are 'hers') so that the appearance in management texts of the non-biological body, the manager untouched by the demands of the flesh, is maintained. He is all man, yet he is unsullied by anything so base as carnal desires. Her mighty endeavours are reduced to the menial tasks of the supportive role – he has disseminated (his seed, his words, his theories) and she has the task of raising them and ensuring his immortality.

Returning to the photograph we can see that this differs from the representations of the other members of the canon not only because of its inclusion of two people, one a woman, but because of the extent of the bodies that is shown. In the British textbook, as I have noted above, we see them almost to their full height, but even the American version of the photograph shows them almost to their waists. Lillian Gilbreth, further, is wearing a dress that reveals her neck and upper chest, in contrast to the men who all wear collars and ties that cover them up to their chins. We have here therefore a signifier of nature and of flesh – the woman is made flesh and, in the context in which this woman is celebrated for her production of 12 children, its inclusion emphasizes heteronormativity. Referring to Marjorie Garber's work, Griselda Pollock writes that 'The representation of two anythings . . . incites the underlying heterosexual binary that unconsciously organises the heteropatriarchy. We see two things, even two pieces of fruit, and they fall into a narrative.' The narrative is that of an 'implicit heterosexing binary' (Pollock, 1999, p. 183). Lillian Gilbreth standing alongside her husband therefore stands as a symbolic representation of all wives – she demonstrates that the men referred to throughout the texts, texts that are largely woman-free and from which all references to biology and thus to sex are eliminated, are heterosexual. More, she symbolizes their sexual potency and their heterosexuality, in that they all have the potential to father 12 children. Lillian Gilbreth thus stands as a symbol of heterosexuality in a managerial world which, rejoicing in the absence of women, could otherwise be construed as homosexual.

The managerial canon is finally, like the painterly canon, a discursive formation which constitutes the objects/texts it selects as the products of artistic/managerial mastery, and which thereby contributes to the legitimation of white masculinity's exclusive identification with creativity, culture and control. The managerial canon normalizes the relations of power and sexuality for it has constructed a visual field for art, whether defined as the painters' definition of art or the art claimed by management, in which feminine inscriptions are not only rendered invisible through exclusion or neglect but are made illegible because of a phallocentric logic which allows voice to only one sex. Management, to paraphrase Griselda Pollock's answer to the question 'What is Woman?' (ibid., p. 99) is *made* by the very discourses and practices which produce and speak this sign. Throughout our lives we are being made and undone as subjects over and over again in our encounters with language, with others and with culture. Texts, images and discursive practices have to be analysed historically as sites where this making takes place. Management, like art, was born into an always already active phallocentrism, and we see, in management's claim to be an art, that it uses that claim to reinforce phallocentrism.

## Conclusion

I concluded the first section of this discussion, where I used Jackson Pollock's work to contrast painters' definition of art with that of the management textbooks, with two readings of management's claim to be an art, one version seeing it as a traducement of the very concept of art, the other seeing both managers and artists as caught up in a constructionist bind whose defining difference is the relationship to the emotional life. In this concluding section I will first explore whether the reading allowed by Griselda Pollock results in a privileging of one or other of these interpretations. It is important to emphasize that I am not using these arguments to develop a gendered understanding of management, but using a gendered understanding to explore how management textbooks both reflect and help to constitute both management and the persons who occupy management roles. In the second part of this chapter I will therefore read the conclusions through a recent work by Martin Parker.

Artists, Pollock argues, project their fantasies and desires onto the canvas. These are taken up by the spectator, who absorbs them, and thus the canon perpetuates the societal status quo. Applied to the canvas of the textbook, we must seek the fantasies and desires of the authors, seek their subjectivities, as these are the realms of their selves that will be given to the student reader in the guise of the self to which they must aspire if they are to become managers. What then are the subjectivities of those who claim that management is an art?

This chapter's analysis of this claim, made through the prism offered by art history, shows that the management textbook projects onto the reader the phantasy of a phallocentric order that celebrates patriarchy and managerialism and abases the maternal, the emotional, the celebration of life over achievement of goals. The difficult transition necessitated by the Oedipus complex has been accomplished, nature has been vanquished, the emotions are strictly controlled. The definition of art as 'the "know-how" to accomplish a desired concrete result' can now be understood. It is the tacit knowledge that ensures perpetuation of patriarchal managerialism, for within patriarchal managerialism there is security, there is safety, there are controls which prevent the always-present fear of decay into anarchy which underpins the rationale for management. The anarchy identified in Chapter 2 can thus now be further understood, for it is not just political anarchy that threatens these writers, but a personal anarchy whereby the emotions may break free into full expression, where nature may win the day over culture, where sexuality may be expressed. Women, gay men, women and men from other cultures, men who wish to be different from this very narrow norm, all would be liberated, and in this liberation the deeply inhibited (anally retentive?) writer on management would be ontologically challenged. The management writer has defined a world in which he feels safe and secure, and he wishes to impose that world upon everyone.

Meanwhile, what of the above issue – are artist and manager one and the same save for their relationship to the emotions, or does management violate the concept of art by claiming for itself the status of an art? To answer this question I will return again to Griselda Pollock. She argues for the need to *difference* rather than to overthrow the canon. She writes that in a culture which suppresses the maternal we must read against the paternal grain and discover the maternal; we must provide

> a territory in which we can both deconstruct the 'great man' myth and then productively read the works of men artists beyond its limited, repetitious refrains, while being able to speak of the myths, figures and fantasies that might enable us to see what women artists have done, to read for the *inscriptions of the feminine*, to provide, in our critical writings, representational support for feminine desires in a space which can also comprehend conflicting masculine desires, liberated from their theoretical encasement in the idealised image of the canonical artist. Furthermore, the differences between men which are currently recognised only in the suppression of all but one group's ideal-ego can be articulated.
>
> (Pollock, 1999, pp. 18–19)

In the context of management, I interpret this as meaning we must seek the liberation of all people, men and women, from the imposition of the 'ideal-ego' of the rational manager operating in a patriarchal, capitalist culture. Management and male artist alike perpetuate their own singular, dominant, ego-laden view of the world, and impose it upon others; these impositions must be shattered if a world more receptive to the talents and needs of all its people is to emerge. Yet I keep being called back to Jackson Pollock's canvases, and to the well of emotion and joy in being alive that they evoke. Sad is a world that can turn such works to the ends of warfare, of capitalism and of managerialism. And management traduces the concept of art when it claims that status for its own.

But to return to the debate I outlined above, of the differences between modernist and post-modernist understandings of art. The former had claimed art's role in 'self-expression', while the latter, forming its ideas around the notion of the decentred artist, argues that art cannot be seen purely as an aesthetic effect, but as implicated in and imbricated with politics, cultural imperialism, racism and sexism. This introduces the theme of the change from modernism to post-modernism I have exposed in my analysis of management textbooks, i.e. the change from the ontologically fixed monad to the culturally constituted and decentred person. The distinction seen in the art world is reflected somewhat in Parker's (2002b) *Against Management*. In this he is critical of the ever-decreasing possibilities of organizing work other than through the aegis of management, a theme that informs this book. This he sees as 'just another oppressive form of commonsense that needs to be addressed more directly' (Parker, 2002b, p. 212). While I am in full agreement with his description of *management*, his description of *managers* is, I find, located within the modernist perspective, in that it presumes, albeit from a critical stance, that managers 'have too much invested in managerialism to make them likely to rebel en masse. They have identities, qualifications, salaries and status through being what they are' (ibid., p. 189). They remain, in Parker's perspective, ontologically fixed monads. I am arguing that managers today have identities that are precariously formed and maintained through such discursively powered mechanisms as can be found in readings of management textbooks, which themselves form part of the wider study of and inculcation into the discipline of management.

I am arguing that the post-modernist interpretation of managers, management and the constitution of managerial identities is a political perspective that offers opportunities for achieving understanding and through that, eventually and hopefully, change. So I do not share Parker's pessimism about the fixedness of managerial identities based upon an economically delineated culture of power. Rather I suggest we must explore how the 'ideal-ego' of the manager is constituted within what Jameson (1991) calls post-modernist capitalism. The textbook's claim that management is an art, read through the lens of feminist art history, reveals something of that ideal-ego, and also posits something of a preferable alternative, while avoiding the dangers of utopian dreaming. As to *management*, that is something different.

# 6  Management as modernity

## Introduction

For Giddens (1991), in a somewhat Foucauldian mood, '[w]ho says modernity says not just organisations, but organisation – the regularised control of social relations across indefinite time–space distance' (p. 16). For Foucault, of course, we all of us belong to organizations and all organizations are alike and take the prison as their model, so we are all imprisoned within a field of organizational power, even when we are sitting alone (Burrell, 1998). Who says organization, we could add, also says 'management', and who says management also says 'masculine'. There is a well-established history of equating modernity with masculinity. Modernity is that world-view whose roots can be found in fourteenth and fifteenth century Europe where '*man*'s conception of the world and his place in it' (Gordon, 1991, p. 17, emphasis added) ushered in an Enlightenment that, in the post-modernist reading, provided the foundations for a modernism which strives after explanation and control. It brought with it the guiding notion that it is only through reason that we can achieve control, with explanation to be sought through a knowledge that is objective and to be striven for through a faculty of reason sharply demarcated from nature. This tight and exclusive view of reality, based within empiricism and rationalism, provides a single standard of rationality against which all actions can be measured. It is a world-view that is profoundly masculine, by which I mean it is imbricated with those attributes that are generally accorded to the male and which serve in the constitution of men's identities.

Women, and female identities, are here the Other, and it is the Enlightenment project which accounts for such a distinction. For Merchant (1983, cited in Nast and Kobayashi, 1996), for example, the Enlightenment saw a dichotomous and mechanistic Man/Nature relation, with the male body regarded, under Descartes' influence, as a machine, while woman's body remained inextricably tied to Nature. This 'ontological hiving off of male from female, Man from Nature' saw Nature constructed in terms of a passive materiality that was controlled by the masculine, rationalizing gaze and hand of science. For 'Nature' read 'woman' and for its now binary opposite, science, read 'man'. Thus organizations, science and the state became masculine domains, the men who inhabit them living a Cartesian dualism which disdains sexuality and emotional life, for the animal nature has, in modernity, to be *controlled* and so, too, the emotions (Seidler, 1994). Male identity is bound up with rationalism and self-control, knowledge is separate from the body and reason is universal and neutral precisely because it is bodiless, and separate from nature and the domain of women (Alcoff, 1996). Man becomes the opposite of woman, so:

> To say that 'reason is male' is more than simply to say that men have been biased against women's capacity to be rational. It is to say that reason has been defined in opposition to the feminine, such that it requires the exclusion, transcendence and even the domination of the feminine, of women and of women's traditional concerns, which have been characterized as the site of the irreducibly irrational particular and corporeal.
>
> (ibid., p. 14)

Thus masculinity and modernity are conflated, and organizations are masculine environments, so both modernity and organizations are constructed through the lens of masculinity. However, queer theory, notably in the work of Judith Butler (1990, 1993, 1997), blows apart the relationship between genitalia and a cultural imputation of gendered identities. The argument from queer theory is of fluid gender identities propelled into abnormal postures within the compulsion of heteronormativity. Characteristics of 'masculinity' and 'femininity' in the post-modern are therefore torn free from their moorings upon male or female bodies, and become free-floating signifiers within power/knowledge complexes that serve to constitute abject subject positions. In this chapter I am using the freedoms allowed by queer theory to explore how managerial identities are gendered in the form of a single, dominant masculinity to which all managers, regardless of their sexual identity, must aspire.

In my borrowings from queer theory, the assumption that modernity and organizations are mimetic of the male is turned upon its head, and the male is seen as constituted through modernity and organizations: the exploration thus turns to a discovery of how masculinity is rendered performative through both male and female bodies, via the discourses which speak through modernity and through organizations. This chapter's aim is therefore that of exploring textbooks and, indirectly, organizations, to discover the ways in which they perpetuate a performative, deracinated masculinity which imposes one gender identity upon all organizational members, regardless of their biological gender. It requires an exploration also of feminist interpretations. The chapter is inspired by Kosofsky Sedgwick's (1991) *Epistemology of the Closet*, which explores how novels of the nineteenth century served in the constitution of the new identity of homosexual. Her aim, which I borrow for this chapter, is 'to attend to performative aspects of texts, and to what are often blandly called their "reader relations", as sites of definitional creation, violence, and rupture in relation to particular readers, particular institutional circumstances' (Kosofsky Sedgwick, 1991, p. 3).

Thus when we explore the confusion in the textbooks about how to adjust to the appearance of women in management, a confusion that goes far beyond issues of equality or discrimination, we must keep in mind Foucault's guidance:

> There is no binary division to be made between what one says and what one does not say; we must try to determine the different ways of not saying such things ... There is not one but many silences, and they are an integral part of the strategies that underlie and permeate discourses. 'Closetedness' [or here the masculinity of organizations] itself is a performance initiated as such by the speech act of a silence – not a particular silence, but a silence that accrues particularity by fits and starts, in relation to the discourse that surrounds and differentially constitutes it.
> (Quoted in Kosofsky Sedgwick, 1991, p. 3)

The Koontz textbook is at a loss as to how to approach women's entry into management. This is seen most obviously in its insouciantly limited exploration of women as managers, for as recently as its tenth edition (1993) it includes the statement that 'In the last decade or so, women have made significant progress in obtaining responsible positions in organizations' (Weihrich and Koontz, 1993, p. 7 and repeated on p. 365). They have achieved this not because of any reasons intrinsic to women, but due, they state, to legislation, changing societal attitudes towards women in the workplace, and the favourable image companies project by placing 'qualified women' in managerial positions. Women, this statement asserts, can become managers not by reason of their qualifications and abilities, but only by others opening up paths for them, just as men have long opened doors for women or carried their new wives over the threshold of the marital home in order to avoid the evil spirits lying in wait. Discrimination, they write, is only 'one reason' for there being not one woman on her way to a chief executive's job in the Fortune 500 corporations. The textbook remains silent about other possible reasons, a silence pregnant with the hoary, venerable and utterly discredited implication that 'women aren't equipped for the public domain'. But this is a silence that Foucault directs us to be alert to, for it says much. I suggest it is saying that just as masculinity is a codeword for modernity, femininity, it follows, is a codeword for something else – for *jouissance*, for pleasure, for exceeding boundaries, all those things that must be kept out of organizations. Thus the attempts to ensure management remains masculine is about far more than keeping women (i.e. those people whose biology allocates to them the designation of 'woman') in order – it is about keeping at bay those things which women are seen to represent. It is about maintaining the logical and rational organizational order.

Women can thus enter management,[1] or at least its lower and middle ranks, but only so long as they are gendered as masculine, i.e. that same sort of masculinity which is the ideal for the organizational man. This requires that women lay aside those characteristics which are regarded as feminine, and perform themselves as masculine. That they are always already female, and thus bound to fail, accounts somewhat for the continuation of inequalities in the workplace. The textbooks now carefully use both male and female pronouns when the plural form cannot be used, but this disguises other methods of reinforcing the masculine, through the use of the charts, diagrams and photographs that now so liberally sprinkle the pages of the textbooks. These construct management as masculine.

Thus the coincidence, in the history of the textbook, in (1) its reaching a satisfied assumption of the legitimate status of management, (2) the introduction of photographs and diagrams to replace the written word and the accompanying 'dumbing down' of the text, and (3) the appearance of large numbers of women in management positions, is more than coincidence. It is again that divide between modernity and post-modernity, but here we apparently see the continuing intrusion of modernity, inscribed upon managers' gendered bodies, into post-modernity, an issue I will explore in the conclusion to this chapter.

This chapter therefore turns to a major aspect of the 'dumbing down' – the replacement of text by photographs and diagrams. Its layout is as follows. I will first explore how management and organizations continue to be constructed as masculine, through analysing first the photographs in the textbooks. The boxes and diagrams are too numerous to allow a coherent analysis, so my focus will be, second, upon organizational charts. My excursion into art history in the previous chapter revealed one of the subtexts of the photographs. In this chapter I will build on that analysis to demonstrate that the photographs and the charts contained in the textbooks are impregnated with an androcentrism that is projected onto the reader and thus onto management. This presentation requires a further borrowing of ideas from art history, specifically Abigail Solomon-Godeau's (1997) interpretation of the male nude in art. The analysis of the charts and diagrams which follows requires a different approach, one that involves taking one example, the organization chart, and its place in organizations and in the text-book, and deconstructing it using methods developed in geography. The organization chart, this exercise reveals, not only symbolizes but contributes to the constitution of management as masculine. Finally, I will place this analysis within the context of the turn to post-modernity, exploring in more depths the reasons for the maintenance of the masculinity of management.

## The photographs in the textbook

A swift glance through management textbooks offered for sale in university bookshops reveals a superfluity of photographs, nearly all showing white men wearing suits, but with a sprinkling of women and black people. The photographs have one of two ostensible purposes: either a portrait of a person whose work is being discussed, or an illustration of a tenet of managerial practice (achieved by showing managers in meetings, giving talks, etc.). In order to discover what these photographs signify I am drawing on Abigail Solomon-Godeau's (1997) study of the disappearance, after a reign of 2,300 years, of the male nude from the French art canon, and its replacement with the objectified female nude. Solomon-Godeau, in focusing upon portrayals of the male, provides a lens that facilitates the identification of the polysemic or multi-signifying functions of the photographs of male managers in the textbooks. These serve, I will argue, a function similar to that of male nudes in seventeenth and eighteenth century classical painting, for in disguising all references to sex they perpetuate a gendered world. Furthermore, in offering images intended for consumption by readers they provide aspirational models. Finally, they represent the values of a 'transcendent and sovereign subjectivity, endowed with reason and judgement, a self-mastering *cogito*' (Solomon-Godeau, 1997, p. 195). This extrapolation from Solomon-Godeau's work allows the discovery of the spectator produced in these images.

Let us start this analysis, however, with a portrayal of the objectified male body that is nearer to us both temporally and spatially, for the 1980s saw the reappearance, through the medium of advertising, of the visual representation of the objectified male body. This occurred at the same time as the turn to the visual in management textbooks, a turn that similarly allowed the visual representation of the male body. Representations of masculinity, Solomon-Godeau argues, are shaped by the presiding terms of gender and gender conflict (ibid., p. 204) and in the adverts of the 1980s she saw produced an avatar of masculinity in the form of the passive, beautiful and seductive youth, presented and posed in ways commonly associated with the display of desirable female bodies (ibid., p. 18). She argues that this current array of ideal masculinities attests, if nothing else, to an iconographic return of the repressed: in other words a desublimation of masculinity in the visual field whereby the masculine body is again, after an absence of two centuries, permitted to be an object of desirous looking (ibid., p. 23). I would suggest that a similar conclusion can be drawn from the photographs in management textbooks, for the males portrayed become 'objects of desirous looking'. The desiring gaze is that of aspirant and practising managers, male and female, who are encouraged to emulate and identify with those they see in the pictures.

In gazing at the photographs in management texts, in perhaps absorbing their symbolic meanings into the subjectivity of the managerial self, the observer sees a privileging of the masculine. Here we see a renaissance, albeit in a different forum, of a tradition in classical art styles inaugurated in fifth century BCE Greece and continued through to Neo-classicism, which provided a visual language for (and of) male supremacy. This tradition established maleness, Solomon-Godeau writes, as the emblem of (ideal) humanity, and relegated femaleness to the realms of alterity, difference and corporeality (the body itself), thus promoting a dichotomy that affirms the equivalence of 'Man' with 'human' and all that that implies (ibid., p. 13). The photographs in the management textbooks, in privileging the male as manager, undoubtedly continue this tradition. They must be contrasted with the male of the advertising legend who is seen often half-naked, holding a baby, and demonstrating, in the projection of male sexual appeal, that side of him which is closest to nature. The males in the management textbooks are, in comparison, active rather than passive, they are involved in doing rather than being gazed at, and they offer their minds rather than their bodies. This division of ideal masculinities into 'hard' or 'soft', phallic or feminized incarnations is, Solomon-Godeau points out, a consistent feature within the larger cultural context of bourgeois and pre-bourgeois ideologies of gender. Thus we see the concurrent development, in the 1980s, of two avatars of masculinity: the 'soft' masculinity of the advertising hoarding that contrasts with the 'hard' masculinity of the management textbook. The juxtaposition of the two offers two versions of masculinity, two versions of lived male subjectivities (and there are many models of masculinity (Haywood and Mac an Ghaill, 1996) and these are but two of them) – the daytime/weekday male who suppresses the body and focuses upon 'the mind'; the nighttime/weekend male who can parade the body and allow its dominance over the mind. Often the 'soft' male is portrayed semi-nude, whereas the 'hard', managerial male is portrayed always in a suit, sexuality stiffly buttoned up and contained, rigidly cordoned off from the most important and always revealed part of the managerial body – the head. It is a male constructed through the host of hidden rules that turn organizations into a discursively masculine world that requires its inhabitants 'to exhibit male-associated characteristics of toughness, competitiveness, aggressiveness and control', concepts that make up part of our understandings of a management 'riddled with notions of masculinity' (Hearn and Parkin, 1986, pp. 78–9). Further, the ethos of organizations has traditionally been male, but a specific type of male – the elite, small in number, who 'put their rules, their stamp, and their model of behaviour on organizational expectations: a pattern extant in today's corporations', one in which the masculine ethos is one of 'masculinity, strength, [and] aggression [which] themselves have become linked to dominance and its micro forms – management and leadership' (Mills, 1992, p. 135).

The manager's suit is prominent in the photographs, as it is in the managerial workplace. J.C. Flugel's analysis of *The Psychology of Clothes* (1930, in Silverman, 1988) is informative here. Flugel shows that a major change in male clothing customs occurred in the late eighteenth century. After centuries of increasing opulence it now became purified of ornamentation, and it took upon itself an appearance of austerity and asceticism which continues to this date. This 'Great Masculine Renunciation', he argues somewhat questionably, assisted the collapse of social and class distinctions between men and the signification of solidarity between male subjects. More convincingly, he sees it as allowing masculine allegiance to the larger social order and man's privileged position therein. The consequence of this, Flugel writes, is that 'modern man's clothing abounds in features which symbolize his devotion to the principles of duty, of renunciation, and of self-control. The whole relatively "fixed" system of his clothing is, in fact, an outward sign of the strictness of his adherence to the social code (though at the same time, due to its phallic attributes, it symbolizes the most fundamental features of his sexual nature)' (Flugel, 1930, p. 113, quoted by Silverman, 1988, p. 25). In this, Silverman indicates, Flugel is highlighting the contradiction between the male clothing allowing the detachment of the male body more and more from sexuality, and at the same time its construction of male sexuality through its phallic representation. Solomon-Godeau concurs in the phallicized ideal of the desirous male body. Within what she conceptualizes as homosociality, or networks of relationships between men that involve both power and desire and which may be expressed in cultural production (Solomon-Godeau, 1997, p. 29), that do not 'necessarily depend on the outright elimination of femininity, but rather, on the more powerful bonds that unite men to one another and which collectively operate to secure the subordinate position of women' (ibid., p. 86), she identifies the desire as political as much as it is sexual. It is a political desire that aspires to the abstract and largely unrealizable ideal that culture and society designate as its masculine norm. It is a phallicized ideal, in Lacan's meaning of the term as a categorical distinction between the phallus and the penis, the merely provisional ability of the latter to represent the former, where the entire male body can represent the phallus and thus masculine power and knowledge. The male nudes analysed by Solomon-Godeau spoke to spectators of the phallic power of the male, just as the photographs in the textbooks speak to readers of the phallic power of the manager.

Thus we recognize the powerful symbolism of the photographs in management texts. The total excision of sexuality allows the besuited manager, opened to the gaze of male readers and portrayed as actively *being* managers, to become phallicized – the photographs signal to readers the power of the manager, of managerial knowledge and thus of the power/knowledge nexus. Here, where the 'exercise of power perpetually creates knowledge and, conversely, knowledge constantly induces effects of power', knowledge and power are integrated with one another so that it 'is not possible for power to be exercised without knowledge, it is impossible for knowledge not to engender power' (Foucault, 1980, pp. 51–2), so the power of the phallus as symbolic signifier of masculine dominance banishes those knowledges that cannot be absorbed into the patriarchal, androcentric order of management.

The whole of the besuited, male body thus becomes a signifier for symbolic knowledge, power and privilege.

What spectator is being addressed (and produced) in such images? The spectator here is the reader of the management textbook, who becomes produced as a supplicant at the altar of heterosexual masculinity. Arousal is sought of his/her narcissistic desire to emulate the active male managers portrayed. S/he is urged to aspire to possess the phallus, for female readers, as many as 50 per cent, if not more, of the readership, are also enjoined to participate in this gendered gaze. What female spectator is being produced? The answer to this question can be found, I suggest, in the timing of the appearance of the photographs. They appeared first in the 1980s, just as women were making their way in large numbers into junior and middle-level managerial ranks, and feminism was proving impossible to suppress. These photographs speak to this 'invasion' of women into male space and perform a function similar to that of the paintings of idealized male nudes at the time of the French Revolution. Where the paintings examined by Solomon-Godeau could symbolize the divide between public and masculine space and private and feminine space, and the banishment of women to the latter, the photographs in management textbooks undertake the symbolic labour of banishing women but using a form of banishment that differs from that of earlier epochs. It is now no longer possible to expel women from the public realm, but it is possible to proscribe that which has been deemed dangerous in women, i.e. a feminine identity that both tempts with its promise of sexuality and arouses psychological yearning with its reminder of the mother. The woman reader gazing upon these photographs of male managers is urged to suppress her sexuality and to become 'male'. She must, if she is to enter the managerial realm, like Lady Macbeth seek to be unsexed, leaving her gendered identity at the organization's door and taking on a masculine gendered identity.

Here we see on the managerial stage an atavistic recourse to the conceptions of gender that informed Shakespeare's comedies, of a continuum rather than a binary divide (Fletcher, 1995). In this perspective sex, like gender, is seen as a 'discursive construction', for it is only within the last two centuries that a dimorphic divide between male and female biology has been recognized. That 'men are men and women are women' needing 'a crow bar to separate them' seems so obvious to our twenty-first century eyes that any denial seems absurd, yet prior to the Enlightenment the sex of humans was regarded not as dimorphic but monomorphic. One sex only was recognized, although some members of this sex carried their genitalia externally, others, seen as inferior, carried identical sexual organs internally. That is, 'men were women with exteriorised sexual organs'. Anatomists saw, where we see difference, different stages upon a teleological journey towards the perfection of the male (Hood-Williams, 1996). Sex was thus invented in the eighteenth century not, Hood-Williams emphasizes, as the result of greater knowledge of the human body, for as knowledge accumulated it supported the one- as much as the two-sex model, but as an outcome of a search for difference.

The photographs in management textbooks therefore symbolize a 'one-sex' model of management, arranged along a continuum from those who possess the phallus on one side, to those who possess the penis and who aspire to possess the phallus in the middle, and those who in their castrated status aspire fruitlessly to possess the phallus at the other end, but must act as if they had such a possession. Masculinized but castrated of the attributes of the woman, women will present no challenge to masculinity. The invitation the photographs send out is for attendance at a managerial party that is strictly predicated upon conformity to the rational, emotionless, masculine norm. Women are allowed entry, but only if they first unsex themselves. Men are allowed entry, but only if they first render themselves devoid of any attributes that do not conform to this one model of masculinity. Research has indeed shown that women entering jobs defined as masculine constantly define and redefine, construct and reconstruct their gender identities to accommodate the interwoven gender regimes of workplaces and home (Grant and Porter, 1994). The management textbooks, we have seen, encourage this construction and reconstruction from the beginning of a woman's training in management. And similarly also for male managers.

Theories of women's management style at first sight contradict this conclusion. Women managers are seen as bringing in a gendered model of management which states that female managers do more 'caring' work for, when compared to male managers, they:

- have a higher percentage of contacts with people;
- have shorter time on desk work;
- spend more time at home on administration work;
- spend more time communicating;
- tour buildings and care for the physical environment more;
- are more likely to use informal styles of communication;
- develop more flexible agendas for meetings;
- increase the chances of co-operative planning during scheduled meetings.

(Adler *et al.*, 1993)

This is a management style which is contrasted with the objective, remote, directive style of traditional management. It appears that women managers are bringing the culture of the home into the workplace. There are two points here. The first focuses upon the apparent paradox that one trend in management thinking extols the value of this supposedly female way of working, a style which is collaborative and consultative, caring, flexible, participative and sharing of power. For many thinkers, including Charles Handy, this is the style of management which should be dominant in this stage of organizational history. We have, it seems, two managerial styles, the male and the female. These are binary opposites defined by each being the antithesis of the other – what one is the other is not. This perspective appears at first sight to be a major development beyond the androcentric bias in management and organization theory. However, closer study of the arguments shows that those who argue in favour of the female management style are not arguing in favour of female managers, but are propounding another management practice which (male) managers should adopt in order to achieve more productive organizations. This is a highly instrumentalist adoption of yet another technique. That these prescriptions are rendered inane by their being decontextualized so that they ignore the reality of organizational and managerial life can be seen from the foregoing discussion. Masculine and feminine are cultural codes which have a psychic dimension and which are deeply embedded in the design and functioning of organizations. Thus organizations are not sets of pre-given, gender-neutral spaces, which are only subsequently occupied by people with gendered identities, but are social constructions that arise from a masculine vision of the world and that call on masculinity for their legitimation and affirmation (Davies, 1995). Organizations thus require us, as adults at work, to act in 'appropriately gendered ways' (Mills, 1992).

The photographs in the textbooks have thus met the incursion of women into the managerial workplace head-on, by giving them the message that in constructing themselves as managers they must constitute themselves as unsexed and gendered as masculine. The words in the textbooks may tell one story, the photographs tell its converse.

## Organizational charts

By the end of this section I wish to have shown that the organization chart symbolizes a projection of the masculine, managerial self of modernity. First, however, I will set the scene by summarizing Munro's (1995) reading of the organizational chart. This, of course, in the rules of academia I am supposed to do, for any theorist worth her salt must, if she is to maintain academic credibility, demonstrate that she has consulted the crops grown by other theorists in her particular field. However, in a chapter that explores the conflation of masculinity, modernity and organizations it behoves the writer to explore whether those crops have been modified by the authors' possession of the masculine gene. Indeed, I must confess to being fascinated that authors who can blithely analyse the most intricate of Derridean, Heideggerean and Foucauldian arguments remain ignorant, perhaps it would be unkind to use the adjective 'blissfully', but ignorant nonetheless, of the powerful critique offered by feminism and gender studies. It seems that the academic world in this sense is as much a 'phallusy' as the world of management described by Hearn (1992), although in academia it is the brandishing of the phallicized theorist (my Derrida is bigger than your Foucault) that adds the necessary inches. But I digress.

Munro's analysis of the organizational chart, steeped in Derrida, Heidegger and Foucault, strangely echoes the harmonious world-view of functionalism, for Munro's chart is a straightforward graphic description of a justly ordered world. He rejects the idea that the organization chart is 'increasingly marginalized as window dressing', that by treating it as 'merely symbolic' it becomes trivialized, for he argues that, as with other examples of 'formal material and devices', it 'interpenetrates everyday social interaction' (Munro, 1995, p. 143) and is indeed at its most powerful when it is being made 'recessive'. He shows that 'hierarchy' (represented by the lines) and 'interaction' (represented by the gaps) are binary opposites, each depending for its existence upon the other. Thus the organization chart, and here Munro is following Robert Cooper, is a 'di-vision' or two visions, with each vision an intrinsic component of a possibly divided reading of the chart as having possibilities of bringing together (symbolized by the lines) or holding apart (symbolized by the gaps) the parts of the organization. One of these will be the 'figure', one the 'ground'; each is co-constituting of the other. Importantly, he rejects the distinction between formal and informal, arguing we produce such differences as 'effects', created by actors. The chart, for actors, is also a symbol of a shared expression, so it is 'more than an incantatory device through which relative positions can be affirmed' for it has the potentially transformative powers of 'all ritual devices', and '[w]hat is interesting is the extent to which each of us can help the other *feel* the occasion to be formal or informal' (ibid., p. 148, emphasis in the original). It is this 'us' that calls up the ghosts of happy functionalists. The chart can thus in Munro's analysis become a 'shared expression' (he does not say shared between whom) which is 'already active'. The organization chart hence prefigures interaction without freezing it, and it sets up one reading rather than another, so it *travels in advance*, allowing the formal to affect the informal and vice versa. Indeed, he argues that contemporary management techniques rely on formal devices such as the chart to interpenetrate the informal, and that people in their everyday organizational situations manage to keep making hierarchy happen.

Following Heidegger, Munro argues that we construct our worlds through making them conform to our representations of it as it should or could be. This, he argues, is the function of the organization chart, to make hierarchy seem first fundamental, then natural and, at the last, normal. Drawing on Foucault he shows that the 'other' spaces, the informal, etc., are all spaces of representation governed by discourse effects. They are all spaces 'in which accounts, re-presentations, are travelling ahead of interaction' (ibid., p. 156). The formal and informal must exist mutually in interaction, and the 'technology' of membership work will therefore involve members making their dualisms appear both specific and foundational. The organizational chart, as a device that 'travels in advance' of interaction, forms one device that members draw on when making divisions. His conclusion that follows from this is important, for his intention is that 'instead of looking to theory to stand "in advance" of our representations, we had much better look at how such theories are already circulating as organizing devices' (ibid., p. 159), for such organizing devices 'animate sociality' and manufacture differences between the formal and the informal.

It is this perspective of Munro's, of the organization chart as a device that animates sociality, that I wish to take forward here, but I seek to explore how the chart undertakes this process of animation. By reading in the issues of gender and power that are missing from Munro's analysis we gain deeper insights into the constitutive process revealed in his analysis.

### The organization chart in textbook and organization

I have in front of me the chart of a new organization, one that was formed out of the recent merger of two large health trusts.[2] It is seemingly innocuous, nothing but a diagrammatic expression of how the organization is structured. Indeed this is how management textbooks treat charts. An organization chart, students who read Daft (1997) as their introduction to the world of management will be told, is the visual representation of an organization's structure (p. 319). It 'merely indicates how departments are tied together along the principal lines of authority' (Koontz and O'Donnell, 1964, p. 379; Weihrich and Koontz, 1993, p. 329). An organization without an organizational chart, the Koontz textbook argues, 'prepar[es] the way for politics, intrigue, frustration, buck-passing, lack of coordination, duplicated effort, vague policy, uncertain decision making, and other evidences of organizational inefficiency' (1964, p. 380; 1993, p. 330 – the only difference between the editions is the insertion of the hyphen in 'buck-passing). Here we have a similar conclusion to that of Munro's, that of the animating powers of the chart to constitute order, regulation and certainty.

This perspective is contradicted by the discrepancy between the certitude of the chart I am examining and the experience of people working in the 'new' organization symbolized by the chart. There is chaos as some managers leave, all move office, some take over the work of two or more managers. Meanwhile medical consultants take on expanded managerial roles or become subjected to managerial control, and the staff who make up the organization writhe under the pressures of uncertainty and too heavy workloads exacerbated by the departures of colleagues who have left in a period when the personnel department is incapable of authorizing replacements. But the new organization depicted by the chart suggests order, clarity, definition, harmony. The new organization operates through several buildings, miles apart, yet the chart writes out of existence the miles that must be travelled between offices by managers seeking to bring together teams from several disparate, factional units. This organization chart is thus a fiction, describing the ought-to-be rather than the what-is. I have another organization chart to hand, that of the university where I work, which 'restructured' itself a couple of years ago. Papers were circulated, working parties drew up various possible structures, meetings were held, staff consulted (or so we were told), committees drafted and redrafted various potential organizational charts, and eventually, after much time and money, the university restructured. My department 'moved' to a new faculty, a veritable 'virtual' move that required only a shuffling about on the organizational chart. I turn right rather than left when I leave my office to go to faculty meetings. That is all that has changed. However, the drawing on the piece of paper that says 'Organization Chart' has changed. This suggests to me that there is something of metaphor about the organization chart.

The most obvious metaphor is that the organization chart is a map, and that is what it undoubtedly is, as it 'reveals to managers and new personnel how they tie into the entire structure' (Koontz and O'Donnell, 1964, p. 380; Weihrich and Koontz, 1993, p. 330). It is a map where,

rather than squiggly lines and coloured blobs symbolizing lakes, moun-
tains, towns and cities, there are straight lines symbolizing departments
and ranks, and where, rather than red, black or yellow lines representing roads and railways, there are straight lines delineating lines of
authority. The boxes in organizational charts represent, we are told,
not people but *positions* to which are attached job descriptions that
speak of certainty, assurance, the omnipotence of the planner of the
organization who knows what needs to be done, where, how and by
which particular position holder. The people who 'fill' these positions
are living, breathing, emoting individuals who buckle under stress, who
jump into political games with more or less enthusiasm, who come to
work after kicking the dog, kissing the children, rowing with partners,
avoiding the neighbours, fuming at the news, taking painkillers for the
headache. The chart represents thus not a simulacrum of reality, nor
even an expression of it; rather it expresses a wish, a hope of a what-
might-be, in the perfectly functioning organizational world. It tells all
people in the organization 'this is the establishment in which you belong,
and you are "here"', just as the map in the middle of town or campus
features, amid the lines and the confusion, a comfortable red arrow
that points to a square and announces, in large, encouraging letters,
'you are here'. It takes years of acculturation to be able to understand
how to project oneself into the map to the place at the tip of the arrow,
and from the canvas back onto the tarmac again, to be able then to
look around and to tread out, more or less purposefully, in the direction that should take the map-readers to their destination. In the West,
we are map-immersed peoples, for maps are to us not alien forms but
'synthesized systems of supersigns we all grew up with' (Wood, 1992,
p. 144). Our acculturation encourages our forgetting of the symbolism
of maps and charts. We forget that they are social constructions (Wood,
1992), that they are contingent, conditional and arbitrary, that they
create boundaries rather than representing 'realities' (ibid., p. 19) and
most of all that they *create ownership at a location* (ibid., p. 21).
We forget that maps are metaphors and that we use spatial metaphors
'in defining concepts through their extension, intension'; we use them
to 'provide the setting for mathematical and logical arguments, and we
make them explicit when talking about "a field of research", "the fron-
tier of knowledge"' etc. (Reichert, 1992, p. 90).

    We forget too that maps embody the interests of their makers and
we forget also that maps are a function of 'the representing mind',
products of the agency of the mapper. They are thus but one perspective on 'the common scene', chosen from among competing interests.
They embody those interests in the map, and the choice of what to
embody is never, and cannot be, objective, for maps always manifest
the interests of their authors. Wood (1992) cautions us to look for the
repressed experience, the suppressed interest, represented in the map.

It is, he argues, the *repression* of the interest that allows the map to masquerade effectively as accuracy and truth. The organization chart, seemingly so accurate and truthful, tells far more than its blankly staring boxes joined by clear, straight lines would at first sight admit. What it does not say is important for the refusal to articulate reveals what is repressed. What remains unsaid in the organizational chart is that in its mapping it draws the world of public spaces that are always the world of heterosexual men, for the map enunciates the public/ private binary divide, a profoundly important ideological concept in liberal western societies (Benn and Gaus, 1983). This argument is so well known that it needs little elaboration here, beyond noting that large organizations, since they emerged in the increasingly homophobic world of the nineteenth and early twentieth centuries, have been worlds where men have gathered in groups which excluded women (Hearn, 1992). Home became and remains the locus of the 'natural', the forum for those acts seen as private and closest to nature, such as the sexual act, the giving of birth (Martin, 1990) and, ultimately, dying. These two binary opposites of public/private equate the private with the female and with nature, and thus with the personal, the emotional, with intuition and subjection; and the public with the male and thus with the political, with justice, reason, philosophy, power and freedom (Pateman, 1983). The many women who throughout have continued to work in the public world of men have been invisible refugees from their 'rightful' place.

A map, furthermore, is formed from myths that are not required to declare themselves in language, and this is the power of the map for in its 'moment of reception, it evaporates' and we see only its neutrality and innocence, an ambiguity that allows the myth to work without being seen (Wood, 1992, p. 104). Maps, in short, 'constitute a semiological system (that is, a system of values) [that] are ever vulnerable to seizure or invasion by myth' (ibid., p. 107). They are codes which legislate how something may be construed as representing something else. Formed simultaneously from semiotics and image that allow a dual signification of language and icon, the map image 'provides a context in which the semantics of the linguistic code are extended to embrace a variety of latent iconic potentials; to the same end, it imposes a secondary syntax that shapes entire linguistic signifiers into local icons' (ibid., p. 124). The map, in presentation attains the level of discourse, that is, it is simultaneously an instrument of communication and persuasion. The organization chart hence signals to us that we who are not senior managers are the little people in the organization, who owe allegiance to the 'big' people in the big boxes at the 'top' of the chart.

Maps also create and reflect space; they 'bind space to the exercise of human will' (Wood, 1992, p. 150). The organization chart, as map, can in this reading be seen as a pictorial sign that reflects the language rather than the landscape of the organization, and the language it reflects is that of the managerial map-maker, imposed upon 'the organization'. This language is implicated by gender bias. The English language covertly (and overtly) demeans or trivializes females, presenting males as normative and females as deviant or secondary (Bonvillain, 1995). The very language we speak allows males to precede and females appear linguistically in second place, always male *and* female, man *and* woman, husband *and* wife. Semantic derogation towards females and linguistic favouritism toward males is implicated in interpretations of the word 'man', supposedly neutral yet imposing meanings by implication, so that even when 'man' is used in generic contexts male images surface and women are filtered out (Bonvillain, 1995). Now this is important when we are discussing *man*agement, for the word has taken on a meaning signalled by its first syllable. This is the syllable which announces the practice of *man*agement and equates it with a practice undertaken by those gendered male. The organization chart expresses this graphically – it can be seen as a projection of the body, with the (male) managerial head at the top, the manager literally 'heading' the organization, and the spreading, earthy, natural world of the non-professional and of women, those who are presumed to work with their bodies rather than their minds, located at the bottom. These are the areas below the collars and ties in the photographs in the textbooks. The charts recall for us the metaphors of 'up' and 'down', remind us always of the superiority of the former and thus tie us into a metaphorical enactment of obedience to those 'at the top' (Johnson, 1987), who are always already gendered male, for Bonvillain's analysis of the gendering of language concludes that:

> All the data uncovered in analyses of English linguistic forms indicate a pervasive, covert ascription of positive and normative qualities to males and negative or secondary ones to females. Continual repetition of English words and expressions, both as speakers and hearers, reinforces cultural evaluations that enhance males' status and disvalue females. These judgments do not originate in the language but arise linguistically to express, supplement, and justify entrenched cultural constructs.
>
> (Bonvillain, 1995, p. 248)

The organizational chart perpetrates graphically that which is achieved through language, for it is, like other maps, a projection of the mind of the map-maker.

Like other maps it 'appropriates and recasts the representations of mental space by concretizing them as part of social life, part of second nature' (Soja, 1985, p. 94). It is a projection of the mental space of the managerial cartographer rather than an objectified representation of the 'organization'. This may explain why, in map-immersed cultures so accustomed to mapping what appears to be 'real' territory, organizational maps do not map the building(s) in which the organization is located but the metaphysical, hierarchical 'structure' of the organization. It explains why the 'box' on the chart that relates to senior management and those boxes that refer to management are not apportioned according to the number of people they represent: the section that maps the workers is no larger than that which represents the senior managers – one box may represent 1,000 workers, another ten senior managers, all are accorded equal space. In this, the managerial mapper is, literally, saying to the worker, 'I'm bigger than you. I take up ten times, a hundred times, the space that you do'. They are perhaps saying more. Hearn argues that organizations are places where men may sublimate their suppressed homosexuality and simultaneously parade themselves as sexually active heterosexuals:

> Organizations . . . give ample opportunity for men's narcissism . . . But most important a large amount of men's contact and discourse in public domains, particularly in organizations, is a deflection from, a sublimation of, or indeed a form of mutual masturbation. Gathering together, as managers and/or workmates, standing up, strutting, performing in public, orating, arguing, saying your piece, in the competitive world of men involves a symbolic waving around of the penis . . . as a display of power to others, women and men, but most importantly men . . . The whole sordid little show is a phallusy – a desperate complex of moves by men to take the public stage by storm, to dominate the material world of reproduction.
>
> (Hearn, 1992, p. 207)

Is the organizational chart therefore a graphic representation of this 'phallusy'? Does it encapsulate visually the striving for the phallus that I explored in relation to The Law? I suggest it does. Not only is the organizational chart encapsulating the phallocentric tendency that allows us to understand seemingly all life forms only in terms of the masculine (Grosz, 1988; Harding, 1991; Calas and Smircich, 1992a, b; Haraway, 1992; Martin, 1996), its phallocentric bias means that when we examine management and organizations we look for and can only see this 'typical' model of male manager as active and dynamic aggressor who differs markedly from the supposedly passive, defenceless female. It is this manager who haunts the organization chart. It is modernity's manager.

Further, the organizational chart, like a map, expresses not a substance but a set of relations between entities that are distributed in time–space (Urry, 1985). These two, time and space, overlap but must be examined separately if we are to grasp the significance of the chart as map.

With regard to time, the dominance in management texts of the problems of change and the seemingly inexorable increase in the speed at which time flows are not reflected in discussions of organization charts. The description of the chart in the Koontz textbook has not changed, save for the inclusion of a hyphen, in 40 years. The organization chart is a static map of the organizational hierarchy, removing fluidity and encapsulating a specific momentary impression for all time. If the organization is mimetic of the manager's body (Dale and Burrell, 2000), then this is a masculine body. The next organizational restructuring results only in a shifting of the boxes on the map – the hierarchical structure remains intact. This is significant, as the juxtaposition of rampant change and time-bound rigidity reveals the contradictions that run through and through management discourses. The photographs and diagrams in their representations symbolize stability and conformity and contradict the warnings in the text of the need for managerial vigilance if survival is to be ensured in times of never-ending, ever-increasing change.

With regard to space, the spaces of the organization are mapped onto the chart by the boxes and the boundary lines. These speak of a space at once imaginary and real: the organic, lived world of the organization which is both an arena of action and that has the potential of enabling further effects, and the captured, paper world of the chart (Lefebvre, 1998). There are at least two space-worlds, two spaces in the organizational chart (the 'informal' organization is a third) – the working space-world and the managerial space-world. In the organization itself, however, ease of movement between the two is restricted: managers in Britain have long engaged in a retreat from direct management of the workforce (Anthony, 1986) and managers remain in their offices for 90 per cent of their working day (Stewart *et al.*, 1994), occupying their own space-world and from there surveying, more Nelson's eye than Panopticon, the world that the textbook through its construction of the managerial consciousness has helped bring into being, one subordinated to the rule of managerialism. The organization chart thus presents an image that differs so much from 'reality' that it offers, like maps, 'a double imposition of force: first in order to maintain a coherence and, later, in the shape of reductionism, in the shape of the strategy of homogenization and the fetishization of cohesiveness in and through reductions of all kinds' (Lefebvre, 1998, p. 411). In the 'territorialising spatial practice' (Duncan, 1996) that is management, the organizational chart thus maps a simplified, reduced world of hierarchical lines that unite the dreamed organization of the manager, devoid of anything but devotion to production, with the lived world of the people who together constitute the organization. This is Derrida's world of the 'ought to be', a projection of the managerial map-maker of the twin desires for orderliness and for a managerial supremacy put beyond challenge.

### Boundary lines – the informal organization

The chart has gaps – in between the boxes and the lines are blank spaces that are as symbolic as the boxes. What can we find in these blanknesses? I suggest more than Munro's binary opposites. Geography teaches us that the spaces within and between the lines on maps are borderlands, i.e. 'social and political constructions that are used to construct differences' and 'relational places where individuals live and construct themselves in relation to each other' (Pratt, 1992, pp. 243–4). Organization charts are formed out of boundary lines which delineate the organization's 'inside' and 'outside', and section the 'inside'. In these 'envelope[s] of space–time' (Massey, 1996) boundary lines are 'saturated with meaning'. They contain 'bounds of convention, limits of the sayable, trace of a dialectic between inside and outside, penumbra in which identity and difference merge, thin line covering vast power, phallolinear mark' (Reichert, 1992, p. 87). This 'phallolinear mark' is something to which I will return.

Management textbooks acknowledge the blank spaces on the chart as 'the informal organization'. Weihrich and Koontz map it onto the chart in 1993 (p. 145) in the form of amoeba-shaped outlines superimposed upon the 'formal' organization, showing routes by which the formal lines of authority are transgressed as department managers have coffee, go bowling and play chess with the vice presidents two ranks above them in the hierarchy. Amoebae, school biology lessons tell us, are single-celled animals that have no brains, that absorb sustenance from their environment and into themselves, but are important in that they contribute to the food chain. This is reflected in the definition of the informal organization that the Koontz textbook borrows from Chester Barnard, as 'any joint personal activity without conscious joint purpose, even though contributing to joint results' (Weihrich and Koontz, 1993, p. 246). Other metaphors in the textbooks suggest, however, that the informal organization is savage and untamed, is perhaps the Freudian id (the unconscious place into which drives and desires are repressed) to the organizational ego (the organized sense of personal identity), with the manager as superego (critic and protector of the ego) (Minsky, 1996). The informal organization (the id) precedes formal organization (the ego), the textbooks tell us, just as the ego and later super-ego is carved out of the id. Communication (that which is buried in the unconscious is inaccessible to the conscious mind) is difficult until formal organization is achieved, but there is a 'gregarious' impulse that leads to the seeking of company (so as to provide the organized sense of identity, or self). Unless controlled the informal organization can challenge the formal, just as the unconscious id so influences conscious behaviour that the ego is permanently precarious. The informal organization can, the textbooks tell us, be tamed, i.e.

coordinated, given a conscious joint purpose and a structure for gaining that purpose, and thus it can become a part of the formal organization, just as the super-ego can work to control the unconscious.

The boxes on the organization chart, it follows, represent the 'cultured' part of the organization, and the spaces in the chart those areas that are unknown and unknowable and which always challenge the organized, conscious world of the manager. The organization chart represents the managerial cartographer's projection of his self-identity onto the organization, so that the organization is literally made in his own image. It is possible to say this because organization charts, like maps, are not empty mirrors but are things that at once hide and reveal the hand of the cartographer; they are fleshly, of the body and of the mind of the individuals that produce them, drawing the eye of the map-reader (Pile and Thrift, 1995). The 'mapping subject' 'is an exclusive structure encoded with a particular gender, class and racial positioning; ... a structure for subjectivity unresponsive to the perspectives of many non-dominant subjectivities, particularly women' (Kirby, 1996, p. 46). This mapping subject both reflects and reinforces ways of conceiving both the subject and space, through a symbiotic shaping of environment and (managerial) self identified by Freud, whereby the self is achieved through the delimitation of an external environment, and the form of the environment thus produced will recursively dictate the shape of the self (ibid.). Charts, like maps, thus represent 'an immutable space organized by invariable boundaries, an a-temporal, objective, transparent space' (ibid., p. 47) that is contiguous with the subjectivity of the map-maker who thus, through the chart that is a projection of the managerial self, shapes organizational subjects and organizational environments in a particular way.

Further, the boxes on the chart symbolize, in their contained rigidity, both the separation of the manager from the natural, the untamed, and the effort of the manager to 'box in' that which does not conform to managerial demands for rationality and order. Maps are framed, marked with text, simplifications, fabrications:

> The map does not simply itemise the world: it fixes it within a discursive and visual practice of power and meaning; and, because it naturalises power and meaning against an impassive and neutral space, it serves to legitimate not only the exercise of that power but also the meaningfulness of that meaning.
>
> (Pile and Thrift, 1995, p. 48)

The organizational chart thus speaks of management's attempt to achieve power over the rest of the organization, establishing the meaningfulness of the meaning of the organization for themselves and others. Even if not visibly present when shut away in their offices, managers are always present, always seeking to tame the non-managerial Other, the id, the 'informal organization' that threatens misrule and gregarious chaos.

### Representing masculine space – the phallolinear mark

Reichert's (1992) notion of the map as 'phallolinear mark' can now be clearly seen. It is a concept that he does not develop, but it alerts us to the gendering of the organization's Other. Maps are inescapably gendered for they presume intertextuality, a prior knowledge of other texts that are always already, in the feminist canon, imprinted upon by patriarchy. Maps form part of the discursive field by which social structures are constituted – our theoretical interpretations can reflect only other interpretations and not a bedrock reality. Our theoretical landscapes are therefore created by, rather than corresponding to, our interpretative schemes and theories. They cannot be seen as hermetically sealed from the broader milieu in which they originate, for as texts they are inextricably intertwined with their context and what is outside them. The organizational chart/map is, like other maps, drawn by male managers who call upon both a history of texts that privilege the heterosexual male and suppress the female and all others not meeting the heteronormative ideal, and a psychological history that is intertwined with the subjectivity of gender and the intense experience of insecurity that is the history of the individual. This latter history calls to them to distinguish themselves from those who are Other, and this is a further symbolic function of the little boxes of the map/chart, which neatly and tightly separate managerial space from the space of the Other, symbolically locking each into their own sections of the (virtual) organization (Young, 1997).

The boxes at the top of the chart thus represent what Hearn and Morgan (1990) refer to as 'hegemonic masculinities', i.e. those forms and practices of masculinity which dominate within societies. These are historically and culturally conditioned, and today's dominant model is white, heterosexist, middle-class and Anglophone. It is a managerial masculinity reflected in preoccupation with control over others for management, by definition, *exists to control others*. In management, the appropriately gendered behaviour is a masculinity shaped around notions of rationality, one that is detached and logical, unemotional and wholly absorbed in the work process. It is a rationality which serves a double purpose, as it provides a manager with an air of superiority over manual workers who are supposedly less rational, and it excludes supposedly irrational females (Mills and Murgatroyd, 1991). It is a rationality embedded deep within Taylorism, where the 'ideal workman would appear to almost lose physical presence, or be a mere disembodied bearer of role, in effect part of a machine system', where a very explicit model of masculinity is given, one of stable, taken-for-granted power and authority, as in the patriarchal family (Hearn and Parkin, 1986, pp. 18–19). This, I suggest, is modernity incarnate, or rather the masculine manager is the materialized metaphysics of modernity.

The organizational chart can thus be read as a 'phallolinear mark', dividing up the territory of the organization in the image of the senior managers who control the territory, and thus defining a *masculine* space.

### Maintaining masculinity

The managerial mapper replicates the masculinist geographers and anthropologists who have written of the 'field' and nature as if they were feminine, and their forays into fieldwork as masculine acts of manly dominance (Sparke, 1996). In organization theory this is seen as the perpetuation by managers of a 'web of rules of masculinity' (Mills, 1992, p. 142). Management textbooks contribute to the sustenance of a gendered world, as can be seen, for example, in Weihrich and Koontz's (1993) discussion of 'factors determining an effective span'. The number of subordinates a manager can effectively manage, they write, depends upon a number of factors, the most important of which is the 'manager's ability to reduce the time he or she spends with subordinates' (ibid., p. 249). A list of factors that 'determine' the amount of time a manager must spend with subordinates is given on p. 250, with the list of attributes that determine that only little time need be spent being the exact opposite of that determining that close supervision is needed. The manager must spend a great deal of time with subordinates who are unwilling to assume responsibility, who are immature, ineffective in meetings and in their interactions, unable to communicate, and who have been little trained, for 'well trained subordinates, require not only less of their managers' time but also less contact with their managers' (ibid., p. 250). The 'good' subordinate, it follows, allows the manager to keep a distance, and is well trained, can undertake well-defined tasks to achieve verifiable objectives, communicates using appropriate techniques, and is mature and willing to assume responsibility. The 'bad' subordinate demonstrates features that are seen as close to nature (untrained, untamed) and thus as violating the heteronormative order. *Rationality*, structure, independence are 'good'; ignorance, ineffectiveness, *emotionality* are 'bad' and must be controlled by close supervision. Rationality is good and results in self-management; emotionality is bad and requires strict, external management. This rationality/emotionality binary reflects the male/female binary divide. Managers must train/tame the feminized members of the organization until they become masculinized so that managers may have their managerial time to themselves, to do the important jobs of management in their own territory of the office or meeting room. The process of training/taming requires their crossing over the boundaries marked on the chart, leaving the box of the manager for that of the 'Other'. In Rose's (1996) terms, it involves them leaving what is to them their 'real' space, one that is fixed and solid, and entering what is for them an 'imagined' space (the space of the informal organization) that is one of flows, fusion and melding, a feminine and a gay space.

This distinction between real and imagined space, one that percolates through geography and cartography, is, Rose argues, drawing on the work of Judith Butler and Luce Irigaray, 'a performance of the male imaginary' that is part of 'prior spatialized male imaginary' (Rose, 1996, p. 73). It is, in Gilmore's (1990) terms, 'man-playing', where the managerial concept of 'masculinity' depends upon how it defines 'femininity' as the castrated male other (Grant and Porter, 1996). Its differential access to power (Haywood and Mac an Ghaill, 1996) allows the construction of a male, managerial self, but one that requires the constantly constructed, negotiated and reconstructed routine social interactions that allow simultaneous processes of differentiation and identification (Collinson and Hearn, 1996) and thus reinforcement of the construction of the manager as masculine.

### Returning to Munro

Munro (1995) argued that the organizational chart is a theory of the organization that 'travels in advance' of interaction and thus constitutes the organization through animating sociality and manufacturing differences between the formal and the informal. My excursion into geography leads me to suggest that the chart should be seen as a metaphor of a map. It is a map that delineates space which, geographers now argue, is relational and constitutive of social processes, and which is a complex web of relations of domination and subordination, of solidarity and cooperation, and is thus 'power-geometry' (Massey, 1992, quoted by McDowell, 1996). The chart symbolically compresses space, excising those aspects of the organization which do not conform to the embodied desires of the managerial map-maker, that is, desires for 'power-geometry', for a world of the managerial ought-to-be, of managerial security in the status of a dominant masculinity that renders all other actors in the organization Other, subject to control by a management which is able to project its omnipresence onto the paper world of the chart and thus disguise its bodily absence from the organic, lived world of the organization. For this world that ought-to-be is one that is a projection of the managerial self-image, of a cultured, rational, masculine subjectivity that rigidly suppresses the natural and the emotional, the worker and thus the *non-masculine*. It is a self-image that has, in elevating a hegemonic masculinity, severely suppressed all aspects that do not conform to this very narrow masculinity. The chart thus, in travelling in advance of interaction, to use Munro's term, constitutes not the organization but the *manager*, and it allows the manager to see the organization as *him-* or *her- (masculinized) self* writ large. In so far as other organizational actors acquiesce in the perspective that is offered by the chart, then I must concur with Munro's analysis that the chart animates the sociality of the organization. This is a sociality, however, that is not that of the happy functionalist who informs Munro's theory, but a sociality imbued, first, with gendered distinctions, and second, with power/knowledge differentials, for managers make a claim to possessing a management knowledge, whose symbolic representation is the organizational chart, that is inseparable from their power.

## Conclusion: queering the textbooks/queering the post-modern

The textbooks, in their turn to the post-modern, work to construct the identities of readers, i.e. how *to be managers*, rather than the passive offering of advice and guidance on *how to do management*. They offer one gender identity to all readers, male or female, and this is the gendered identity, inscribed in the photographs, diagrams and charts, of one particular form of masculinity, a masculinity not attached to genitalia but to discourse. This is a masculinity which embodies modernity and thus modernity, represented through masculinity, is inscribed upon the bodies of both male and female managerial bodies.

There are two themes in this conclusion which now need to be explained and explored. The first of these is that in the above discussion I have drawn largely upon feminist theories, but alluded throughout to queer theory, and the potential it offers for arguing that gender identities may be divorced, to a greater or lesser extent, from the biologically sexed body. The second is the insistence upon modernity being inscribed, as it were, upon managers' bodies and through managerial identities, an insistence that seemingly contradicts my assertion, through many of the previous chapters, that the textbooks underwent a post-modernist turn, towards the constitution of identities, from the 1980s. The following analysis is predicated upon the post-modern rejection of the 'either/or' and the acceptance instead of the 'both/and'. Queer theory allows a rejection of the *either* male *or* female, so that we can read individuals as *both* male *and* female, and similarly it introduces the necessity of rejecting the sharp distinction between the modern and the post-modern, and to see the post-modern as having *both* the modern *and* the post-modern collapsed into each other.

## Queering the textbooks

I am going beyond feminist theorizing and into queer theory as the latter allows me to argue that both male and female managers have to gender themselves according to a dominant model of masculinity, an argument made possible by queer theory's demonstration that gender arises from the performativity of gendered behaviours, or, in Judith Butler's words:

> The regulatory norms of sex work in a performative fashion to constitute the materiality of bodies and, more specifically, to materialize the body's sex, to materialize sexual difference in the service of the consolidation of the heterosexual imperative ... Thus, the fixity of body is fully material, but materiality is seen as the effect of power, as power's most productive effect. Thus 'sex' is not simply what one has, or a static description of what one is: it will be one of the norms by which the 'one' becomes viable at all, that which qualifies a body for life within the domain of cultural intelligibility.
>
> (Butler, 1993, p. 2)

Butler's work is famously inaccessible, a reputation belied somewhat by a paper published in 1996 in which she summarizes the arguments of her various books. In this paper she argues:

1  Following Foucault, that identity categories tend to be instruments of regulatory regimes, whether as the normalizing categories of oppressive structures or as the rallying points for a liberatory contestation of that very oppression (Butler, 1996, p. 180).
2  Her suspicion of identity categories. She argues (ibid., p. 181) that in the construction of the 'I' there is much that must be excluded, left outside. What is excluded is a radical *concealment*, for whatever terms we use to describe ourselves the meaning of the term is, first, always indeterminate and, second, imposed by others. Power thus comes into play in this use of a label, so that one side of the label is 'good' (e.g. heterosexuality) and the other side 'bad' (e.g. transvestite).
3  However, the 'good' depends upon the 'bad' to know what it, the good, is and so although it looks as if the 'bad' is derived from the good, it is the other way around.
4  She then uses 'drag' to develop her thesis. In drag, a person *performs* a sexual identity, or plays at a sexual identity. Butler argues that we all do this, *perform* or *play* out our sexual identities. We are now at the heart of Butler's thesis. She suggests, referring to herself:

This is not a performance from which I can take radical distance, for this is deep-seated play, psychically entrenched play
*and this 'I' does not play its lesbianism as a role*. Rather, it is
through the repeated play of this sexuality that the 'I' is insist-
ently reconstituted as a lesbian 'I'; paradoxically, it is precisely
the *repetition* of that play that establishes as well the *instability*
of the very category that it constitutes. For if the 'I' is a site of
repetition, that is, if the 'I' only achieves the semblance of identity through a certain repetition of itself, then the I is always
displaced by the very repetition that sustains it. . . And if the 'I'
is the effect of a certain repetition, one which produces the
semblance of a continuity or coherence, then there is no 'I' that
precedes the gender that it is said to perform; the repetition,
and the failure to repeat, produce a string of performances that
constitute and contest the coherence of that 'I'.

(ibid., p. 183)

5   She concludes (ibid., p. 185) that drag constitutes the mundane
way in which genders are appropriated, theatricalized, worn and
done; it implies that all gendering is a kind of impersonation and
approximation. If this is true, it seems, there is no original or
primary gender that drag imitates, but *gender is a kind of imitation for which there is no original*; in fact, it is a kind of imitation
that produces the very notion of the original as an *effect* and consequence of the imitation itself. In other words, the naturalistic
effects of heterosexualized genders are produced through imitative
strategies; what they imitate is a phantasmatic ideal of heterosexual
identity, one that is produced by the imitation as its effect. In this
sense, the 'reality' of heterosexual identities is performatively constituted through an imitation that sets itself up as the origin and the
ground of all imitations. Heterosexuality is always in the process
of imitating and approximating its own phantasmatic idealization
of itself – *and failing*.

6   The very possibility of becoming a viable subject requires that a
certain gender mime be already under way (ibid., p. 187). The
'being' of the subject is no more self-identical than the 'being' of
any gender; in fact, coherent gender, achieved through an apparent
repetition of the same, produces as its *effect* the illusion of a prior
and volitional subject. In this sense, gender is not a performance
that a prior subject elects to do, but gender is *performative* in the
sense that it constitutes as an effect the very subject it appears to
express. It is a *compulsory* performance in the sense that acting
out of line with heterosexual norms brings with it ostracism,
punishment and violence, not to mention the transgressive pleas-
ures produced by those very prohibitions. In short, 'there is no

performer prior to the performed, that the performance is performative, that the performance constitutes the appearance of a "subject" as its effect'.

In this exploration of gendered identities, Butler's work radically destabilizes the binary divide between male and female for she shows that *all* gender identities are performative and depend not upon genitalia, nor indeed upon social construction whose base is the materiality of the body, but upon the iterative performance of a norm that does not exist. From this, it is possible to explore managers, whether women or men, as having a gender identity in that part of their lives when they are managers achieved through the performativity of iteration: this performative identity is the deracinated masculinity demanded of managers. It is facilitated by the textbooks which engage the reader in demonstrating the required masculinity.

Further, queer theory challenges 'the regulatory power of the category of the normal' (Seidman, 2001, p. 358), and offers the potential to 'queer' broader aspects of our lives. Diana Fuss (2001), taking forward this potential, argues that 'heterosexuality' requires 'homosexuality' in order to define itself. The opposition of 'heterosexual/homosexual' is, for Fuss, constructed on another related opposition, the couplet 'inside/outside', a binary opposition which permeates and in so doing helps define Western culture and indeed the Western psyche, where identity is relational, constituted through reference to an outside or other which defines the boundaries of the me and the not/me. But, she asks

> how do outsides and insides come about? What philosophical and critical operations or modes produce the specious distinction between a pure and natural heterosexual inside and an impure and unnatural homosexual outside? Where exactly, in this borderline sexual economy, does the one identity leave off and the other begin?
> (Fuss, 2001, p. 348)

In relation to my foregoing argument, we can similarly ask where, in a culture of fragmented identities that are constantly in the process of being generated, and where women and men share many characteristics, does the identity of 'masculine' end and the identity of 'feminine' begin, and indeed where does the category of 'manager' end and 'worker' begin? Further, however, Fuss's questions bring to mind Parker's adoption of Kosofsky Sedgwick's metaphors to recommend a practice of queering academic discourses to achieve 'an unceasing exposure of what was secreted away, and at the same time a closeting of some other term' (Parker, 2001, p. 49), i.e. a refusal of the either/or and the acknowledgement of the both/and.

This insistence upon the 'both/and' does not arise solely from queer theory, of course, but is fundamental to much of, for example, Derrida's work. However, in our attempts to periodize the modern and the post-modern it is too easy to assume it is *either* one *or* the other (and indeed to assume that both exist). We find this, most obviously, in Cooper and Burrell's exposition in 1988 of two opposing conceptual positions on organizations, modernism and post-modernism, a necessary peda-gogical device at a time when post-modernism was somewhat new and strange to many studying organizations and management. Jameson has been bothered for more than a decade by the problem of how the post-modern emerged. In 1991 (p. xiii) he wrote 'The name itself – post-modernism – has crystallized a host of hitherto independent devel-opments which, thus named, prove to have contained the thing itself in embryo and now step forward richly to document its multiple genealogies'. By 2002 (p. 24) he is exploring 'a twofold movement, in which the foregrounding of continuities, the insistent and unwavering focus on the seamless passage from past to present, slowly turns into a consciousness of a radical break; while at the same time the enforced attention to a break gradually turns the latter into a period in its own right'.

This, of course, is what I have been doing for, informed by such works as Cooper and Burrell's (1988), I have been programmed, as it were, to look for such a break and to try to understand how the modern gave way to the post-modern. I was at the start of this project somewhat flummoxed by the continuities in management: much of the textbook remains unchanged and the manager's uniform of suit and tie is little different at the beginning of the twenty-first century from the uniform of managers at the opening of the twentieth century. It seemed that all was continuity, that management was a modernist redoubt in a post-modern world until a closer reading suggested that there was such a break, that the textbooks turned from describing *how to do management* to *creating managers*. The exception appears to be that of the manager as Enlightenment rationality in motion. This suggests the following interpretations:

1   The possibility of continuity of aspects of the modern into the post-modern.
2   An identity that appears to be modern but is in fact a post-modern simulacrum of a modern identity.

I suggest that it is the second of these, for if we are truly in a post-modern age then all is simulacrum. The inscription of Enlightenment rationality upon the manager's gendered body is thus distinct and sepa-rate from the managerial enactment of Enlightenment rationality in the modern era. There the manager's role was to *do management*, today it is to *be the manager*, and the model for 'the manager' emerged, in the modern era, out of older ideas of control, older ideas of the need for control (Protevi, 2001).

I will turn to Fredric Jameson (1991) to explain this. He argues (Jameson, 1991, p. 12) that in post-modernism depth is replaced by surface, or by multiple surfaces, and that the alienated subject of modernity is displaced by the fragmented subject (ibid., p. 14). Rather than the ideas of a ruling class forming the dominant (or hegemonic) ideology of bourgeois society, the advanced capitalist countries today are 'now a field of stylistic and discursive heterogeneity without a norm' (ibid., p. 16). Rather than original artworks there is now nothing original, nothing new, but all is pastiche. 'Pastiche is, like parody, the imitation of a peculiar or unique, idiosyncratic style, the wearing of a linguistic mask, speech in a dead language. But it is a neutral practice of such mimicry, without any of parody's ulterior motives, amputated of the satiric impulse, devoid of laughter ... the producers of culture have nowhere to turn but to the past: the imitation of dead styles, speech through all the masks and voices stored up in the imaginary museum of a new global culture' (ibid., p. 17). It is this last point I wish to address here, and suggest, following Foucault, that pastiche applies not only to the more traditional definition of cultural artefacts, but to ourselves, as the works of art which we make of ourselves. Foucault asked: 'Couldn't everyone's life become a work of art? Why should the lamp or the house be an art object, but not our life?' (Foucault, in Rabinow, 1986). And just as in other works of art there is no original work, nothing but pastiche, so, in the works of art that we make of ourselves, we can do nothing but make pastiche. The manager is thus *both* a post-modern simulacrum of modernity *and* a reminder of the promise of modernity. And so the manager who has the Enlightenment rationality of modernity inscribed upon his/her body is not a modern monad whose identity lies somewhere within, an essentialist core in a grey suit, but a pastiche of the idea of what the manager is. The textbooks provide one of the patterns for knitting this pastiche together.

# Part III

# Reconstruction

The social construction of management

# 7   The managerial self

## Introduction

The eruption and dissemination so widely of a discourse as influential as that of management must, it would seem, in this post-modern age where the self is regarded as a discursive production, in some way influence the formation of persons, particularly the persons who have become managers and/or who have studied management. In what ways is the subjectivity of the manager constituted through the enactment of 'dumbed-down' male rationality using expressionless art, unscientific science and the law of the phallus? This chapter seeks to discover what expressions of the self are made possible or inhibited through the study and practice of management.

This is not the place to rehearse the numerous theories of the 'self', but discussions that ignore *definitions* of the self fall into an endlessly recursive word-play that allows the concept at the centre of the debate to disappear, untouched and underanalysed. I will thus provide below a short overview of some of the debate in order to contextualize the current analysis, noting that the disputations within the humanities and social sciences as to the ontology and epistemology of the self offer such intricate mazes that the pursuer of the 'self' is likely to become lost. The self used here follows Butler (1997, pp. 10–11) in seeing it as that which takes occupation of the locus of the subject and thus assumes its, the self's, subjectified identity. The subject is a linguistic category, a 'structure in formation', a 'site' that is occupied by individuals. From this, the 'self' becomes a discursive construction that draws upon multiple discourses in its processes of formation and re-formation: each of us is multiple selves. The multiply selved self cannot be an essentialized self. This is important, for the limitations of language may at times predispose the reader of this chapter to presume that the managerial self who emerges from the analysis is an essentialized entity formed solely out of management discourse. Such a presumption will be erroneous, if only because the data reveal that managers themselves recognize in themselves several selves. (The clumsiness of that last sentence demonstrates in advance the difficulties of this project of exploring the managerial self.)

How does one discover the managerial self? In previous chapters I have used as my data the contents of a long series of management textbooks, but now I wish to explore how they have served to constitute the world. Published data will not suffice, and so I have undertaken a series of interviews with managers and gathered data from a semi-public meeting, the results of which form the basis of this chapter. Foucault allows us to use texts or transcriptions of talk as our data, to read what has been said in such a way as to reveal the discourses that enable practices of the self to occur. There are, however, limitations to using Foucault when discovering how discourses constitute the self, for he fails to show how discourses come to be taken up by the subject (Butler, 1997), and therefore Foucault forms the inspiration but not the guidance for this chapter. To facilitate this analysis, I am using a model of discourse analysis based on the theories of Bollas (1993, 1995), Harré (1998) and Mühlhäusler and Harré (1990). Bollas, a psychoanalytical theorist working in the objects-relations school, offers what seems to me the most intuitively persuasive of arguments about how we constitute ourselves from moment to moment, taking with us into our futures the imprints of our past. Unfortunately, Bollas' only guidelines on how to gain access to the objects that subjects use when constituting themselves require the researcher to act as psychoanalyst to the subjects' analysands, a process that is beyond the reach of a social scientific research project. Harré (1998) and Mühlhäusler and Harré (1990) offer a method of gaining insight into the phenomenology of the managerial self, and I have built on their analysis of personal pronouns to construct a model of discourse analysis that focuses upon the way that subjects explore who they are as an 'I' and a 'me'. This model allows the discovery of how management discourse becomes part of the 'I' or the 'me'. In this, management discourse is seen, in Bollas' (1993) terms, as an 'object' that becomes constitutive of the self.

This model involves a psychologization of the self which Newton (1998) has argued, in his critique of the work of Knights and Willmott, invokes precisely that which Foucault appeared keen to avoid. Foucault, however, is on record as saying his works are 'tools' he offers to others to use as they think fit (Martin *et al.*, 1988). He did not see his theories as biblical texts that should stand for all time, as the one, single truth, and thus he never ruled out the potential to use his work as a basis for a psychologization of the self.

The analysis reveals that managers are multiply selved, the managerial self forming one part of the complex that is their selves: the managerial self is imbricated through and through with the discourse of the organization. Managerial texts too form part of the discursive construction of the managerial self. The role of management education in constituting the managerial self is not what I, as a teacher of (critical) management, had anticipated.

## Theories of the self

Theorists of the self working in the shadow of Descartes see the self as an experience located in an idea of interiority, where the self resides within the body but remains separate from it. This is an idea conditioned by culture, technology, intellectual development in general, and by ideology. The self of Western cultures which has a strong sense of autonomy and individualism is distinct from the self recognized in other cultures and other epochs. This Cartesian self continues to structure many of our practices. The 'hard' sciences still argue that the scientist is separate from that she studies with her mind (Harding, 1991); medicine and psychiatry carve out their respective territories of body and mind (Harding and Palfrey, 1997). Even those who attempt to struggle free from the dualist bindings can fall into an alternative, albeit weaker, version (Scott, 1997). This Cartesian self informs the 'everyday' theory of the self which operates as a form of 'common sense' (Parker, 1997). It is a self located firmly within the body, a self which feels ontologically secure in the knowledge of continuity of self-identity (Giddens, 1990). There is something about this Enlightenment self that inspires its critics to metaphor. Kirby, a geographer, perhaps naturally uses the metaphor of the map, seeing this Cartesian subject as 'a closed circle: its smooth contours ensure its clear division from its location, as well as assuring its internal coherence and consistency. Outside lies a vacuum in which objects appear within their own bubbles, self-contained but largely irrelevant to this self-sufficient ego' (Kirby, 1996, p. 45). Burkitt (1991) sees these monadic selves as 'self-contained unitary individuals who carry their uniqueness deep inside themselves, like pearls hidden in their shells' (p. 1).

Post-modernism, in killing rational Western 'man', has robbed us of these ontological certainties. The post-modern self is, like the post-modern landscape which it projects, 'a *derealization* of space, its plasticity, its tendency to become an infinite semiosis with no resting point'; the post-modern self is one where there is an 'interpenetration of space and body and the connection of body and psyche', where there is a 'crisis of boundaries' so that 'space' can penetrate 'me' (Kirby, 1996, p. 52). The inspiration of Foucault, Lacan and the turn to discourse in the social sciences open the way for the self to become seen as a function of discourse. Lacan, and here I am simplifying drastically and drawing only on secondary texts, saw the 'I' as the conscious subjectivity of the person, constructed within the symbolic realm of signs and language, and distinct from the hidden, undifferentiated, pre-categorical and pre-ontological unconscious out of which it had emerged (Burkitt, 1991). Lacan studied the emergence of the individual, Foucault the individual as a member of a population subjected to governance. From a Foucauldian perspective, however, the psychoanalytical discourse upon which Lacan calls is itself one of the discourses that constructs the individual (Rose, 1989; Parker, 1997).

Discourses, for Foucault (1972, p. 49) are practices that systematically form the objects of which they speak. They are the dominant, organizing principle of the social domain; the individual is constructed through discourse, a product of power/knowledge wherein the self, or the soul as he calls it, becomes subjectified. The power that subjectifies also forms the self, forms what 'one' is through discursive conditions that condition our ability to articulate an 'I', a 'me' or a 'we'. The selves that we know are therefore fundamentally dependent 'on a discourse we never chose but that, paradoxically, initiates and sustains our agency' (Butler, 1997, pp. 1–2).

It is no surprise therefore that theorists working in this tradition attempt to show how particular discourses construct the individual 'self'. For instance, Kirby (1996), whose work I have quoted above, argues that cartography, standardized as a science in the Enlightenment, was both an expression of Cartesian subjectivity and a technology that allowed, perhaps caused, Enlightenment subjectivity to coalesce. She sees the 'mapping subject' as an 'exclusive structure encoded with a particular gender, class and racial positioning' unresponsive to the perspectives of many non-dominant subjectivities (Kirby, 1996, p. 46). Within psychology scholars are engaged in a reflexive urge to analyse how psychological discourses have formed the modern subject. Rose (1989) argues that the 'psychological sciences' work in the service of the state to govern the 'soul'. They structure our reality, providing 'technologies of subjectivity' that 'exist in a kind of symbiotic relationship with what one might term "techniques of the self"'; the ways in which we are enabled, by means of the languages, criteria, and techniques offered to us, to act upon our bodies, souls, thought, and conduct in order to achieve happiness, wisdom, health and fulfilment. Through self-inspection, self-problematization, self-monitoring and confession, we evaluate ourselves according to the criteria provided for us by others. Through self-reformation, therapy, techniques of body alteration, and the calculated reshaping of speech and emotion, we adjust ourselves by means of the techniques propounded by the 'experts of the soul' (Rose, 1989, pp. 10–11). The manner through which psychoanalytic discourse constitutes the subject has been traced by Parker (1997), who explores how it runs through and structures contemporary common sense and so becomes a form of representation and practice which positions subjects and thus constructs forms of subjectivity. The therapist is part of the regime of truth that defines what subjectivity must be like, that constructs 'us', and is a medium through which we speak to each other about ourselves.

As noted earlier, the model of the self I am using here comes from Judith Butler (1997), whose Foucauldian perspective sees the self as that which takes occupation of the locus of the subject and thus assumes its, the self's, subjectified identity. To Foucault's list of discourses that form the subjectified self – medicine, discipline, madness and sexuality – others have been explored and added. In this chapter I will add another, that of managerial discourse, a term which encompasses the language provided by management textbooks and those incorporated (or perhaps not?) into the self through management education and training, and the practice of management.

## The analytical model

How, then, to discover the managerial self? Foucault has been extra-ordinarily influential in allowing us to explore the constitution of the self through discourse, but he does not provide a methodology for analysing our present-day, lived world experiences. His influence here is as a stimulus in our search for the discourses that are involved in the practices of the self. He leaves us in the dark as to how the discourses we so discover have become embedded in the constitutive practices of the self. Butler (1997) holds out a promise of a useful methodology, in her attempt to meld Freud with Foucault, but she deviates into the highways and byways of Nietzsche and Althusser, offering insights for the philosopher but not perhaps the social scientist. Rather than Freud I find the psychoanalytical theories of Freudian interpreter Christopher Bollas (1993, 1995) more conducive to an exploration of how discourses are incorporated into the ongoing project of the multiply selved self, for Bollas adopts a post-modern definition of the self, allies this to Freud's theories of dreams and locates his theory within object-relations theory, and thus takes forward fruitfully the work of Freud in seeking to understand the constitution of the self.

The self, for Bollas (1995), is a continuously moving experience, a psychic texture formed over many years by countless experiences that contribute to a store of mental contents, some of which cannot be put into words and may not even be easily accessible by the conscious mind. These mental contents comprise introjected objects. Objects can include people, pieces of music, items of writing, experiences, etc. He suggests that each of us begins life 'as a peculiar but unrealized idiom of being, and in a lifetime transforms that idiom into sensibility and personal reality. Our idiom is an aesthetic of being driven by an urge to articulate its theory of form by selecting and using objects so as to give them form' (Bollas, 1995, p. 151). Here we have the link with Foucault, for the dominant discourses of Foucauldian analysis become the 'objects' of which Bollas speaks; the discourses/objects become absorbed into the idiom of the self. The discourses of management, and the experiences of working in management become, 'inner presences' in the selves of managers. But, the self 'does not seem to arise out of a person's episodic experiences' (ibid., p. 160), it is not the sum of its parts, rather it is 'an aesthetic intelligence' (ibid., p. 166) or an 'aesthetic movement that can be felt psychically' (ibid., p. 172). The self is an 'internal object' that is 'fashioned from several sources: from an inner feel of the authorizing aesthetic that gives polysemous (not unitary) shape to one's being; from an inner feel of internal objects which are the outcome of the other's effect upon one's self; from the shape of discrete episodes of self experience' (ibid., p. 173).

This 'internal object', this 'phenomenon of the real', is, he argues, the result of our moving through our lives as a unique set of evolving theories that generate insights and new perspectives about ourselves, but through the various experiences we meet we are raised into increasing sets of questions about who we are (ibid., p. 69). The theories arise from the effect of objects upon us: people, music, artworks, artefacts, whatever, they 'move through' us like ghosts, inhabiting our minds, and conjured up when we evoke their names (Bollas, 1993, pp. 56–7) as we may do in the conscious or unconscious thought processes through which we dream ourselves into being. Thoughts of objects indeed form countless trains, thousands of ideational routes, leading to an explosive creation of meanings which meet up with new units of life experience (Bollas, 1995, p. 55), mostly when we are, literally, 'lost in thought'. We are thus inhabited by inner structures which form highly condensed psychic textures, and so we can be 'substantially metamorphosed by the structure of objects; internally transformed by objects that leave their traces within us' (Bollas, 1993, p. 59).

In this reading management texts become objects that may, in some way or another, become part of the psychic structures of the manager. Bollas provides no guide to gaining evidence of how such objects become part of the dreamings of managerial selves. How then do we gain access to the 'I' who is dreamed into being? For this task I will turn to Harré (1998) and Mühlhäusler and Harré (1990).

Harré is not perhaps a post-modernist, he is more indeed a critical realist, yet his work is heavily informed by the turn to discourse. In 1998 he argued that the self, as the singularity we each feel ourselves to be, is not an entity but a grammatical fiction, a necessary characteristic of person-oriented discourses (Harré, 1998, pp. 3–4). He suggests that what 'people have called "selves" are, by and large, produced discursively, that is in dialogue and other forms of joint action with real and imaged [*sic*] others. Selves are not entities, but evanescent properties of the flow of public and private action' (ibid., p. 69). This definition is similar enough to Bollas' to allow an intermingling of their two perspectives, yet both ignore the issue of power to which Foucault, via Butler, makes us so very aware: it is a concept that cannot be forgotten in this analysis. Singularities of self, for Harré, are not to be explained as the consequence of the existence of a Cartesian ego, a unique person substance but rather as 'patterns of discourse, the spatio-temporal uniqueness of personal embodiment anchoring expression to person through the indexicality of the personal pronouns' (ibid., p. 147). In earlier work (Mühlhäusler and Harré, 1990), he had argued that the 'transcendental ego, the "inner self", is not an empirically presented entity, but a shadow cast on the mind by the grammatical forms used in the practices of self-reporting, avowing, etc., deriving from indexical properties of pronouns and their equivalents' (ibid., p. 5). The self is thus not an object but the leading concept of a theory of what one is as a person (ibid., p. 89).

Harré (1983, 1998) and Mühlhäusler and Harré (1990) provide, in their emerging theory of how people use pronouns, a method of exploring how people construct the theories about or grammatical fictions that *are* their 'selves'. The model encourages an analysis of the slippages between the use of the 'I' and the 'me' and the 'you', this last used to refer to the third person singular and plural and also to the first person. Combining insights from Bollas allows an intense phenomenological understanding of the processes of thought and imagination, revealing the fleet trajectories of thought which stimulate changes in referents that become signified by the various pronouns. We thus have a model that allows us to explore the construction of the managerial self.

I differ in one respect from Harré and Mühlhäusler in that they state that the use of pronouns involves the deployment of one's philosophical theories of what one is (Harré and Mühlhäusler, 1990, p. 16), for the following analyses suggest, in a grammatical impossibility, that persons have philosophical theories about what 'one are', in that they recognize the existence of two or more selves (if only the distinction between the 'at work' and the 'outside work' selves). I am seeking respondents' philosophical theories of the several selves they see themselves as being. In Hughes' (1999) words, 'It is inadequate to talk about *a* discourse constituting *a* self; this is both misleading and partial . . . Rather than there being merely a mind and body . . . there are a number of *minds, bodies,* and *selves* . . . [W]e must look at the discourses and discursive practices occurring in particular discursive configurations which operate in the constitution of particular (and multiple) subjects', i.e. at selves that are formed through configurations of discursive practices.

The model for analysis thus involves an examination of the moment-by-moment significance of pronoun use. Where the first person singular is used, it is instructive, following Harré and Mühlhäusler (1990), to explore how it is used, for they show that although there may appear to be only one speaker there may be two or more voices, belonging to different versions of the 'I', in any speech act. The 'I', they postulate, is the human agent, and the 'me' is that agent's beliefs about itself. (Their use of the term 'agent' ignores the issues of power.) The agentive 'I' is the indexical 'I', the 'I' that can be identified as pondering upon and developing a theory of the self.

The 'you' is an impersonal pronoun that can refer to other people or to other versions of the self, and people's use of it as a first person singular suggests a transcendence of the personal and some relationship between the speaker and certain persons or objects. This is supported by philosophers such as Heidegger (cited in Harré and Mühlhäusler, 1990) who have noted that the switch to '*one*'-type pronouns signals a change in the very concept of self in modern societies, a change to reduced responsibility and individuality. We come to be not ourselves but rather exist in reference to others, alienated, average and distanced from authentic being. Everyone becomes the other, and no one is the self, so that the being that *is* us is 'eroded into commonality', a 'oneness' within a collective, public, herd-like 'theyness' (Harré and Mühlhäusler, 1990).

Finally, the use of the first person plural (we) can allow the speaker not only to integrate with the audience, but to diminish the speaker's responsibility for what is said (ibid., p. 175).

That then is the model used here. It will allow me (or my academic self) to pursue the 'internal object' that represents the managerial self and reveals how dominant discourses are enacted within constructions of the multiple self, through identifying how the unconscious works to assist the process and how the discourses of the managers reveal their articulations of their multiple selves and, notably, of their managerial self.

## The managerial self at work

The business world in general, and the NHS in particular, is currently beset by mergers, with a score of them taking place annually in the NHS. The subjects of this study have been involved in one such merger and I have taken advantage of this disruption in interviewees' lives to explore with them how they see themselves, the organization, the merger and their post-merger world, perceptions that were tossed to the surface in this eruption in which they have been forced to remake their worlds. Six managers have been interviewed, one a junior manager taking on a more senior role for the first time, two of them middle level managers moved horizontally across the new organization, one of them a senior manager who again moved horizontally into her desired post, one an experienced manager about to be made redundant, and one a senior manager who did not secure a job in the merged organization and is now working in a senior management post in another organization. Four women and two men were interviewed: I use feminine pronouns throughout so as to help maintain confidentiality. The interviews each lasted an average of one hour, were tape recorded and transcribed verbatim.

The data reveal that managers recognize a sharp distinction between an 'at-work' managerial self and their 'outside-work' selves. The managerial self is permeated with the organization and the organization with the manager. The managerial self is one that can be 'switched off' outside work, and the outside-work self needs to be protected from the organization. The managerial self is one that has to be publicly displayed in the realm of the organization; it has to be seen to be *doing* management yet what management is is only vaguely apprehended. The manager has absorbed the Foucauldian gaze and as s/he enacts and re-enacts the managerial persona s/he constantly checks to ensure the managerial performance is that which is expected.

### The managerial self is constructed through discourse

I will begin this analysis by exploring whether there is such a thing as a managerial self. In the following quote the respondent refers to the 'I' and the 'me':

> *I* think that it's taken *me* about almost a year to fully absorb the organization's culture and values and things like that. [On] Monday this week . . . [One of my colleagues] came up to *me* and said 'I'm really proud of you, you spoke like a true [member of this organization]', and that really you know sort of meant a lot to *me* because it demonstrated and I think I'm now absorbed into the organization. I'm now an ABC person.

This piece of discourse can be deconstructed, using the model discussed above, as shown on page 172.

Other respondents use the metaphors of the organization's blood running through their veins, and speak of being an organization person 'born and bred'. The managerial self is therefore that part of a manager's subjectivity which is imbricated with the organization.

How does Bollas explain how the organization can become this 'object' that is absorbed into the self? In 1993 Bollas explored the nature of the subjective world, examining deeply the significance of the occupation of our minds by constantly flowing streams of thoughts, thoughts conjured up through some seemingly insignificant allusion, hints that arise from our previous experiences of objects. In Bollas' poetic description:

| | |
|---|---|
| *I* think that | The 'I' here signifies the human agent analysing itself and seeking self-understanding through developing a theory of the self. |
| it's taken *me* about almost a year to fully absorb the organization's culture and values and things like that. | The 'me' is the theory of the self that emerges from the analysis. Here the 'me' is permeable – the organization is an 'object' that enters through the skin and becomes part of the self. |
| [On] Monday this week . . . [One of my colleagues] came up to *me* and said 'I'm really proud of you, you spoke like a true [member of this organization]', | The colleague too is an object, an important one in that the interaction with this colleague has now become the 'psychic texture' of an episode in this manager's life history (Bollas, 1995, p. 153). |
| and that really you know sort of meant a lot to *me* because it demonstrated and I think I'm now absorbed into the organization. I'm now an ABC person. | The speaker's sense of the 'me' as being formed by the organization has received external validation. The organization has been absorbed into her being, and similarly she is absorbed into the organization, so closely that she cannot distinguish herself from the organization. |

we consecrate the world with our own subjectivity, investing people, places, things, and events with a kind of idiomatic significance. As we inhabit this world of ours, we amble about in a field of pregnant objects that contribute to the dense psychic textures that constitute self experience. Very often we select and use objects in ways unconsciously intended to bring up such imprints; indeed we do this many times each day, sort of thinking ourself out, by evoking constellations of inner experience. At the same time, however, the people, things, and events of our world simply happen to us, and when they do, we are called into differing forms of being by chance. Thus we oscillate between thinking ourself out through the selection of objects that promote inner experience and being thought out, so to speak, by the environment which plays upon the self.

(Bollas, 1993, pp. 3–4)

Through exploring the transformational accomplishment of an 'object of effect' we can deepen our understanding of the nature of human life. The effect of the object may be negative and lead to trauma, or positive and thus generative. The thinking of our self into being, its constant construction and reconstruction through millions of sequential 'I's, allow, through the sense of familiarity with objects, an illusion that the self is a unity (ibid., p. 30).

The above speaker has absorbed the organization into her self, and she is, she says, absorbed into the organization. From Bollas' theoretical perspective the organization has become a '*mnemic* object', a lexical function that 'speaks' our self. In psychoanalytical terms, we project ourselves into objects, and when we use that object something of the self we have stored in it will arise. So, we project ourselves upon objects and absorb the object and its projections back into our self, thus eliciting inner experiencings. *Structural* objects, in contrast, through their intrinsic character create a particular self experience, so a piece of music may evoke a particular reaction, a book another, and so on. The object world is, for Bollas, 'an extraordinary lexicon for the individual who speaks the self's aesthetic through his precise choices and particular uses of its constituents' (ibid., p. 21). The organization becomes part of the aesthetic of the self. Interactions with colleagues, of the kind remembered by the above speaker, become part of the 'psychic texture' (Bollas, 1995, p. 153) of a person's aesthetic.

More is revealed in the following quote from the interviews, which shows not only discrepancies in power between an individual manager and an organization but also something of the way in which the organization is built into the concept of the managerial self:

I suppose for a while when I sort of made that made that sort of leap out um there was a sense of you know do I have value, um you know, have I been kidding myself for so many years that I'm good at what I do and stuff like that. But one of my mentors actually said that the key thing to keep you going is that you you you never forget or doubt your own value.

This statement shows that the manager on leaving the organization loses the organizational 'me', and that when the organizational self has disappeared only the 'I', and thus not a whole person, is left, one who ponders over whether she has 'value' any more. This can be seen by identifying the several voices that belong to different versions of the 'I' in this speech act. Here there are two 'I's evident, the 'I' who is thinking about the past, and the remembered 'I' who had worked in the old organization and ultimately left it. There is a speedy interchange between the two 'I's, as the speaker jumps first into one version and then into the other. The dialogue between the two parts of herself (have I been kidding myself?) suggests she is anxious that, without the managerial self, she is worthless. We then see the introduction of the third person singular, where she is using 'you' to refer to herself, but this is a part of the self that could break down ('stop going') without the outside validation that is implicit in the need to refer to a third person for expression of her value. This can be seen more clearly if we break this piece of text down further, as shown on page 175.

It is perhaps necessary, however, when leaving one organization to 'kill' the managerial self that had been structured by the old organization, for later this respondent referred to her time in the old organization as 'my other existence': this other existence is one that belongs in the past, so the phrase can be translated as 'the 'I' that I used to be but who no longer exists, having been superseded by the 'I' who is now working in the new organization. In the new organization she has, in absorbing another organization into the self, become a new person.

'Normality' for managers, these interviews demonstrate, is a state of being fully absorbed into the organization, so much so that the boundaries between the manager and the organization disappear. Only in times of distress do managers apprehend this and wish a clearer distinction between themselves and the organization, as demonstrated by the respondent whose reply to the question of what she would like to see have happened in the organization in the next year, was 'that the boundaries that we have are very clear'.

Should managers revolt against being totally absorbed into the organization, the period of resistance to the organization's percolation throughout the self is, it seems, short-lived and thus futile:

I suppose sometimes I think you need to do something for you not just for this organization and not just for others. And six months

| I suppose for a while | Here the respondent is the indexical 'I' who is pondering ('suppose') upon herself in the past. |
| --- | --- |
| When I sort of made that made that sort of leap out | This is the remembered 'I' who had belonged to the old organization but now has left it – this section acts as the marker that divides the 'old' self from the one who is now organization-less. |
| um there was a sense of you know do I have value, um you know, have I been kidding myself for so many years that I'm good at what I do and stuff like that | The 'I' may be valueless without the part of the self that belongs to the organization. The indexical 'I' returns and ponders upon the 'I' who used to work in the old organization. |
| But one of my mentors actually said that the key thing to keep you going is that you you you never forget or doubt your own value. | Here she refers to herself in the third person 'you'. This 'you' is a separate part of the self, one that exists only in reference to others. It is a part that is in danger of breaking down, failing to keep going. It is so fragile that she cannot maintain it without the support and validation of another person. This, I suggest, is the 'managerial self' that could cease to have any existence now it is outside an organization. It can literally cease to keep going. |

ago I would have said that even more strongly. You know I will no longer do anything for anybody else. I will do it for me. Well already that edge is knocked off. So it's interesting isn't it how you change and come back to being normal really.

In the first sentence the 'I' referred to is the indexical 'I' who is thinking and theorizing about the self. There are two 'yous' operating in that sentence, the passive recipient and the active doer, but both are distinct and separate from the organization. The second sentence heralds a suddenly strong 'I' whose introduction signals a strengthening in her resistance to the organization. The use of the phrase 'you know', in this context, suggests that the strong 'I' is here addressing the 'you' the speaker was a few months ago, giving the order which follows, where the strong and active agentive 'I' states that she will no longer do anything for anybody else, but only for the 'me'. The 'me' is the core 'me', the one that does not belong to the organization. In the final sentences 'Well already that edge is knocked off. So it's interesting isn't it how you change and come back to being normal really', the 'you' is the normal 'you', the one that 'normally' exists, that is, following Heidegger, part of the managerial crowd. It is a passive you, one that can be overruled by the managerial self (i.e. the self imbricated with the organization) who keeps the 'you' in a position of passive receptivity. Individuality is lost to the commonality of the managerial herd.

The managerial self can thus keep other parts of the self under control, bringing them back into submission after periods of revolt. Even when managers appear unhappy with the managerial self they will make offerings that demonstrate their positive perspective. One respondent, when asked about how she had learned to be a manager after having trained and worked as a nurse, said:

> It's something you are never trained to do. Um. And suddenly you are asked to do it and you continue I mean over this ten years it is now really but the things that I have been asked to do have not always sat very comfortably and I have always in my own mind had to find a way around why I am actually doing it and what what I can achieve for patient care by doing it and you know try to find that as a way through. Um but I suppose I don't know how you learn to be a manager I really don't. I think you start off as a ward sister the leader of the ward and you have to manage that group of staff and sometimes I think it's quite an art to be a manager.

There are four versions of the self operating here, and there is also here the first example of what I am calling 'the Bollasian pause' (BP), i.e. a pause in a discourse which signals that the respondent is engaged in an internal dialogue devoted to theorizing the self. Bollas explores how psychoanalyst and analysand select narrative and mental objects to bring about inner states in one another. I suggest that the theory of personal pronoun use articulated here allows the theorizing 'I' to, so to speak, take the roles of both therapist and analysand in selecting narrative and mental objects that ponder on and thus develop the inner state of the 'me'. The 'um' and other forms of pauses signal that this process is taking place through a remarkably fleet process of thought. An encounter, Bollas writes (1993, p. 29), 'solicits us, lifts us up from our unconscious nuclearity', showing 'an aspect of the self to the I'. This experience is 'only ever partly thinkable: the experience is more a dense condensation of instinctual urges, somatic states, body positions, proprioceptive organizings, images, part sentences, abstract thoughts, sensed memories, recollections, and felt affinities, all of a piece'. It is during the pauses, the 'thinking spaces', that these 'only ever partly thinkable' experiences are taking place, allowing the 'I' to comprehend an aspect of the self and to take itself forward, in a linearly experienced world, into the next 'I'. The text can now be deconstructed, as shown on page 178.

This person is obviously not happy being a manager as it requires her to undertake things that she feels are not quite honourable. She therefore divides her workplace self into the person who does things she is unhappy about (I(One)), the weak part of her self who is unable to resist the orders she is given but cannot learn how to do the job, and who is referred to throughout as 'you', and the person who finds a way to justify her actions to herself by retreating into the premanagerial version of the self (I(Two)). I(Three) is the indexical 'I' who is developing this theory. The Bollasian pause here signifies a reconstruction of the self, as the manager considers the import of what she has just said. The narration that is spoken is of a person who was doing an honourable job, who was ordered away from that job into the world of the manager, a role she dislikes because of its unethical aspects, and she can only justify what she does as a manager by returning to that original, pre-managerial part of herself.

The second appearance of I(Three) bears witness to the need for a deeper interpretation, for here we see, signalled by the second Bollasian pause, a positive reconstruction of the managerial self. Now there is 'quite an art to be[ing] a manager'. This use of the metaphor 'art' recalls my earlier discussion, and it adds to our understanding of the art of management for *it signifies the speaker's apprehension that the manager is, like a piece of work in an art gallery, on public display*. Any disillusion she has with her managerial job has to be kept out of sight (literally, for it must be kept in her 'own mind'). In this reading, the above section of speech can be interpreted as saying:

When I was a nurse I did an honourable job. Suddenly I found myself doing the job of management, which I find less honourable. But as

| | |
|---|---|
| It's something you are never trained to do. | You |
| Um | BP |
| And suddenly you are asked to do it and you continue | You |
| I mean over this ten years it is now really but the things that I have been asked to do have not always sat very comfortably and | I (One) |
| I have always in my own mind had to find a way around why I am actually doing it and what what I can achieve for patient care by doing it and you know try to find that as a way through. | I (Two) |
| Um | Second BP |
| but I suppose I don't know ... I really don't ... I think | I (Three) |
| how you learn to be a manager | You |
| you start off as a ward sister the leader of the ward and you have to manage that group of staff | You |
| and sometimes I think it's quite an art to be a manager. | I (Three) |

I am a manager I am constantly on display, and so I have to disguise the feelings of disillusion beneath the façade of the manager.

Goffman (1969), it would seem, is an appropriate reference here, as we appear to be developing a dramaturgical presentation of the managerial self. This illusion is in error, for this self is more Foucauldian than Goffmanesque, more an evanescence of power/knowledge plays than a social product apprehensible only in relation to a functionalist social context.

## *The managerial self is an ideal which has to live up to the textbook image of the manager*

Managers, these data reveal, carry around with them an image of what the manager should be. The manager should be totally devoted to the organization, impervious to pressure, and the managerial self should mirror the textbook in that it has a head but no body, is culture rather than nature, mind rather than body, rational rather than emotional.

That the manager should be totally devoted to the organization is revealed in the following extract, which contains the illuminating metaphor of the organization as the 'outfit', i.e. something that is worn that disguises the nakedness of the body beneath:

> Sometimes you can find yourself being absorbed by the work, you know, the kind of work that I'm involved with now you can just like do it every waking hour if you if you uh were so inclined um but I think my the organization I work for now recognizes that there is a working existence and there's an outside working existence. Didn't really get that feeling in my old job as strongly I mean clearly there was but I think my new my new outfit is um is better in that respect.

The following table contains a deconstruction of this piece of text. However, first let me focus on the phrase 'you know'. 'You know' is sprinkled through all these texts: it is a seemingly innocuous figure of speech that dusts many of our conversations. Is it a request for affirmation or agreement addressed to the interviewer/listener, or a signal that the speaker is addressing the internal 'I', albeit one that appears to be projected onto the interviewer/listener? It could of course be either of these things, depending upon the context in which it is used. However, an analysis of its appearance throughout these pieces of text shows that it very often precedes an idea best described as a visual image being cast upon the 'mind's eye', as if a film were being projected upon a screen. Its use signals that the speaker is about to describe something in words that are but sorry representations for the pictorial representations evoked in a flash in the mind of the speaker. They suggest what Bollas calls 'psychic intensities' full of latent thoughts that become condensed into single images, much like dreams condense the events of an entire day (Bollas, 1995, pp. 51–5 *et passim*). An evocative object (such as the question I have posed to the speakers) evokes a tumble of virtually simultaneous thoughts, and 'this concrescence of factors transcends any single element, transforming the episode into a meditation full of questions'. These moments are 'saturated with simultaneously evoked planes of unconscious ideation' (ibid., p. 56) that have the structure of dreams. Dreams are projections during sleep of images onto the mind's eye; here we have what Bollas describes as the waking dream where thoughts are evoked in such a rush they have to be rendered comprehensible through an image. The 'you know' signifies that this process is occurring in the speaker, and the image is then rendered available somewhat to the listener through the convenience of poverty-stricken words.

This speaker, happy in her managerial work, shows how the self can become so totally absorbed by the organization that any other aspect of the self can disappear. The organization must take on responsibility for the separation of the manager from the workplace.

The managerial self should be impervious to pressure and should never let any emotions show. The following extract exhibits the use of the 'you' to signify the managerial self who is under pressure and the 'I' that is theorizing about the managerial self. The 'um' after the second sentence (the Bollasian pause) signals the introduction of the 'I' and the immediate return to the 'you' signals the very speedy thinking processes that seem to have occurred during the course of speaking that sentence. The managerial self cannot be emotionally weak and here the speaker appears to be gathering her stock of internal objects that tell her she is not 'emotionally weak'. The result is a denial of the earlier sentences – the signs of emotional weakness have occurred rarely and not for some time. Managerial self honour is restored in the last sentence:

> And that just has then demonstrated this is getting to you now just 'drop a gear a bit an' and do what you do and there's things that you're not going to be able to do. Stop trying to you know clear your in-tray in the course of a day. Um. And that's probably bothered me, thinking right, I've never been, I've never been an emotionally weak person and that that begins to worry you. But it's only on a couple of occasions and it's not been recent. I think I've become a sort of tougher character really, because I've been more resilient.

Most tellingly, as the following extract shows, the managerial self should mirror the textbook in that it has a head but no body, is culture rather than nature, mind rather than body, rational rather than emotional. The restructuring meant that managers had to apply for new posts, and present themselves for interview. The speaker demonstrates the perspective of themselves managers felt had to be presented if they were to be offered a job they wanted, or indeed if they were to be offered any job:

> If you get you know 80 marks out of 100 following your interview you will get your preference, your top preference. If you come somewhere down here [gestures to mid chest/heart level with both

| | |
|---|---|
| Sometimes you can find yourself being absorbed by the work, | The work can suck you into it, take over your entire being. |
| You know, | Image-making process is occurring, where the speaker is seeing herself at her desk until very late in the evening. |
| The kind of work that I'm involved with now | Clear separation of the 'I' and the 'you'. Here the 'I' is the 'I' doing the theorizing, and the theory is about the work (how absorbing it is) and the organization. |
| You can just like do it every waking hour if you if you uh were so inclined | This 'you' is separate, it's the one that is involved in the work – it's the managerial self. |
| Um | The Bollasian pause, here signalling that the speaker realizes that she could be denigrating the new organization. It signals a refusal of the apparent defamation. |
| But I think my the organization I work for now recognizes that there is a working existence and there's an outside working existence. | Change from what was to have been 'my organization' wherein there is no distinction between the self and the organization, to the one she works for now, showing there is a distinction between the two. There are two 'existences' but it is the organization that has to remind the manager that this is so, for the managerial self can be totally taken over by work. |
| Didn't really get that feeling in my old job as strongly I mean clearly there was but I think my new my new outfit is um is better in that respect. | The absence of any reference to 'I' at the beginning of this sentence suggests the speaker is unable to remember what it was like to be an 'I' in the previous organization. |

arms] you'll just be farmed out to wherever is left, and it felt very much like a cattle market then. I perceived it to be a cattle market type of approach.

Here the manager, the 'I', is contemplating the procedure all managers went through during the restructuring. The 'you' is used to refer to herself as representative of all the managers going through the process. Her gesture demonstrates the managerial assumption of how a manager's worth is calculated. This worth is measured against the body, with that part above the middle of the chest (mostly the head and shoulders) the part that marks the person out as a manager. Below this is only the animal level, revealed in the extremely suggestive metaphor of the farm. The person valued only for their body/meat and not their brain is 'farmed out' to be sent eventually to a 'cattle market'. Compare this with my discussion in Chapters 5 and 6 about the photographs contained in management textbooks, where the body is noticeable in its absence. The dominant metaphor of the manager in those photographs was of male rationality as embodied in the head. Here we see how that metaphor informs the thinking of practising managers; how they can call on it in times of crisis to explain and understand their managerial world.

### The distinction between the managerial self and the outside-work selves

Speakers distinguished between their work selves and their outside-work selves. The following quote illustrates interestingly the dualism that is inherent in this division of the selves. From a manager who has become disillusioned with the managerial job, it shows that management is associated with being seen to be at the workplace, with 'doing everything', with working oneself to the point not of exhaustion but of death. The outside-work self is somewhere where there is 'life'. This is where 'personal' rather than organizational values are to be found:

> You can't do everything. But you know I leave work at half past five, six o'clock every day now which I didn't do before because I've got a life and I can only do so much in a day and I'm not you know I don't want to die young because I've given everything to the job because I've discovered that it's not worth doing that. So perhaps personally it's done quite a lot for me if I'm going to be honest. Having gone through the trauma that I did I think it's actually made me re-evaluate what my own personal values are and perhaps probably very good. Because there are people you know with young families who are sat behind their desk at nine ten o'clock at night and I'm not doing that.

In this quote the managerial self is referred to here as the 'you', suggesting distancing from this unwelcome self. Following Heidegger's observation given above, this is now seen as the part of the self that is indistinguishable from the common herd (of managers). The 'I' is the self that has values, that has 'a life'. It is here dictating to the managerial self – 'you know'. 'You know' is used three times in this short piece of speech. Each signals the emergence of a strong visual image – the manager can be seen leaving work; lying in her coffin; observing other people sitting at their desks and working by lamplight while their children sleep at home. The first one is, however, somewhat disturbing to a manager, for it suggests a slippage in the managerial role that requires the manager to continue to work after non-managers have gone home. The next two instances of the use provide justification for this desertion through appealing to the commitment of far greater crimes that are avoided through her commitment of this comparatively lesser crime. The 'you know' thus has a multiple function. It signals that a thought coded in vision rather than words is appearing in the speaker's mind; it signals that the speaker is talking to her 'self' and justifying her actions and statements. This speaker is thus signalling that deviation from the managerial norm must be justified, and justification can be found only through appeals to the avoidance of far greater crimes (her own death, familial neglect).

Several respondents demonstrated through the use of metaphor that the managerial self is one that can be 'switched' on or off, except under conditions of duress:

> On-call has been introduced ... And that's a seven day a week, 24 hour a day commitment. We've got the mobile phone that doesn't stop ringing about issues and you think can I ever switch off?

This metaphor of 'switching off' alerts us to how the managerial self is constituted: it is, following Bollas, the result of an inner dialogue that can normally be turned off in order to allow other parts of the self to emerge through different dialogues. Under conditions of stress and distress, however, the managerial self dominates all internal dialogues, suppressing other parts of the self. This is seen very strongly in the next extract, where the 'I' is used to refer to the pre-stressed managerial self. Significantly pronouns virtually disappear from the references to the current, stressed self, symbolizing the disappearance of any aspects of the self other than the managerial self:

> So it's making a more concerted effort to just totally switch off and go do something else. Whereas I used to just love work, enjoy it, and it wasn't an issue. I could go home and it didn't buzz round

in my head. But sleepless nights, early morning wake-ups, just thinking about what you've to do and your deadlines. Um. And that is difficult to cope with.

The second extract reinforces this observation. Here, the 'home life' is affected by the managerial self that cannot be switched off. The 'I' finds that 'very stressful':

It does have an effect on your home life because you just you can't switch off from work you're so nervous and worried about wanting to deliver and get on with your new job and make a difference, make an impression, but people were not really being helpful or facilitating that. So I found that very stressful.

This dominance of one internal dialogue and the suppressing of others is, for Bollas, indicative of a lack of an 'unconscious freedom necessary for creative living' (1995, p. 71). The dominance of one internal dialogue represents an obsession that signifies a deadening of the self and the psyche. Such a 'terminal object' ends 'the natural forward movement of those departing trains of thought that are the elaborations of any person's idiomatic experience of life' (ibid., p. 75).

### The manager works to maintain the managerial self

The manager works actively to maintain a self-image of herself as a manager. This self-image, the aspired to managerial self, is revealed when, in *extremis*, it is challenged and another managerial self becomes dominant, as seen in the displayed material on pages 185–6.

### When the managerial self is stripped away, very little is left

I interviewed these managers at a time shortly after they had been through a period of great upheaval in their working lives, one that was leaving them evincing distress and vulnerability, as is implicit throughout these extracts. The managerial self, so many of the interviews revealed, is one that is kept distinct and separate in many ways from the 'non-work' selves, especially at a time when the managerial self is feeling profoundly damaged and distressed. For some managers, however, their managerial selves can become their whole selves, so when the former is challenged to the point of erosion there is nothing left. To explain this, I am focusing on only one of the interviewees. She had applied for and won the post which she most wanted in the new organization, so she has, it would seem, what she wishes, and has neither grudges to bear nor axes to grind. However, she was extremely distressed throughout our discussion. Here therefore we have a manager who

| | |
|---|---|
| I've found myself very recently in the last couple of weeks because of the pressure I've been under . . . | 'I've found myself' here signifies the contemplative 'I' who discovered almost accidentally a lost part of her 'self', a part brought to the surface because of the stresses she's been under. |
| My director has had me in a couple of times and given me a total carpeting . . . | The metaphor here is one from childhood, where the pupil is called to the head teacher's study for disciplinary action. The self has been stripped back to this vulnerable, defenceless, child-like 'me'. |
| I go back to my team then become almost Theory X and sort of transactional you know. 'If this happens again, you know, we're gonna be in serious bother, you know, we're going to have action taken against us', | In this section the respondent is calling upon her management degree to explain her actions, a process that signifies, as I will show below, that she is observing herself. She is here standing outside her body to observe her actions when she, whose adult person has just been laid bare, has to return to the team and act as its manager. |
| And I've gone away and thought '*Oh God,* this is just not you. I can't believe I'm saying this.' | She has now projected herself back into the person she is after she has acted in a way that contradicts her managerial self-image. Her call to an external observer (the omnipresent deity) signifies that the self-examination is confessional: she has looked at herself and denied the possibility that her managerial self is different from that self she aspires to and works to maintain. |
| Where you feel that threat tactics is the only way to get people delivering for you and I have never ever worked in that | The swift transition between selves here reveals the distancing from this self that has been revealed. It is a 'you' not a 'me' |

| | |
|---|---|
| way before, and I think that's 'cos of the pressure that's put on me that you just snap an' an' and become a lot more Theory X in that you're not delivering and you've not done this and almost like been more, using more threat tactics. | that uses threat tactics, who works in a way that the 'I' disagrees with. The 'I' is theorizing and contemplating the self (the revealed 'me') who she now realizes can 'snap', or fracture into several pieces that act in different ways. |
| And I think [pause] | The transitional phase, the Bollasian pause, where the parts of the self are re-formed into the 'I' that ponders upon itself. |
| It probably culminated last Friday when I had had a very difficult week, I had one of the worst weeks I've ever had last week . . . , and I went home at the weekend and just went through a period of reflection and I thought | The managerial self has been stripped bare because of the pressures. |
| You know 'for God's sake, Barbara, don't change into, don't emulate what your director's doing. For goodness sake you know keep a sense of balance and er, | Here various parts of the self are speaking to each other, the self who is known by her first name; the self who is doing the thinking, the self who is talking to Barbara. |
| And I had a lot of sort of long discussions with myself in my head last weekend to say | This section shows even more strongly the existence of several 'selves', sufficient in number to participate in several discussions. |
| This is not you. Don't get pushed so far down the line where you start duplicating or reinforcing that sort of behaviour on the staff that work with you. | The section finishes with a theory of the managerial self. This manager has a strong idea of how she wishes her managerial self to behave, this part of the self that is not the 'me', but the 'you', the managerial self who is distinct from the core 'me'. |

should be revelling in the new opportunities opening up for her in a job that she values, but who instead is extremely distressed. I am focusing upon her because when I analysed the transcript of our discussion I found that she used neither the third/first person singular (you) nor its equivalent 'one'. She used 'me' only where it was grammatically impossible to use any other phrase. She is stripped down, it seems, to the essential 'I'. The following extract encapsulates this perfectly, for it shows that she can see no existence other than that of a manager or someone who, in a sexist, ageist society, is seen as being utterly worthless, i.e. the 'old lady'. But here she distinguishes two types of manager, the ruthless and financially driven general manager, and the unsaid opposite of the 'Theory Y', human relations-oriented manager. There is now no room in the organization for the latter, and so she is doomed to become the 'little old lady':

> Maybe I'm too soft, maybe I'm not made for this, maybe I'm not a ruthless general manager sssss that's financially driven. But I do accept that. But maybe I'm just an old lady now who just needs to [pause] go away and knit in a corner or something but I, that's what makes me sad.

### Summary: the managerial self and the organization

In the ongoing project of the self, the managerial self is but one part of a multiply selved individual. The managerial self is the 'at-work' self, a self whose psychic texture is indistinguishable from the organization. This self may dominate all other selves. The manager projects this self onto the organization, sees no distinction between at-work self and organization, implying that managers see the organization as the managerial self writ large.

Outside work, the managerial self can be 'switched off', for the internal dialogue that is dominated by the manager/organization can be suppressed to allow expressions of other parts of the self to dominate. At work, managers have to constantly display the façade of the manager, disporting themselves as culture rather than nature, rationalists devoid of emotion, mind rather than body, totally loyal, impervious to pressure. The metaphor of the comic-book hero, Superman, comes to mind. The managerial self is thus extraordinarily vulnerable to any demonstration that the organization is distinct from the managerial self, that it has power over them and can render them disposable. This extreme vulnerability, I suggest, shows there is more at work here than the mere play of raw power: this vulnerability is rather an index of inherent instabilities in the social construction of the manager.

Now it is time to return to the study of the textbooks that have dominated this book so far, to explore how they contribute to the construction of the managerial self. But first I wish to suggest what managers may anticipate is achievable through education or training in management.

## Returning to the texts: anticipations of education and training – the case of the chief executive

I will here use one piece of text to explore how programmes in management (and leadership) are perceived in the world of managers contemplating a course of study. Management courses, it seems, offer the promise of ontological security.

The NHS recently called for tenders to carry out a development programme for experienced chief executives. A working party of ten (of a total of about 450) chief executives developed the ideas which informed the tender documents. A representative of the working party, who had been a chief executive for eight years, spoke at a meeting held to provide information to interested organizations. She described her experience of education and training opportunities in her job, and the training needs of chief executives in general as follows:[1]

> The first point I should make is that for most of that time it has been pretty much self-directed stuff. We have seen the odd flurry of coherence coming out of regional office about development. People like me are used to thinking for ourselves what our development needs are and putting stuff together. My accountability is to board chair, appointment of secretary of state. I have worked for four different chairs. All these chairmen they have lots of strengths but I cannot say that appraisal of me, performance management and a development programme, all of that process I cannot say that that has been a strong feature of my experience.
>
>   So what I have been doing to develop myself has been patchy and I have had flurries, but then I have drowned in day to day things when I couldn't get my head up. There is not the coherence.
>
>   But an odd, short-term short course, intensive, something like 'strategic thinking in the 90s', you know the sort of stuff, lasts two to three days, pretty expensive, quite enjoyable.
>
>   A major vehicle has been around learning sets. Most chief execs of my vintage have usually been involved in learning sets, usually self-formed and rarely facilitated, and dependent upon the individuals involved to keep them going.

She continued by describing the outcome of a further example of her previous training, when she had managed to get some money to go on a three-week training programme in the US, which resulted in publicity in the local paper about the waste of taxpayers' money.

The dominant metaphor in this text is that of the mother and child. We have an account of someone who has no one who can look into her and identify her needs. She therefore is left to her own devices, and the results are first, chaos: 'I have drowned in day to day things when I couldn't get my head up', and second, failure. Every time she has organized her own training the result has been unproductive or, at worst, embarrassing. In the mother/child relationship the mother (or other caretaker) can look at the child and know its needs without its articulating them, something of which it is anyway, before its access to language, incapable. Without the mother, the child's world is one of chaos and of a fear of drowning in the bombardment of sensations and experiences that assault the growing infant.

The reference to 'I', to the self, disappears in the third and fourth paragraphs. The 'I' of the first paragraph is a person who is looking at herself in her job – speaking at this meeting, observing regional office, liaising with the board chair. This is a person who is very much in control and who is critical of those technically above her in the hierarchy. The 'I' of the second paragraph is a different person. Here reference to the 'self' is made: 'So what I have been doing to develop myself' can be read as 'So what I have been doing to develop my "self"' with the self as something that is owned by, is a property of, the 'I'. This self is experiencing the threat of dissolution through 'drowning' in the job. The way out of this is through developmental courses. In this she is repeating one of the major outcomes sought by the proposed programme, i.e. participants should be able to separate better their organizational and home lives. The 'I' disappears from the final two paragraphs of the above account that refer to the development courses the speaker has already experienced. This absence is meaningful, for it suggests that the speaker has attended courses that have had no impact on the 'I' or on the self. The use of the metaphor of the vehicle is illustrative: all that happens on such courses is that the body, as the vintage vehicle that carries the 'I', goes along to indulge itself in luxury (the courses are expensive) and fun (the courses are 'quite enjoyable'). The learning sets, meanwhile, are 'self-formed' and, it seems, lacking in success, for the selves that form these sets are acknowledged to be lacking.

This account, and that contained in the tender documents which formalize this account, shows that NHS chief executives seek from academia training, mentoring and guidance that will not only make them better 'leaders' and change their working lives, but will also save and develop their 'selves'. The manager/leader who has not received academic training in management is perceived as being in danger of annihilation of the self under the demands of managerial work. Immersion in academic managerial discourse is sought as it is believed to prevent or eradicate personal as well as organizational chaos.

What a promise is thus held out by the management textbook, a promise of complete ontological security. Is this why so many students flock to study degrees and other qualifications in management? It is time to explore the effect on the managerial self of immersion in management education at masters degree level, to discover the extent to which this promise is fulfilled.

## Returning to the texts: education and training – the outcome of participating in management degrees

Five of the six managers interviewed had studied for masters degrees in management or were currently engaged in such pursuits at the time of the interviews. The first section of text I will analyse arose in reply to my asking one speaker what studying for a masters degree had meant to her. Her reply is contained in the left-hand column of the table.

Three versions of the self are operating here, incorporating:

| | |
|---|---|
| I think the course has made me recognize you know | I |
| it's it's sort of filled in the knowledge gaps as it were because you can go through life doing things and you have no idea why or what the theory is behind it. | You |
| So I suppose because I'm much better read now | I |
| I can recognize you know just what I'm about and how my mind's working and what I'm doing. So that's what the course has done for me. | Me |

The 'I' referred to in this account is the indexical 'I', the 'I' that is pondering upon and developing a theory of the self. The 'you' is an impersonal pronoun, that can refer to other people or to other versions of the self. Here, the section 'you can go through life doing things and you have no idea why or what the theory is behind it' refers to the past, to the pre-study self, and it can thus be read as a reference to the state of being uneducated, which is one where the individual lacks individuality, is one of the herd, so to speak. The masters degree in management serves therefore to lift a person out of the commonality, to provide uniqueness. This unique person has complete understanding – 'I can recognize you know just what I'm about and how my mind's working and what I'm doing', whereas previously s/he seems to have been walking around as if an automaton, performing actions without knowing the reasons why. The theory of the self that is the 'me' ('so that's what the course has done for me) is therefore the theory of a self that has deep self-understanding about her actions in her managerial world.

The following extract takes us a little further into understanding the effects of management education upon the manager:

| | |
|---|---|
| I had felt I had got to a stage at Medicine at [Trust B] where I was on top of my job, knew all the consultants, got on well with them, and had respect within the Trust, | I1A |
| Um | Bollasian pause |
| I had been doing my masters degree and my dissertation was on job satisfaction in middle managers in an NHS Trust, and I had actually done that with Elizabeth Jones [new chief executive] as my sponsor. | I2A |
| So I actually felt I had just hit a sort of pinnacle really where I'd I'd got some sort of I suppose recognition and acknowledgement in the Trust that I was doing a good job. I was efficient and I was on lots of Trust working groups. | I1B |
| I was invited on a lot of Trust working groups. | Bollasian pause |
| Partly through what I'd done, partly also I think because I had been doing the masters course | I1B |
| and people actually think 'God, she's actually doing some academic study' and it's that feeling of self-esteem, of value and recognition achievement that we all want. | I2B |

Here there are two 'I's evident, the managerial 'I' and the student 'I', with the swing between the two signalled by the Bollasian pauses. The second of these is in the form of a repeated statement rather than an 'um' or other signifier, but repetition allows the miniscule amount of time needed for thought processes to take place. The speaker is judging each of these two aspects of the self, and, in I1B and I2B, pronouncing them a success. I1B is the judgemental 'I', who is making the self visible to herself in order to assess it (and here pronouncing it a success). While the speaker refers (I2B) to a self that is observed and judged by other people, and again is pronounced a success, she is engaged in standing outside herself and looking at herself in the way that she imagines others do. Here we see Foucault's 'power of the gaze' in process, with the judgemental, internalized gaze undertaking its examination. Success is judged not by the tasks that are undertaken but by *visibility*, by being known and by being in the right places. This 'gaze' is checking that the manager is acting as a manager should act and is climbing up the hierarchical ladder.

The next extract comes from the same speaker, who has now moved forward in time in her narrative to her present, post-merger job, which is causing her great problems.

In this extract we have the use of the first person singular, I, the first person plural, we, and the second person singular, you, which can also be read as second person plural. The 'self' now adopts different forms:

| | |
|---|---|
| Interestingly enough people I've been on the [masters degree] with who worked at [Trust A] when I was at [Trust B] I'm now sort of working among them and there's a more of a support mechanism there. | I |
| People like Jane Stevens who was in the same cohort as me is now a divisional nurse in another area but we both came through this cohort together so knew each other from the [university], | We |
| and you know you can just drop in and have coffee and say how is it for you and you both sit there looking bedraggled and tired and you have a real, so you can have a mega chelp to each other and just get it off your chest. | You |

The 'I' as used here feels herself lost in an alien world (the other Trust) save for her fellow students with whom she has a shared identity, as can be seen in the use of 'we' in the second section of this quotation. Her cohort of students has therefore become one of her internalized objects, showing one way in which education programmes become part of the psychic texture of the self. It is the third section that is particularly striking, where 'you' replaces references to the first person. This, it can be seen, is a verbal strategy that distinguishes one part of the self from another, the private from the public. This is a private 'you', which has dropped into an office occupied by someone going through exactly the same traumas, with whom it is thus safe to reveal the private self, the 'you', the one who is not available to the public gaze. The 'you know', as noted above, signals a visual image, a very strong one of the manager who looks 'bedraggled and tired' and totally unlike the manager who is allowed to be shown in public, who complains and pours out troubles, but only in the safety of an office tucked away and out of sight. The judgemental gaze cannot operate here. The manager is again seen to be a self that is put on display and offered to the public gaze. The private self is a refuge, a place where the manager can escape from the demands of being in the public eye.

Together, these two speakers suggest that a higher degree in management provides a means of checking on the self to ensure that one is conforming to how a manager should appear to be, i.e. one who reflexively obeys the rules encoded in management education. Our third speaker confirms this. Without prompting, she referred on several occasions to the coordinator of the degree programme, who I've here called Anne Williams. For instance, at one point she said 'You know, if you share this with Anne and I don't recommend that you do, for she'll probably say that I'm a very tut tut poor time manager. I actually don't think I am.' Later she said:

> I don't sleep very well. I tend to wake up around 4 o'clock most days. But much of that is about, I've got so much work to do and the anxiety levels. And I do work very late. However, again, to be very, very fair, [pause], and I'll blame this on Anne Williams, um, I did my MA with Anne, Anne led the MA that I did and finished in whenever it was, and I did my MA in the middle of the night. So, um, I'm quite used to working late at night. Um, that's not a problem for me.

These repeated references to the director of the management degree, Anne, are located within references to judgement and assessment, with the inference that Anne is symbolic of someone who is constantly checking on what the respondent is doing. The course director has thus become symbolic of management discourse, and is thus the disciplinary gaze of

Foucault's *Discipline and Punish*, she is the jail-keeper in the Panopticon, always potentially watching. She has been internalized by the subject, and she is thus symbolic of management degrees and their discourses. The respondent shows that she is failing to achieve her managerial objectives, and she does not wish the course director to know about this. This is better seen by deconstructing the quote so as to discover the articulation of the pronouns. It has three sections in which three versions of 'I' are operating, the change from one to the other signalled by Bollasian pauses in the form of the words 'however' and 'so' and the more common pauses that allow time for thought:

| | |
|---|---|
| I don't sleep very well. I tend to wake up around 4 o'clock most days. But much of that is about, I've got so much work to do and the anxiety levels. And I do work very late. | I1 |
| However, again, to be very, very fair, [pause], and I'll blame this on Anne Williams [masters degree coordinator], um, I did my MA with Anne, Anne led the MA that I did and finished in whenever it was, and I did my MA in the middle of the night. | I2 |
| So, um, I'm quite used to working late at night. Um, that's not a problem for me. | I3/Me |

I1 is the confessional 'I', the 'I' that is admitting to being a failure as a manager. Work is now so demanding that the subject is anxious and cannot sleep. The second 'I' is the one that is thinking about what she has just said, is considering its implications, and realizing that she has said something amiss which signals that she is failing as a manager. I have shown above how any evidence of failure requires the manager to adjust her speech so as to avoid constructing the failed managerial self. The repeated references to the course director/managerial discourse signal that she is examining herself through the lens of the managerial discourse she absorbed as she took on her managerial self during her studies. The final 'I', qualified by the 'me', that then appears and which is interrupted by two Bollasian pauses, is rejecting her earlier statement. Working late at night is 'not a problem for me' because the managerial me has learned how to work late at night in order to fit in the demands that cannot be dealt with during the working day. The interjection of the repeated references to the course director have resulted in this significant shift, from a failing manager to one who can cope with all the demands of the managerial job. The course director personifies the judgemental gaze; her appearance in the mind of the speaker requires the speaker to adjust her statements and to deny that she is failing as a manager.

## The manager's management of the managerial self

In earlier chapters I distinguished between the modernist and the postmodernist eras in the textbooks. This chapter's study was undertaken in the early twenty-first century, so its findings are those of the postmodern. Thus it is a study of how managers construct their identities and constitute the practices of management, having stepped into the subject position of management.

It can be seen that those who have studied management over a prolonged course of study do not become the rational, logical controllers of chaos promised in the textbooks, but they absorb into their selves the necessity to become such bulwarks against chaos, establishing for themselves the necessary rules of self-conduct (conduct of the self) that should be followed by persons occupying this place. They present a public self that appears to conform to the all-controlling manager, and constantly monitor themselves to prevent deviation from the role in public. Any aberration occurs in private or must be denied. They have absorbed 'the managerial gaze', reified in the bodies of management teachers, into their very beings. Nowhere in our interviews did respondents report that their studies had changed the way they worked as managers. Throughout the emphasis was upon the self and how this had changed. It seems that rather than managing others their prime role is managing their selves.

This conclusion is supported by another finding. I asked each respondent to describe for me their day and the tasks that their managerial job required of them. Without exception, beyond a few vague nods at tasks, they were unable to put names or labels to what they did. One manager, for example, when asked what she had to do in her job, provided a list of hospital services for which she is 'overall general manager', mentioned the people who report to her and their responsibilities, and listed the organizational aims that she must ensure the people who report to her must achieve. She described it as a 'huge' job. A second, when I asked her what her job involved, told me I would have to tell her to 'shut up' because her reply would be so long, but could focus not on what she actually did but on the amount of time she spends working (11–12 hour days). A third described her job in relation to the status that comes with it, the issues that are dealt with, and the people and networks with which she liaises and is linked as a result of the job. Again, the number of hours worked were listed.

Try as I might, I cannot in interviews get managers to describe what they do in anything other than very, very superficial detail.

In some ways this is not surprising, as the long list of studies, dating from the 1950s, into the reality of management shows. Management is about talk. As recently as 1994 Rosemary Stewart and colleagues reported on a study of British and German middle managers which showed that over 90 per cent of each British manager's day was spent in their offices. It is difficult to see how days spent in the retreat of the office allow fulfilment of what their interviewees saw as the manager's role in Britain: to oversee and to motivate. Similarly, the British manager's view of the organization, they found, is that it is a village, with work as a pseudo-social activity, and management as personality driven (Stewart *et al.*, 1994, p. 116), yet it is a very small village that can be squashed into the confines of an office. Their role is not so much to deal with technical problems as the 'human problems of teamwork, motivation, development and so on' (p. 120), but it seems that these 'socially complex' tasks can be undertaken from the privacy of the managerial den. Stewart *et al.*'s work appears in one way to confirm Anthony's earlier conclusion (1986) that British management has long been engaged in a retreat from involvement with the worker, a retreat which means the manager by definition does not manage. Alternatively, such a perspective assumes that the textbooks set the standard against which managers should be measured. Managerial life-worlds follow different rules – the managerial job is not a series of overlapping tasks which can be summarized under terms such as planning, organizing and leading, staffing, coordinating and controlling. Rather, my arguments lead to the conclusion that the tasks of management consist of *being* the manager and thus symbolizing the battle against chaos, and second, with *maintaining* that subject position. Managers' prime function is thus control of the managerial self, for the managerial self is mimetic with the organization, and by controlling their selves they symbolically control the ever-threatening organizational chaos. Control is thus inscribed upon the managerial body. Being subjected and subjectified within the power/knowledge nexus, managers are safe, unchallenging, unthreatening to the social order.

# 8 Conclusion
## The social construction of management

The foregoing analyses lead to the conclusion that the textbooks serve to construct the subject position of management, a space in which the identity of manager is achieved. The empirical study showed that managers enact a managerial role that involves portraying themselves as managers, maintaining the visual façade of management, controlling themselves strictly to prevent the mask slipping, and so carrying out the symbolic role of manager. The subject position contained within the textbooks is thus reconciled with that occupied by managers. They symbolize rationality, culture, control. They symbolize the phallus, the law, the enactment of science. They symbolize order, the keeping in abeyance of chaos, the necessity for a structured world. They symbolize modernity. The textbooks, and management degrees, proffer a judgemental gaze for internalization.

However, to be a manager requires that there be a managerial Other, and a managerialized order requires the denigration of other participants in the organization and the arrogation of others' rights to self-determination. In this managers symbolize a world devoid of trust, a world gone mad, where no one (not even managers) can be credited with the power of self-control, motivation to work or enjoyment of their labour, where everyone is seen as slothful, ignorant, chaotic, and only those occupying the subject position of management can ensure that the world continues to function as the organization writ very large.

It is time now to conclude this exploration of the social construction of management, as seen largely through the pages of management textbooks, through drawing together the above threads to offer a theory of the construction of the subject position of management and thus the social construction of the subjects who occupy that position. In Chapter 1 I defined social constructionism as an interpretivist epistemology which, at any point in intellectual history, draws upon the panoply of whatever interpretivist intellectual movement is seen as avant-garde and radical. The emphasis here is upon interpretivism and upon an exploration of the workings of power as a theoretical endeavour to understand how 'the social worlds' we study are constituted in their moment to moment iterations of what passes for reality. In this concluding chapter I will return again to Judith Butler's theories, drawn upon also in previous chapters, but here I will use the potential offered by her theorizing of the performativity of gender, and of matter, to conclude this exploration. Through using Butler's work I will thus explain this distinction between subject position and subject, and thus show how texts enter the social world. What I cannot do in this conclusion, for that would be another study entirely, is explore how we, the non-managers, the managerial Other, concur in and thus contribute to such a construction of management, for even though we may despise it and seek in various ways to undermine it, we are all implicated in the maintenance of this socially constructed mode of organizing.

Earlier, I used the distinction between two definitions of the word 'performative' to distinguish between modernist and post-modernist readings of the construction of management. In this chapter I will focus only upon the latter definition, i.e. I will explore how management is a *performative* achievement, in the sense that Judith Butler uses the term when she argues (1990) that gender is performative. 'Performative' means the absence of any ontological status apart from the various acts which constitute a seeming reality, so that acts and gestures, articulated and enacted desires, create the illusion of an interior and organizing core, an illusion that is discursively maintained (Butler, 1990, p. 136). In other words, such acts, gestures, enactments, generally construed, are performative in the sense that the essence or identity that they otherwise purport to express are fabrications manufactured and sustained through corporeal signs and other discursive means. 'Performative', it follows, suggests a dramatic and contingent construction of meaning (ibid., p. 139), where the various acts of, in Butler's example, gender, create the idea of gender, and without those acts there would be no gender at all. For Butler, gender is thus a construction that regularly conceals its genesis; the tacit collective agreement to perform, produce, and sustain discrete and polar genders as cultural fictions is obscured by the credibility of those productions – and the punishments that attend not agreeing to believe in them; the construction 'compels' our belief in its necessity and naturalness (ibid., p. 140). In this book I am concerned with the credibility of the production of 'the manager', through the configurations of power that construct the subject of management. This has an added significance when seeing both gender and management as discursive productions, for the discursive production of management is percolated through and through with a *gendered* signification, although I have argued that for 'gender' we should read 'modernity'.

Butler argues that the 'being' of gender is *an effect*, an object of a genealogical investigation that maps out the political parameters of its construction in the mode of ontology. Management, in my reading, differs in that it reveals a world constituted epistemologically through the textbooks and management teachings. Her inquiry is a genealogy of gender ontology, which seeks to understand the discursive production of the plausibility of the binary relation between the 'real' and the 'authentic'. My study is a genealogy of epistemology which thus follows Parker (1992) in recognizing the epistemological status of moral/political objects that have been called into being through discourse, and which pretend to represent something as 'real', as taking the status of an object of knowledge, but which rather have been constructed in a political rhetoric. This leads me to conclude that 'management' is a performative epistemology, in that a social theory constructs the discursive space, management, into which managers climb to *perform and thus construct themselves as managers*, and which thus renders their Other, the worker or non-managerial member of staff, as Abject.

## Judith Butler, gender trouble and management as performative

For Butler, a political genealogy of gender ontologies requires the deconstruction of the substantive appearance of gender into its constitutive acts. This involves first an analysis of that which disrupts our taken-for-granted acceptances of the world as we know it. Butler analysed drag artists; for my argument it involves bringing together arguments from the foregoing chapters that reveal managers as disruptive, first, as both creators and controllers of chaos, and second, as both managers and workers. Where Butler explores the embodiedness of gender I will bring together my earlier arguments about the embodiedness of *the* manager and the organization as the projected embodiment of the manager. The essential incompleteness that Butler discovers in gender I have discovered in management as that incompleteness between the product of the text, i.e. the model of how the manager should be, and the lived worlds of the manager, but there is also the incompleteness of a subjectivity that must erode aspects of humanity deemed vital in other areas of life, such as a capacity for joy, empathy, compassion, feeling, intellectual endeavour, pleasure in embodiedness, etc.

### Disruptions

Butler, in seeking to *disrupt* our understanding of gender in order to develop its genealogy, looks for that which disrupts our taken-for-granted acceptance of our worlds in order to understand the transgressed order. Applied to management, the first of these disruptions may be found within the binary opposites of manager and worker. The structure of the organization is predicated upon the existence of these two, indeed the very definition of management as getting things done through other people illustrates managerial dependence upon the existence of the worker, thus management constructs the Other (workers) to consolidate its identity. (Worker dependence upon the manager is not so clear cut, although it is constructed such that we can think of no other.) Yet managers too are workers, dependent upon monthly salaries paid in exchange for their labour power. This status of managers as both worker and manager disrupts conventional ideas of the binary divide for managers-as-workers may threaten the body of capitalism. The unspoken emphasis throughout the texts on managers' reliability, the texts' refusal to acknowledge the possibility that managers may not conform to the expectations placed upon them, is indicative of a suppressed fear of its opposite, the power of managers to overturn the organizational apple cart. It could be this censored fear that has been the motivation behind the ever-more sophisticated attempts at control of the manager, such as preventing them from learning powers of critical thought. Taylorism brought into being the manager, but the textbook helps bring into being the rigidly controlled manager, one who has 'internalized the gaze', is ever watchful over the managerial self, and who ensures full self-compliance with the tenets of managerialism. Some of this compliance is of course brought about by 'hygiene factors' such as high salaries and other inducements, but these of themselves, as Herzberg showed but for other purposes, are not sufficiently powerful control mechanisms. Rather, the control mechanisms are to be found in the constitutive mechanisms of the manager, those that persuade managers of ways in which they may behave as they construct and reconstruct their managerial identities, in an ongoing production of a managerial self. This takes me to the question of whether or not we can conceive of managers as drag artists, the disruptive transgressors so influential upon Butler's thinking. I find in this an analogy that is most useful.

Drag artists dress themselves up as members of the opposite sex, some seeking verisimilitude, others parody, but all seeking somehow to transgress the ultimate binary divide of the two sexes. Drag artists enable Butler to make her breakthrough in her theory of gender as performative as, she argues, drag, in imitating gender, 'implicitly reveals the imitative structure of gender itself – as well as its contingency' (Butler, 1990, p. 137). She denies the existence of an original which such parodic identities imitate, arguing that the parody is of the very notion of an original, an imitation without an origin. To be more precise it is a production which, in effect – that is, in its effect – postures as an imitation (ibid., p. 138). Rather than asking if we can conceive of managers as drag artists it may therefore be more apposite to ask if they are engaged in a parody of an original which itself does not exist. Is this what managers are doing when they shave off their beards so as to excise all signs of nature, and dress in suits which symbolize their devotion to the principles of duty, renunciation, self-control and adherence to the social code? The social code of management involves a denial of sexuality and emotion, and the appearance of rationality and culture. It involves the enacting of the archetypal male. This male, who is foundational to the management textbook, is a construct brought into being in order to represent the control of ever-threatening chaos, but he is a male so devoid of any human characteristics that he is non-human, an archetype, someone who can never exist. Further, from Butler we know that as a gendered male he is involved in performing the gender of masculinity, and thus the gender which symbolizes modernity, and I have shown that women managers are compelled to perform that gender too. The manager therefore enacts a parody of masculinity, using mechanisms derived from received meanings which originate at least in part in the management textbook, and based upon imitative practices which construct the illusion of an interior, primary self.

Finally in this list of illuminative disruptions, I have identified management textbooks as both creating chaos and bringing into being the controllers of that chaos – the manager. Is this work of the textbooks a mere rhetorical, justificatory flourish, or does it, in its disruptive potential, signify something deeper? Giddens (1990) suggests that ontological insecurity is a characteristic of the age of what he calls late modernity. We live in an era of risk, where there is no one upon whom to place specific blame for those dread factors that plague us, yet in a secular age no one to whom we can turn for comfort in the face of the feared apocalypse. He draws upon psychoanalytical thought to reach understanding of his sociological perspective, yet psychoanalytical theories speak of similar dread risks, although here they emanate not from the wider society but from childhood. They are carried unconsciously and plague our emotional lives and intimate relationships in adulthood. The writers of the textbooks, from this perspective, can be seen as projecting their own fears, emanating perhaps from both sociological and psychological discourses, onto the text. Giddens identifies four responses to these risks. Pragmatic acceptance involves a concentration upon surviving through focusing upon day-to-day problems; sustained optimism entails a continued faith in the possibilities of science to solve all problems; cynical pessimism where the emotionally neutralizing nature of cynicism takes the sting out of pessimism, and radical engagement, which is 'an attitude of practical contestation towards perceived sources of danger' (Giddens, 1990, p. 137). This involves mobilizing to reduce the impact of or to transcend major problems, and is, Giddens points out, most closely associated with social movements. I suggest that Giddens' analysis is too narrow, for he ignores the all-important realm of organizations, and the response of the power/knowledge nexus of patriarchal managerialism to this risk. I contend that the writers of management textbooks have not only projected their own feelings of ontological insecurity onto the text but have constructed their own solution by bringing into being the ought-to-be organization, one seemingly washed clean of any uncertainty by an omnipotent management.

Earlier I defined the art of management as the meeting in the social worlds of organizations of the subjective worlds of managers, the managed, and teachers and students of management, meetings which are presented to us, through rhetoric, in such a way as to mystify the relationship between management and organization, giving authority to management as possessors of a social power that informs the subjectivity of managers, employees, and teachers and students of management. This meeting of the social worlds occurs within a power/knowledge nexus formed by patriarchal managerialism and academia, for patriarchal managerialism is legitimized by the knowledges arising from academia, and academia requires patriarchal managerialism to supply both students and the world on which it has built its theoretical edifice. The meeting takes place, however, in an ontologically virtual organization, created by management textbooks in conjunction with those management scientists upon whose work the textbooks draw (very) selectively. This 'virtual' organization is one that is researched into and upon which lectures are based, but that exists largely in the pages of the textbooks and in the mental maps and symbolic codes of writers and researchers on management. It is, however, being formed through the nexus of power and knowledge, a powerful organization that is laid like a matrix over the lived organizations of managers and other workers, organizations that, as the discursive turn in the social sciences reveals, have multiple realities. The organizational world of the management textbook becomes only one among many worlds.

It is, however, an organizational world that also calls upon science for not only its legitimation but also the desired safety from uncertainty. The management textbooks claim a scientific status for management, but later ignore this claim when they offer prescriptions for managerial practice that are founded largely in anecdotes and hypothetical examples rather than science. Indeed, science is denigrated. The powerful claim to developing management as a science, one that has shaped the development of the discipline, is replaced by folk wisdom, gossip and 'common sense', and science disappears from the discussion save in the vestigial form of recourse to a limited number of rather elderly references. The result, I have suggested, is the penetration of the managerial psyche with a chaos wrought from such contradictory demands, which thus renders the manager malleable and controllable.

The organizational world so constituted is symbolized by the organization chart. This, I have argued, can be read as a projection of modernity, and the masculine (i.e. either male or female) managerial self is a projection of an organization made in the manager's own image and the manager is made in the organization's, and thus modernity's, image. It is a projection of the mental space of the managerial cartographer rather than an objectified representation of the 'organization'. The organizational chart can be read as a 'phallolinear mark', identifying masculine space and dividing the territory of the organization in the image of the senior managers who govern it. In its mapping of a simplified, reduced world of hierarchical lines that unite the dreamed organization of the manager, devoid of anything but devotion to production, with the lived world of the people who together constitute the organization, it symbolizes management's ought-to-be world, of the twin desires for orderliness and for a managerial supremacy put beyond challenge. The boxes on the organization chart represent the 'cultured' part of the organization, and the spaces, which as I have shown represent the 'informal' organization, those areas that are savage and untamed, unknown and unknowable, and which always challenge the organized, conscious world of the manager.

It is a map of modernity, and it offers a pastiche of and for the manager.

The power/knowledge nexus is reinforced by the law that is enacted within organizations which in patriarchal managerialism have become juridified. Law, whether at the state or organizational level, is a discourse of power/knowledge in that it is a complex apparatus or mechanism of power which produces and is produced by the hegemonizing knowledge and truth necessary for the existing order. Rules of law should be seen as cultural signifiers of power struggles, as a form of domination, and constitutive of modern forms of power including a patriarchal managerial discourse within the juridified workplace. Patriarchal managerialism constitutes a judicial system at the level of the organization mimetic of that of the state system, a legal system in which managers form the law-makers, judiciary, police officers and investigators. In making the claim that the legitimacy of managerial authority rested in law, the textbooks first made the connection between law and management, one which heralded the discursive leap that sees the juridification of the workplace. In this organizational legal system laws are passed that establish standards of self-discipline required under modernity. That is, this form of law lays down rules which state that behaviour inside the enterprise should be serious, disciplined and unlike that which could be acceptable or forgivable in other fora. Nothing is allowed to upset the orderly world constituted by management as a defence against chaos.

The normative, idealized narrative of this juridified workplace is of the 'ought-to-be' workplace where emotion and nature are eliminated and the manager is in total, rational control. Employees who introduce emotions, the physical world of the body and irrationality into the workplace can be tried for indiscipline and judged against this ideal. Where they bring their emotions and their indiscipline into the courtroom of the disciplinary hearing they must be silenced (the hearing suspended) until they have learned to deport themselves in the acceptable, controlled manner. Here, 'the law' of the workplace is homologous with laws of modern societies. Organizations, through the law of the enterprise, reach out their tentacles into their workers' private lives, seeking to ensure employees discipline themselves in their personal lives. Employees should conform to an exemplar of the 'ought-to-be' worker – an automaton totally committed to rational organization. This ought-to-be worker is, importantly, constituted within a law that is one form of a phallicized rationality that dominates all women and all men, although the degree of domination experienced by men will vary according to their position of power. The phallicized law, in subordinating workers, symbolically castrates them, reduces them to the status of the feminine. What can be seen as 'masculine' behaviours (horseplay, etc.) are seen as chargeable offences – only a specifically defined male behaviour, that of the manager, is allowed at the workplace, so one form of masculinity attempts to subordinate and indeed to denigrate the other, which it sees as capable of displaying emotions and symbolizing nature, and thus of reminding the manager of the inescapably natural, sexual self that pervades masculinity just as much as it does femininity (Seidler, 1994).

It is difficult, sometimes, to see where, if at all, the 'organization' ends and the manager 'begins'. The organization chart can be read as a projection of the aspired-to managerial ego onto the page and onto the organization. The *scientific* organization is one that is constructed in the textbooks and projected onto the life-worlds of organizations, just as the manager is constructed in the textbook and 'real-life' managers are expected to conform to the textbook model. In the ongoing project of the self, I have shown that the managerial self, the 'at-work' self, is a self whose psychic texture is indistinguishable from the organization. The manager projects this self onto the organization, sees no distinction between at-work self and organization, implying that managers see the organization as the managerial self writ large. The managerial self is rational, organized, non-emotional, masculine, in control. The organization thus is rational, organized, a place where emotions must be suppressed, a masculine, modern but thus post-modern place.

The ought-to-be organization and the ought-to-be manager are each projections of the other, and each is both reflected in and projected out of the management textbook.

## Embodiedness

While it may be easy, at first sight, to see the necessity for analysing embodiedness when undertaking a study of gender, it is not perhaps so obvious when analysing management. However, the managerial body has haunted the pages of the previous chapters. It is there within the photographs in the textbooks, speaking messages to readers that instruct them how they should construct themselves as managers. They should excise all elements of sexuality, of nature and of the emotions – they should maintain themselves as rigidly 'buttoned up' as the severely collar-and-tied representatives of the managerial canon portrayed in the photographs in the texts. The manager's besuited, clean shaven body is a cultural sign.

Furthermore law is inscribed upon the bodies of managers (see Chapter 4). Within the context of the Freudian/Lacanian perspective of the law as a symbol of phallic power, the inscribing of the law upon the manager's body means that that very body becomes the phallicized symbol of the power of the Law, and thus of patriarchal relationships. The corporeal enactment of the manager, as bearer of the phallic power of law, can be seen, in Butler's terms, as synecdochal for the social system per se. Further, managers are subjectified within this symbolically inscribed body that they occupy when at work, for intrapsychic processes are an affect of the surface politics of the body (Butler, 1990). Following Mary Douglas in exploring interiority and exteriority, Butler argues that what appears as the 'internal fixity of the self' is suspect, and so we must explore in what language 'inner space' is figured. Butler argues that acts, gestures, articulated and enacted desires, all contribute to the creation of an illusion of an interior and organized gendered (managerial) core. When students gaze at the photographs of managers in textbooks, or when managerial readers see the photographs of successful managers in *Management Today*, *Harvard Business Review* or other management journals, they may presume a core that is a reflection of the exterior, an exterior upon which we are taught to read 'rational, in control, non-emotional'.

This core, Butler argues in terms of gender, is an 'illusion maintained for the purposes of the regulation of sexuality within the obligatory frame of reproductive heterosexuality' (Butler, 1990, p. 136). In terms of management the managerial 'core' becomes an illusion required in the regulation of the *manager* so as to ensure an organizational control that the manager herself may otherwise find intolerant. As Butler (1990) reminds us, where political and discursive origins of identities can be experienced as part of a psychological 'core', then an analysis of the political constitution of the (managerial) subject and its fabricated notions about the ineffable interiority of its identity (as manager) or of its true identity (as part of the workforce) is put beyond reach. Yet the textbook or the management journal holds out the promise of reaching this unreachable managerial core, of absorbing it into one's self, of becoming that managerial person.

Where gender is an act and gender reality created through sustained social performance, so thus must management be 'a ritual social drama' through which processes of signification are enacted. Signification, Butler argues, does not determine the subject, but provides 'a regulated process of repetition' within the 'orbit of the compulsion to repeat' that produces substantializing effects. In enacting the law of the workplace, in signifying it and symbolizing it upon their bodies, the manager thus enters voluntarily into a self-identity that requires that s/he conform to the requirements of constructing the phallicized law of the workplace both within the managerial self and within the workplace. In so doing, the manager engages in a set of repeated acts within a highly rigid regulatory frame that congeals over time to produce the appearance of substance, of a natural sort of being (Butler, 1990, p. 33). Earlier I showed that managers hide themselves away from observers at times when they feel they cannot maintain this achieved being. Thus just as the substantive effect of gender is performatively produced and compelled by the regulatory practices of gender coherence, so also is management performatively produced. It is a public act, a public production, that constitutes the identity it is purported to be.

Modernity's patriarchal managerialism requires a managerial actor who embodied rationality, logic and order, who exhibited no emotions and who excised their exhibition from the organization. It closes down the abilities to meditate, to contemplate, to ponder the meaning of life; it defines subjectivity out of existence and facilitates totalitarianism. The 'art' of management can be seen as a public display of the manager performing the role of the symbol of control of chaos. Managers are, just like pieces of art in a gallery, on display. On their post-modern bodies are inscribed the requirements of modernity's managerialism; through the repetition of their actions they perform this pastiche.

### Incompleteness

As in other ritual social dramas, Butler argues, the action of gender requires a performance that is *repeated*. This repetition is at once a re-enactment and re-experiencing of a set of meanings already socially established; and it is the mundane and ritualized form of their legitimation (Butler, 1990, p. 140). Bodily gestures, movements, and styles of various kinds, the everyday mundane ways of acting, constitute the illusion of an abiding gendered self. Gender should thus be conceived as a constituted 'social temporality'. The

> *appearance of substance* is precisely that, a constructed identity, a performative accomplishment which the mundane social audience, including the actors themselves, come to believe and to perform in the mode of belief . . . The abiding gendered self will then be shown to be structured by repeated acts that seek to approximate the ideal of a substantial ground of identity, but which, in their occasional

*dis*continuity, reveal the temporal and contingent groundlessness of this 'ground'.

(ibid., pp. 140–1)

Further, it 'would be wrong to assume in advance that there is a category of "women" that simply needs to be filled in with various components of race, class, age, ethnicity, and sexuality in order to become complete. The assumption of its essential incompleteness permits that category to serve as a permanently available site of contested meanings (ibid., p. 15).

These conclusions apply equally to management. There is a category of persons labelled 'managers' but our unknowingness about them, the discursive silences into which they fall when pressed to describe what they do, the silences in the textbooks that cannot equate observational studies of managers with what the textbooks say they should do, the always 'rather nebulous character of managerial work' (Townley, 1994, p. 60) enable an essential incompleteness that allows management to remain as a permanently available site of contested meanings, one that is written upon by managers themselves, by management scientists, critical management theorists, the law, students, government and, indeed, by workers. Each can construct the manager in its own desired image.

The textbook authors and management scientists write their image of the manager. The organizational chart/map that symbolizes the manager calls upon a psychological history that is intertwined with the subjectivity of gender and the intense experience of insecurity that is the history of the individual. The management writer has defined a world in which he feels safe and secure, and he wishes to impose that world upon everyone. However, the safety and security is not set in concrete, and it threatens to break up and allow expression of a personal anarchy whereby the emotions may break free into full expression, where nature may win the day over culture, where sexuality may be expressed. Suppression requires them to distinguish themselves from those who are Other, and this is a symbolic function of the boxes of the map/chart, which neatly and tightly separate managerial space from the space of the Other. Yet managers too are Other, for they are both workers and managers; they are people who experience emotions and who live lives redolent with nature. The manager of the textbook is incomplete, having gaps where parts of her humanity should be.

In Chapter 5 I suggested that as both the work of artists and of managers has been used and misused for the political ends of American capitalism, managers and artists both are caught up in a paradox of existence, wherein they construct themselves according to the labels they apply to themselves, the label produces the meaning, and meanwhile capitalism, in selling products that in a dialectically reflexive irony produces these constructions of the artistic and managerial selves, benefits. The labels managers may apply to themselves are found in the figurative works of the textbook which animate the homosociality of the organization. The manager adheres strictly to the social code of modernity, even though the besuited and clean-shaven body of the manager is phallicized, in Lacan's meaning of the term as a categorical distinction between the phallus and the penis, the merely provisional ability of the latter to represent the former, where the entire male body can represent the phallus and thus masculine power and knowledge. The photographs in management textbooks open the male manager to the gaze of readers, for the photographs signal to them the power of the manager, of managerial knowledge and thus of the power/knowledge nexus. The power of the phallus as symbolic signifier of masculine dominance banishes those knowledges that cannot be absorbed into the patriarchal, androcentric order of management. The whole of the besuited, clean-shaven male body thus becomes a signifier for symbolic knowledge, power and privilege. Arousal is sought of the spectator's narcissistic desire to emulate the portrayed active male managers. He is urged to aspire to possess the phallus. Female readers see a world in which womanhood is proscribed as dangerous, and so they must abandon their sex if they are to gain entry. Readers are thus invited to project their own desires onto the manager, to write the manager as the person they wish themselves to be.

Managers are also written upon by the law. The 'managers' constituted through the discourse of law are not so much involved in having their position legitimized by law but in being themselves, as managers, constituted by law. Managers here become the corporeal enactment of phallic law. The law is inscribed upon their bodies and it renders them docile, just as they in turn attempt to render workers docile. Rather than the law being a resource for managers, the subject position that is the managerial self is constituted, at least in part, by the law. Managers are made docile for, just as the prisoner in the Panopticon is formulated through a discursively constituted identity as prisoner, is *made* through her/his subjection to the organization within which s/he is incarcerated, so too is the manager activated or formed as a subject by the juridified organization. The discourse of law within the organization is one that brings into being the patriarchal and phallocentric manager who is at the same time subjectified and impotent.

This duality of managers I found also when deconstructing management textbooks' claim that management is a science. The recourse to this claim on the one hand removes management from the political realm and puts it beyond challenge – management is a regime of truth so powerful that even those who seek to challenge it can fall under its thrall. On the other hand there is always the possibility that managers may 'write themselves' and become a threat to the social order. Containment of this potentiality is achieved through the constitution by textbooks and management scientists of a world of organizations and of management that is laid like a matrix over the lived worlds of organizations and of management. These worlds are not politically neutral but serve to ensure that managers too become enmeshed in discourses that render them impotent and unthreatening. *Mainstream/ malestream degrees in management and business, and the research upon which they are based, can thus be seen as in themselves forms of disciplinary practice.* This conclusion was supported by the empirical research I reported on in Chapter 7. In exploring how managers constitute their 'selves' I used a definition of the self that follows Butler (1997, pp. 10–11) in seeing it as that which takes occupation of the locus of the subject and thus assumes its, the self's, subjectified identity. The subject is a linguistic category, a 'structure in formation', a 'site' that is occupied by individuals. From this, the 'self' becomes a discursive construction that draws upon multiple discourses in its processes of formation and re-formation: each of us is multiple selves.

Managers, these data reveal, carry around with them an image of what the manager should be. Management is associated with being seen to be at the workplace, with 'doing everything', with working oneself to the point of exhaustion, although never showing that exhaustion. The manager should be totally devoted to the organization, impervious to pressure, and the managerial self should mirror the textbook in that it has a head but no body, is culture rather than nature, mind rather than body, rational rather than emotional. Managers are *like pieces of work in an art gallery, on public display.* The managerial subject is, however, something that has to be actively maintained by the manager. The manager works to maintain a self-image of herself as a manager. This self-image, the aspired-to managerial self, is revealed when, in *extremis*, it is challenged and another managerial self becomes dominant. It is a self that, except during times of duress, can be switched on or off. In this constant construction and reconstruction of the managerial self, there is therefore an incompleteness. The 'manager' is a subject so incomplete that the organization becomes part of the identity, for the managerial self revealed by interviewees was one whereby the organization had become part of the managers' subjectivity, and the self of the manager absorbed into the organization. The boundaries between the manager and the organization disappear.

## Conclusion

Management education, I have shown, can be sought due to its promise of providing ontological security through prevention or eradication of personal as well as organizational chaos, but the experience of that education does not change the way managers work. Rather, a prolonged course of education at higher degree level results rather in the internalization of the Foucauldian judgemental gaze. This 'gaze' checks that the manager is acting as a manager should act, constituting his/her identity according to the desired model of the managerial identity, and achieving the portrayal of the manager that should be portrayed. Rather than managing others, managers' prime role is managing their selves.

Those who have studied management over a prolonged course of study therefore do not become the rational, logical controllers of chaos promised in the textbooks, but they absorb into their selves the necessity to become such bulwarks against chaos, establishing for themselves the necessary rules of self-conduct (conduct of the self) that should be followed by persons occupying this place. They present a public self that appears to conform to the all-controlling manager, and constantly monitor themselves to prevent deviation from the role in public. Success is judged not by the tasks that are undertaken but by *visibility*, by being known and by being in the right places. Any aberration occurs in private or must be denied.

The textbooks therefore offer their readers a pattern by which they can construct themselves, a pattern based on an original manager who has no origin, who has never existed. The textbook readers are drawn in, through the seduction of the text, to a construction of a managerial self that involves portraying themselves as managers, maintaining the visual façade of management, controlling themselves strictly to prevent the construction slipping, and so become the pastiche of the modern manager. To repeat what I said earlier: they symbolize rationality, culture, control, the phallus, the law, the enactment of science, order, the control of chaos, the necessity for a structured world. They symbolize all others as Other, as carriers of irrationality, nature, chaos, disorder, etc. The manager is constructed as the sole bulwark against anti-capitalism, anti-modernity.

Managers' prime function is therefore not planning, organizing, staffing, leading or controlling, but, through the necessity of constructing themselves through this dense system of symbols, of revealing themselves as the embodiment of modernity, their prime function is the constitution of and control over their managerial selves. Managers too are subjected and subjectified within the power/knowledge nexus. Management is thus distinct from the manager, for management is constructed by the textbook and by management scientists, while the manager climbs into the space of management and constitutes herself to fit that space. The manager is thus a subject who is both subjectified by and subject to the power of management.

Here then is the distinction between 'management' and 'managers', for although the two are often seen as interchangeable they must be seen as distinct, with the one, 'management' regarded as the subject, and the manager as the individual who comes to occupy the site of the subject. The 'subject', Butler argues (1997) should not be confused or regarded as interchangeable with 'the person' or the 'individual', for genealogically, the subject is a

> linguistic category, a placeholder, a structure in formation. Individuals come to occupy the site of the subject ... and they enjoy intelligibility only to the extent that they are, as it were, first established in language. The subject is the linguistic occasion for the individual to achieve and reproduce intelligibility, the linguistic condition of its existence and agency. No individual becomes a subject without first becoming subjected or undergoing 'subjectivation'.
>
> (Butler, 1997, pp. 10–11)

In the constructed world of post-modernity's managerialism managers are involved in performing themselves, as managers, so that they conform to the textbook model of the manager. The function of *management*, one created by the textbooks, is therefore a discursive epistemological space, one into which the *manager* must climb. It is prior to and distinct from the manager, but it constitutes the manager who comes to occupy that space. Management is thus performative in that it has no ontological status apart from the various acts, undertaken by managers, which constitute its reality. The job of managers is to undertake this performative function and embody the theory of management. Management is thus a social construction that has rendered us incapable of dreaming of other ways of running the organizations in which we belong. Management's power subjects and subjectifies the worker, and we are all of us workers. But management's power subjects and subjectifies the manager too.

# Notes

## 2 Management as text

1 In the interests of reducing monotony, I am referring to the textbook throughout as either 'the Koontz textbook' or 'Koontz and O'Donnell'. This means Weihrich's name rarely appears in my text, for which I apologize.

## 3 Management as science

1 Anyone who has been involved in preparing for the Teaching Quality Assessment in the UK's Higher Education system will recognize this framework, as it is now applied to the objectives of each lecture which must fit into the objectives of the module which must fit into the objectives of the degree which must fit into the objectives of the department which must fit into the objectives of the university.

2 Page 152 contains a full-page diagram.

## 4 Management as legal authority

1 The metaphor of impotence is striking, given Hearn's (1992) description of management as a 'phallusy'.

2 I am grateful to Mark Learmonth for this observation.

## 5 Management as art

1 The loss of this last text, on managerial authority, is significant, as I show in Chapter 4 on management's claim to a status in/as law.

2 I am grateful to Kahryn Hughes for this observation.

## 6 Management as modernity

1 I need at this point to insert a reflexive note. This chapter relies heavily on the 'f' word – feminist theories. There is an androcentric, and indeed phallocentric, bias throughout management and organization studies (Calas and Smircich, 1992b; Gherardi, 1995; Collinson and Hearn, 1996), as through the arts, humanities, physical and social sciences (Calas and Smircich, 1992b). I experienced the lash of that bias when earlier drafts of this chapter were reviewed, for they were heavily criticized for using feminist theories that were charged with being 'outdated': I was told I was saying nothing new. I, of course, beg to differ, for my aim is to use feminist theories because of the intellectual expertise they offer and the delightful way

in which they allow a deep intrusion into the subtexts of management. 'Man-bashing' is far from my aim, yet that seemed to be the assumption of the reviewers. I had discussed this book previously with someone, a good Marxist, who had taught me many years previously when I was an undergraduate, and he advised me to avoid any use of feminist theories. Those critics suggested he was offering wise words. However, I disagree utterly with anyone who dismisses a complex, multidisciplinary, multiply theorized, internally disputatious and constantly evolving perspective of thought, staffed by extremely clever and insightful academics, on the grounds of its label or its presumed bias rather than the quality of its analyses. I am therefore ignoring that advice, and challenging any anti-feminists to overcome their bile and assess this chapter on its merits.

2   A 'trust' was the name given by the Conservative government in Britain, during one of their periodic restructurings of the National Health Service in the 1980s, to what had been known as hospitals, clinics and other forms of health organizations. The label has remained.

## 7   The managerial self

1   It was impossible to tape the proceedings of this public meeting, so the text that follows is a shorthand record of the presentation. I am capable of keeping up with an average speaking rate for short bursts, but this technique necessarily omits some of the richness of data that are gathered through tape recording, notably the pauses and hums that proved so useful in the above analysis.

# Bibliography

Adler, Sue, Laney, Jenny and Packer, Mary (1993) *Managing Women*. Buckingham: Open University Press.

Ahmed, Sara (1995) Deconstruction and Law's Other: Towards a Feminist Theory of Embodied Legal Rights. *Social and Legal Studies*, 4, 55–73.

Alcoff, Linda Martin (1996) Feminist Theory and Social Science. New Knowledges, New Epistemologies. In Duncan, Nancy (ed.) *Body Space*. London: Routledge, pp. 13–27.

Alvesson, Mats (1993) *Cultural Perspectives on Organizations*. Cambridge: Cambridge University Press.

Alvesson, Mats and Willmott, Hugh (2002) Identity Regulation as Organizational Control: Producing the Appropriate Individual. *Journal of Management Studies*, 39:5, 619–44.

Anthony, P.D. (1986) *The Foundation of Management*. London: Tavistock.

Anthony, P.D. (1994) *Managing Culture*. Buckingham: Open University Press.

Arksey, Hilary (1994) Expert and Lay Participation in the Construction of Medical Knowledge. *Sociology of Health and Illness*, 16:4, 448–68.

Armstrong, Peter (1996) The Expunction of Process Expertise from British Management Teaching Syllabi: An Historical Analysis. In Glover, Ian and Hughes, Michael (eds) *The Professional-managerial Class. Contemporary British Management in the Pursuer Mode*. Aldershot: Avebury, pp. 269–301.

Ashe, Marie (1995) Mind's Opportunity: Birthing a Poststructuralist Feminist Jurisprudence. In Leonard, Jerry D. (ed.) *Legal Studies as Cultural Studies. A Reader in (Post) Modern Critical Theory*. New York: State University of New York Press, pp. 84–132.

Bacharova, Ljuba (1999) Personal communication.

Ball, Stephen J. (1990) Management as Moral Technology: A Luddite Analysis. In Ball, Stephen J. (ed.) *Foucault and Education: Disciplines and Knowledge*. London: Routledge, pp. 153–66.

Benn, S.I. and Gaus, G.F. (1983) The Public and the Private: Concepts and Action. In Benn, S.I. and Gaus, G.F. (eds) *Public and Private in Social Life*. London: Croom Helm, pp. 3–30.

Benton, Lauren (1994) Beyond Legal Pluralism: Towards a New Approach to Law in the Informal Sector. *Social and Legal Studies*, 3, 223–42.

Berger, Peter L. and Luckmann, Thomas (1967) *The Social Construction of Reality*. Harmondsworth: Penguin Books.

Berle, A.A. and Means, G. (1932) *The Modern Corporation and Private Property*. New York: Macmillan.

Best, Steven and Kellner, Douglas (2001) *The Post-modern Adventure. Science, Technology, and Cultural Studies at the Third Millennium*. New York: Routledge.

Best, Victoria (1999) *Critical Subjectivities. Identity and Narrative in the Work of Colette and Marguerite Duras*. Oxford: Peter Lang.

Bollas, Christopher (1993) *Being a Character. Psychoanalysis and Self Experience*. London: Routledge.

Bollas, Christopher (1995) *Cracking Up. The Work of Unconscious Experience*. London: Routledge.

Bonvillain, Nancy (1995) *Women and Men: Cultural Constructs of Gender*. Englewood Cliffs, NJ: Prentice Hall.

Bourdieu, Pierre (1998) *Practical Reason*. Cambridge: Polity Press.

Braverman, H. (1973) *Labor and Monopoly Capital: The Degradation of Work in the Twentieth Century*. New York: Monthly Review Press.

Buchanan, David and Huczynski, Andrzej A. (1997) *Organizational Behaviour: An Introductory Text*. London: Prentice Hall.

Burack, Elmer H. and Mathys, Nicholas J. (1983) *An Introduction to Management. A Career Perspective*. New York: Wiley.

Burkitt, Ian (1991) *Social Selves. Theories of the Social Formation of Personality*. London: Sage.

Burr, Vivien (1995) *An Introduction to Social Constructionism*. London: Routledge.

Burr, Vivien (1998) *Gender and Social Psychology*. London: Routledge.

Burrell, Gibson (1998) Modernism, Post-Modernism and Organizational Analysis: The Contribution of Michel Foucault. In McKinlay, Alan and Starkey, Ken (eds) *Foucault, Management and Organization Theory*. London: Sage, pp. 14–28.

Butler, Judith (1990) *Gender Trouble: Feminism and the Subversion of Identity*. London: Routledge/Chapman & Hall.

Butler, Judith (1993) *Bodies That Matter*. New York: Routledge.

Butler, Judith (1996) Imitation and Gender Insubordination. In Morton, Donald (ed.) *The Material Queer; A LesBiGay Cultural Studies Reader*. Boulder, CO: Westview Press, pp. 180–92.

Butler, Judith (1997) *The Psychic Life of Power*. Stanford, CA: Stanford University Press.

Calas, Marta B. and Smircich, Linda (1992a) Voicing Seduction to Silence Leadership. *Organization Studies*, 12:4, 567–602.

Calas, Marta B. and Smircich, Linda (1992b) Re-writing Gender into Organizational Theorizing: Directions from Feminist Perspectives. In Reed, Michael and Hughes, Michael (eds) *Rethinking Organization: New Directions in Organization Theory and Analysis*. London: Sage.

Campbell, Jan (2000) *Arguing with the Phallus*. London: Zed Books.

Carr, Adrian and Hancock, Philip (eds) (2003) *Art and Aesthetics at Work*. Basingstoke: Palgrave.

Chalmers, Alan (1990) *Science and its Fabrication*. Milton Keynes: Open University Press.

Chandler, A.D. (1977) *The Visible Hand: The Managerial Revolution in American Business.* Cambridge, MA: Harvard University Press.

Chia, Robert (1994) The Concept of Decision: A Deconstructive Analysis. *Journal of Management Studies*, 31:6, 781–806.

Clark, Timothy and Salaman, Graeme (1998) Telling Tales: Management Gurus' Narratives and the Construction of Managerial Identity. *Journal of Management Studies*, 35:2, 137–57.

Clegg, Stewart (1998) Foucault, Power and Organizations. In McKinlay, Alan and Starkey, Ken (eds) *Foucault, Management and Organization Theory.* London: Sage, pp. 28–48.

Cockcroft, Eva (1999) Abstract Expressionism. Weapon of the Cold War. In Frascina, Francis and Harris, Jonathan (eds) *Art in Modern Culture. An Anthology of Critical Texts.* London: Phaidon Press, pp. 82–90.

Cole, G.A. (1995) *Management. Theory and Practice.* 4th edition. London: DP Publications.

Collinson, David and Hearn, Jeff (1996) 'Men at Work': Multiple Masculinities/ Multiple Workplaces. In Mac an Ghaill, Mairtin (ed.) *Understanding Masculinities.* Buckingham: Open University Press, pp. 61–76.

Cooper, Robert and Burrell, Gibson (1988) Modernism, Post-modernism and Organizational Analysis: An Introduction. *Organization Studies*, 9:1, 91–112.

Cornell, Drucilla (1995) Time, Deconstruction, and the Challenge to Legal Positivism: The Call for Judicial Responsibility. In Leonard, Jerry D. (ed.) *Legal Studies as Cultural Studies. A Reader in (Post) Modern Critical Theory.* New York: State University of New York Press, pp. 231–66.

Daft, Richard L. (1997) *Management.* 4th edition. Orlando: The Dryden Press.

Dale, Karen and Burrell, Gibson (2000). What Shape Are We In? Organization Theory and the Organized Body. In Hassard, John, Holliday, Ruth and Willmott, Hugh (eds) *Body and Organization.* London: Sage, pp. 15–30.

Davies, Celia (1995) *Gender and the Professional Predicament in Nursing.* Buckingham: Open University Press.

Derrida, Jacques (1995) *Archive Fever. A Freudian impression.* Chicago: University of Chicago Press. Trans. Eric Prenowitz.

Derrida, Jacques (1998) *Monolingualism of the Other OR The Prosthesis of Origin.* Stanford, CA: Stanford University Press. Trans. Patrick Mensah.

Douzinas, Costas, Warrington, Ronnie and McVeigh, Shaun (1991) *Postmodern Jurisprudence. The Law of Text in the Texts of Law.* London: Routledge.

Dreyfus, Hubert L. and Rabinow, Paul (1982) *Michel Foucault. Beyond Structuralism and Hermeneutics.* Brighton: Harvester.

Du Gay, Paul (1996) *Consumption and Identity at Work.* London: Sage.

Duncan, Nancy (1996) Renegotiating Gender and Sexuality in Public and Private Spaces. In Duncan, Nancy (ed.) *Body Space.* London: Routledge, pp. 127–45.

Easthope, Anthony (1990) *What a Man's Gotta Do. The Masculine Myth in Modern Culture.* Boston: Unwin Hyman.

Fineman, Steven and Gabriel, Yiannis (1994) Paradigms of Organizations: An Exploration in Textbook Rhetorics. *Organization*, 1, 375–401.

Fitzpatrick, Peter (1992) *The Mythology of Modern Law.* London: Routledge.

Fletcher, A.J. (1995) *Gender, Sex and Subordination. England 1500–1800.* London: Yale University Press.

Ford, Jackie and Harding, Nancy (2002) Aestheticised Maps as Powers of Resistance. Paper given at the 20th Annual International Labour Process Conference, University of Strathclyde, Glasgow.

Ford, Jackie and Harding, Nancy (2004, forthcoming). Invoking Satan, or, Re-reading the Psychological Contract. *Journal of Management Studies.*

Foucault, Michel (1972) *The Archaeology of Knowledge.* London: Routledge. Trans. A.M. Sheridan-Smith.

Foucault, Michel (1973) *The Birth of the Clinic.* London: Routledge.

Foucault, Michel (1980) *Power/Knowledge.* London: Harvester Wheatsheaf. Ed. Colin Gordon. Trans. Colin Gordon *et al.*

Foucault, Michel (1994) *Aesthetics. The Essential Works.* London: Allen Lane/ The Penguin Press. Ed. James Faubion.

Fournier, Valérie and Grey, Chris (2000) At the Critical Moment: Conditions and Prospects for Critical Management Studies. *Human Relations,* 53:1, 7–32.

French, Robert and Grey, Christopher (eds) (1996) *Rethinking Management Education.* London: Sage.

Frosh, Stephen (1997) *For and Against Psychoanalysis.* London: Routledge.

Fuery, Patrick and Mansfield, Nick (2000) *Cultural Studies and Critical Theory.* Oxford: Oxford University Press.

Fuss, Diana (2001) Theorizing Hetero- and Homosexuality. In Seidman, Steven and Alexander, Jeffrey C. (eds) *The New Social Theory Reader. Contemporary Debates.* London: Routledge, pp. 347–52.

Gabriel, Yiannis (1999) *Organizations in Depth.* London: Sage.

Gergen, Kenneth J. (1985) Social Constructionist Inquiry: Context and Implications. In Gergen, Kenneth J. and Davis, K. (eds) *The Social Construction of the Person.* New York: Springer-Verlag.

Gergen, Kenneth J. (1991) *The Saturated Self Dilemmas of Identity in Contemporary Life.* New York: Basic Books.

Gergen, Kenneth J. (1998) Constructionist Dialogues and the Vicissitudes of the Politics. In Velody, Irving and Williams, Robin (eds) *The Politics of Constructionism.* London: Sage, pp. 33–48.

Gergen, Kenneth J. (1999) *An Invitation to Social Construction.* Thousand Oaks, CA: Sage.

Gherardi, Silvia (1995) *Gender, Symbolism and Organizational Culture.* London: Sage.

Giddens, Anthony (1990) *The Consequences of Modernity.* Cambridge: Polity Press.

Giddens, Anthony (1991) *Modernity and Self-identity: Self and Society in the Late Modern Age.* Cambridge: Polity Press.

Gilbert, Nigel and Mulkay, Michael (1980) Contexts of Scientific Discourse: Social Accounting in Experimental Papers. In Knorr, Karin D., Krohn, Roger and Whitley, Richard (eds) *The Social Process of Scientific Investigation.* Dordrecht: D. Reidel, pp. 269–94.

Gilligan, Carol (1997) In a Different Voice: Women's Conceptions of Self and Morality. In Meyers, Diana Tietjens (ed.) *Feminist Social Thought.* New York: Routledge.

Gilmore, David D. (1990) *Manhood in the Making: Cultural Concepts of Masculinity.* New Haven: Yale University Press.

Goffman, Erving (1969) *The Presentation of Self in Everyday Life*. London: Allen Lane/The Penguin Press.

Gordon, Scott (1991) *The History and Philosophy of Social Science*. London: Routledge.

Grace, C. and Wilkinson, P. (1978) *Sociological Inquiry and Legal Phenomena*. Middlesex: Collier Macmillan.

Grant, Jan and Porter, Paige (1996) Women Managers: The Construction of Gender in the Workplace. *Australian and New Zealand Journal of Sociology*, 30:2, 149–64.

Grey, C. (1999) 'We are all Managers Now'; 'We Always Were': On the Development and Demise of Management. *Journal of Management Studies*, 36:5, 561–85.

Grey, Christopher and French, Robert (1996) Rethinking Management Education: An Introduction. In French, Robert and Grey, Christopher (eds) *Rethinking Management Education*. London: Sage, pp. 1–16.

Grey, Christopher and Willmott, Hugh (2002) Context of CMS. *Organization*, 9:3, 411–18.

Grosz, E.A. (1988) In(ter)vention of Feminist Knowledges. In Caine, Barbara, Grosz, E.A. and de Lepervanche, Marie (eds) *Crossing Boundaries. Feminism and the Critique of Knowledges*. Sydney: Allen and Unwin.

Guba, Egon G. and Lincoln, Yvonna S. (1998) Competing Paradigms in Qualitative Research. In Denzin, Norman K. and Lincoln, Yvonna S. (eds) (1998) *The Landscape of Qualitative Research. Theories and Issues*. Thousand Oaks, CA: Sage, pp. 195–220.

Guilbaut, Serge (1999) The New Adventures of the Avant-Garde in America. In Frascina, Francis and Harris, Jonathan (eds) *Art in Modern Culture. An Anthology of Critical Texts*. London: Phaidon Press, pp. 239–51.

Hacking, Ian (1998) On Being More Literal about Construction. In Velody, Irving and Williams, Robin (eds) *The Politics of Constructionism*. London: Sage.

Hacking, Ian (1999) *The Social Construction of What?* Cambridge, MA: Harvard University Press.

Haimann, Theo and Scott, William G. (1970) *Management in the Modern Organization*. Boston: Houghton Mifflin.

Haraway, Donna J. (1992) *Primate Visions: Gender, Race and Nature in the World of Modern Sciences*. London: Verso.

Harding, Nancy and Palfrey, Colin (1997) *Confused Professionals? The Social Construction of Dementia*. London: Jessica Kingsley.

Harding, Sandra (1991) *Whose Science? Whose Knowledge? Thinking from Women's Lives*. Milton Keynes: Open University Press.

Harré, Rom (1983) *Personal Being*. Oxford: Basil Blackwell.

Harré, Rom (1990) Some Narrative Conventions of Scientific Discourse. In Nash, Cristopher (ed.) *Narrative in Culture: The Uses of Storytelling in the Sciences, Philosophy and Literature*. London: Routledge.

Harré, Rom (1998) *The Singular Self. An Introduction to the Psychology of Personhood*. London: Sage.

Haywood, Christian and Mac an Ghaill, Mairtin (1996) Schooling Masculinities. In Mac an Ghaill, Mairtin (ed.) *Understanding Masculinities*. Buckingham: Open University Press, pp. 50–60.

Hearn, Jeff (1992) *Men in the Public Eye*. London: Routledge.

Hearn, Jeff and Morgan, David H.J. (1990) *Men, Masculinities and Social Theory*. London: Unwin Hyman.

Hearn, Jeff and Parkin, Wendy (1986) *'Sex' at 'Work': The Power and Paradox of Organization Sexuality*. Brighton: Wheatsheaf Books.

Hood-Williams, John (1996) Goodbye to Sex and Gender. *Sociological Review*, 44:1, 1–16.

Hughes, Kahryn (1999) *From Anorexia Nervosa to Anorexic Practices: The Process of Subject Constitution in the Therapeutic Encounter*. Unpublished PhD thesis. University of Leeds.

Hunt, Alan (1993) *Explorations in Law and Society*. London: Routledge.

Hunt, Alan and Wickham, Gary (1994) *Foucault and Law. Towards a Sociology of Law as Governance*. London: Pluto Press.

Jacques, Roy (1996) *Manufacturing the Employee: Management Knowledge from the 19th to 21st Centuries*. London: Sage.

Jacques, Roy (1997) Review of: Early Management Thought. In Wren, D.A. (ed.) *Electronic Journal of Radical Organizational Theory*, 3:2. http://www.mngt.waikato.ac.nz/Research/ejrot/Vol3_2/jacques.asp.

Jameson, Fredric (1991) *Post-modernism, or, the Cultural Logic of Late Capitalism*. London: Verso.

Jameson, Fredric (2002) *A Singular Modernity. Essay on the Ontology of the Present*. New York: Verso Books.

Jeffcutt, Paul (1994) The Interpretation of Organization: A Contemporary Analysis and Critique. *Journal of Management Studies*, 31:2, March, 235–49.

Johnson, Mark (1987) *The Body in the Mind. The Bodily Basis of Meaning, Imagination and Reason*. Chicago: University of Chicago Press.

Kellner, Douglas (1989) *Post-modernism/Jameson/Critique*. Washington: Maisonneuve Press.

Kerr, C. *et al.* (1962) *Industrialism and Industrial Man*. New York: Heinemann.

Kerruish, Valerie (1991) *Jurisprudence as Ideology*. London: Routledge.

Kirby, Kathleen M. (1996) Re-mapping Subjectivity. Cartographic Vision and the Limits of Politics. In Duncan, Nancy (ed.) *Body Space*. London: Routledge, pp. 45–55.

Knorr-Cetina, Karin D. (1981) *The Manufacture of Knowledge: An Essay on the Constructivist and Contextual Nature of Science*. Oxford: Pergamon Press.

Koontz, Harold and O'Donnell, Cyril (1955) *Principles of Management: An Analysis of Managerial Functions*. New York: McGraw Hill.

Koontz, Harold and O'Donnell, Cyril (1959) *Principles of Management: An Analysis of Managerial Functions*. New York: McGraw Hill.

Koontz, Harold and O'Donnell, Cyril (1964) *Principles of Management: An Analysis of Managerial Functions*. New York: McGraw Hill.

Koontz, Harold and O'Donnell, Cyril (1968) *Principles of Management: An Analysis of Managerial Functions*. New York: McGraw Hill.

Koontz, Harold and O'Donnell, Cyril (1972) *Principles of Management: An Analysis of Managerial Functions*. New York: McGraw Hill.

Koontz, Harold and O'Donnell, Cyril (1976) *Management*. New York: McGraw Hill.

Koontz, Harold and O'Donnell, Cyril (1980) *Management*. New York: McGraw Hill.

Koontz, Harold and Weihrich, Heinz (1984) *Management*. New York: McGraw Hill.

Koontz, Harold and Weihrich, Heinz (1988) *Management*. New York: McGraw Hill.

Kosofsky Sedgwick, Eve (1991) *Epistemology of the Closet*. New York: Harvester Wheatsheaf.

Krauss, Rosalind E. (1996) *The Optical Unconscious*. Cambridge, MA: The MIT Press.

La Monica, Elaine and Morgan, Philip (1994) *Management in Health Care: A Theoretical and Experiential Approach*. Basingstoke: Macmillan.

Laclau, E. (1990) *New Reflections on the Revolution of Our Time*. London: Verso.

Latour, B. (1987) *Science in Action*. Milton Keynes: Open University Press.

Laudan, Larry (1995) *Beyond Positivism and Relativism. Theory, Method and Evidence*. Boulder, CO: Westview Press.

Learmonth, Mark (1998) Managerialism and Public Attitudes to UK NHS Managers. *Journal of Management in Medicine*, 11:4, 214–21.

Lefebvre, Henri (1998) *The Production of Space*. Oxford: Blackwell.

Leonard, Jerry (1995) Foucault and (the Ideology of) Genealogical Legal Theory. In Leonard, Jerry D. (ed.) *Legal Studies as Cultural Studies. A Reader in (Post) Modern Critical Theory*. New York: State University of New York Press, pp. 133–51.

Lewison, Jeremy (1999) *Interpreting Pollock*. London: Tate Gallery.

Lincoln, Bruce (1989) *Discourse and the Construction of Society: Comparative Studies of Myth, Ritual, and Classification*. New York: Oxford University Press.

Linstead, Stephen and Höpfl, Heather (eds) (2000) *The Aesthetics of Organization*. London: Sage.

Lynch, Michael (1998) Towards a Constructivist Genealogy of Social Constructivism. In Velody, Irving and Williams, Robin (eds) *The Politics of Constructionism*. London: Sage, pp. 13–32.

McDowell, Linda (1996) Spatializing Feminism. Geographic Perspectives. In Duncan, Nancy (ed.) *Body Space*. London: Routledge, pp. 28–44.

MacIntyre, Alasdair (1981) *After Virtue. A Study in Moral Theory*. London: Duckworth.

MacKinnon, Catherine (1989) *Towards a Feminist Theory of the State*. Cambridge, MA: Harvard University Press.

McLeod, John (1997) *Narrative and Psychotherapy*. London: Sage Publications.

Martin, Emily (1996) The Egg and the Sperm: How Science has Constructed a Romance Based on Stereotypical Male–Female Roles. In Sargent, Carolyn F. and Brettell, Caroline B. (eds) *Gender and Health: An International Perspective*. London: Prentice-Hall, pp. 29–43.

Martin, Joanne (1990) Deconstructing Organizational Taboos: The Suppression of Gender Conflict in Organizations. *Organization Science*, 1:4, November, 339–59.

Martin, Luther H., Gutman, Huck and Hutton, Patrick H. (eds) (1988) *Technologies of the Self. A Seminar with Michel Foucault*. Amherst: University of Massachusetts Press.

Massey, Doreen (1996) Masculinity, Dualisms and High Technology. In Duncan, Nancy (ed.) *Body Space*. London: Routledge, pp. 109–26.

Meecham, Pam and Wood, Paul (1996) Modernism and Modernity: An Introductory Survey. In Dawtrey, Liz *et al.* (eds) *Investigating Modern Art.* New Haven: Yale University Press, pp. 1–34.

Meltzer, Bernard N., Petras, John W. and Reynolds, Larry T. (1975) *Symbolic Intractionism: Genesis, Varieties and Criticism.* London: Routledge.

Mills, Albert J. and Murgatroyd, Stephen J. (1991) *Organizational Rules.* Milton Keynes: Open University Press.

Mills, Albert J. (1992) Organization, Gender, and Culture. In Mills, Albert J. and Tancred, Peta (eds) *Gendering Organizational Analysis.* Newbury Park, CA: Sage, pp. 93–111.

Minsky, Rosalind (ed.) (1996) *Psychoanalysis and Gender.* London: Routledge.

Morrison, Wayne (1997) *Jurisprudence: From the Greeks to Post-Modernism.* London: Cavendish.

Mühlhäusler, Peter and Harré, Rom (1990) *Pronouns and People: The Linguistic Construction of Social and Personal Identity.* Oxford: Basil Blackwell.

Mulkay, M., Potter, J. and Yearly, S. (1983) Why an Analysis of Scientific Discourse Is Needed. In Knorr-Cetina, K.D. and Mulkay, M. (eds) *Science Observed.* London: Sage, pp. 171–204.

Munro, Rolland (1995) Managing by Ambiguity: An Archaeology of the Social in the Absence of Management Accounting. *Critical Perspectives on Accounting*, 6, 433–82.

Myers, G. (1990) *Writing Biology: Texts in the Construction of Scientific Knowledge.* Madison: University of Wisconsin Press.

Nast, Heidi J. and Kobayashi, Audrey (1996). Re-corporealizing Vision. In Duncan, Nancy (ed.) *Body Space.* London: Routledge, pp. 75–96.

Newton, Tim (1998) Theorizing Subjectivity in Organizations: The Failure of Foucauldian Studies? *Organization Studies*, 19:3, 415–47.

O'Doherty, Damian and Willmott, Hugh (2001) Debating Labour Process Theory: The Issue of Subjectivity and the Relevance of Poststructuralism. *Sociology*, 35:2, 457–76.

Parker, Ian (1992) *Discourse Dynamics: Critical Analysis for Social and Individual Psychology.* London: Routledge.

Parker, Ian (1997) *Psychoanalytic Culture.* London: Sage.

Parker, Martin (2001) Fucking Management: Queer, Theory and Reflexivity. *Ephemera. Critical Dialogues on Organization.* 1:1, 37–53, www.ephemeraweb.org.

Parker, Martin (2002a) Utopia and the Organizational Imagination: Outopia. In Parker, Martin (ed.) *Utopia and Organization.* Oxford: Blackwell, pp. 1–8.

Parker, Martin (2002b) *Against Management.* Cambridge: Polity Press.

Pateman, Carole (1983) Feminist Critiques of the Public/Private Dichotomy. In Benn, S.I. and Gaus, G.F. (eds) *Public and Private Social Life.* London: Croom Helm, pp. 281–303.

Peters, T. and Waterman, R.H. (1982) *In Search of Excellence.* New York: Harper and Row.

Pile, Steve and Thrift, Nigel (1995) Mapping the Subject. In Pile, Steve and Thrift, Nigel (eds) *Mapping the Subject.* London: Routledge, pp. 13–51.

Pollock, Griselda (1999) *Differencing the Canon. Feminist Desire and the Writing of Art's Histories.* London: Routledge.

Pospisil, L. (1971) *Anthropology of Law: A Comparative Theory*. New York: Harper and Row.

Potter, Jonathan (1996) *Representing Reality Discourse, Rhetoric and Social Construction*. London: Sage.

Pratt, G. (1992) Spatial Metaphors and Speaking Positions. *Environment and Planning D: Society and Space*, 10:3, 241–43.

Prior, Lindsay (1997) Following in Foucault's Footsteps. Text and Context in Qualitative Research. In Silverman, D. (ed.) *Qualitative Research: Theory, Method and Practice*. London: Sage.

Protevi, John (2001) *Political Physics*. London: The Athlone Press.

Rabinow, P. (1986) *The Foucault Reader*. Harmondsworth: Penguin.

Reichert, D. (1992) On Boundaries. *Environment and Planning D: Society and Space*, 10:1, 87–98.

Roberts, John (1996) Management Education and the Limits of Technical Rationality: The Conditions and Consequences of Management Practice. In French, Robert and Grey, Christopher (eds) *Rethinking Management Education*. London: Sage, pp. 54–75.

Rose, Gillian (1996) As if the Mirrors had Bled. Masculine Dwelling, Masculinist Theory and Feminist Masquerade. In Duncan, Nancy (ed.) *Body Space*. London: Routledge, pp. 56–74.

Rose, Nikolas (1989) *Governing the Soul. The Shaping of the Private Self*. London: Routledge.

Sabine, G.H. (1951) *A History of Political Theory*. London: Harrap.

Sarbin, Theorore R. and Kitsuse, John I. (1994) Preface. In Sarbin, Theorore R. and Kitsuse, John I. (eds) *Constructing the Social*. London: Sage, pp. x–xiii.

Scott, Anne (1997) The Knowledge in Our Bones: Standpoint Theory, Alternative Health and the Quantum Model of the Body. In Maynard, Mary (ed.) *Science and the Construction of Women*. London: UCL Press, pp. 106–25.

Seidler, Victor J. (1994) *Unreasonable Men. Masculinity and Social Theory*. London and New York: Routledge.

Seidman, Steven (2001) From Identity to Queer Politics: Shifts in Normative Heterosexuality. In Seidman, Steven and Alexander, Jeffrey C. (eds) *The New Social Theory Reader. Contemporary Debates*. London: Routledge, pp. 353–60.

Shotter, J. (1985) Social Accountability and Self Specification. In Gergen K.J. and Davis, K.E. (eds) *The Social Construction of the Person*. New York: Springer Verlag.

Shotter, John (1993) *Conversational Realities. Constructing Life through Language*. London: Sage.

Shotter, John and Gergen, Kenneth J. (1989) *Texts of Identity*. London: Sage Publications.

Silverman, Kaja (1988) *The Acoustic Mirror. The Female Voice in Psychoanalysis and Cinema*. Bloomington: Indiana University Press.

Skultans, Vida (1999) Narratives of the Body and History: Illness in Judgement on the Soviet Past. *Sociology of Health and Illness*, 21:3, 310–28.

Smart, Carol (1989) *Feminism and the Power of Law*. London: Routledge.

Soja, Edward W. (1985) The Spatiality of Social Life: Towards a Transformative Retheorisation. In Gregory, Derek and Urry, John (eds) *Social Relations and Spatial Structures*. Basingstoke: Macmillan, pp. 90–127.

Solomon-Godeau, Abigail (1997) *Male Trouble. A Crisis in Representation.* London: Thames and Hudson.

Sparke, Matthew (1996) Displacing the Field in Fieldwork. Masculinity, Metaphor and Space. In Duncan, Nancy (ed.) *Body Space*. London: Routledge, pp. 212–32.

Spivey, Nancy Nelson (1997) *The Constructivist Metaphor. Reading, Writing, and the Making of Meaning.* San Diego: Academic Press.

Stewart, R., Barsoux, J.-L., Kieser, A., Ganter, H-D. and Walgenbach, P. (1994) *Managing in Britain and Germany.* Basingstoke: St. Martin's Press.

Stillar, Glenn F. (1998) *Analyzing Everyday Texts. Discourse, Rhetoric and Social Perspectives.* Thousand Oaks, CA: Sage.

Strati, Antonio (1999) *Organization and Aesthetics.* London: Sage.

Stratton, Jon (1996) *The Desirable Body.* Manchester: Manchester University Press.

Synott, Anthony (1993) *The Body Social. Symbolism, Self and Society.* London: Routledge.

Thomas, Alan B. and Anthony, Peter D. (1996) Can Management Education be Educational? In French, Robert and Grey, Christopher (eds) *Rethinking Management Education.* London: Sage, pp. 17–35.

Thomason, George (1988) *A Textbook of Human Resource Management.* London: Institute of Personnel Management.

Townley, Barbara (1994) *Reframing Human Resource Management. Power, Ethics and the Subject at Work.* London: Sage.

Townley, B. (1998) Beyond Good and Evil: Depth and Division in the Management of Human Resources. In McKinlay, Alan and Starkey, Ken (eds) *Foucault, Management and Organization Theory.* London: Sage, pp. 191–210.

Urry, John (1985) Social Relations, Space and Time. In Gregory, Derek and Urry, John (eds) *Social Relations and Spatial Structures.* Basingstoke: Macmillan, pp. 20–48.

Van Gennep, Arnold (1960) *Rites de Passage.* London: Routledge and Kegan Paul. Trans. M.B. Vizedom and G.L. Caffee.

Velody, Irving and Williams, Robin (1998) Introduction. In Velody, Irving and Williams, Robin (eds) *The Politics of Constructionism.* London: Sage, pp. 1–12.

Watt, Ian (1996) *Myths of Modern Individualism. Faust, Don Quixote, Don Juan, Robinson Crusoe.* Cambridge: Cambridge University Press.

Weihrich, Heinz and Koontz, Harold (1993) *Management. A Global Perspective.* New York: McGraw Hill.

Wilkinson, Adrian and Willmott, Hugh (1995) Introduction. In Wilkinson, Adrian and Willmott, Hugh (eds) *Making Quality Critical.* London: Routledge, pp. 1–32.

Willmott, Hugh (1993) Strength is Ignorance; Slavery is Freedom: Managing Culture in Modern Organizations. *Journal of Management Studies*, 30:4, 515–50.

Wolpert, Lewis (1992) *The Unnatural Nature of Science.* London: Faber and Faber.

Wood, Denis (1992) *The Power of Maps.* New York: The Guilford Press.

Wood, Paul (1996) Jackson Pollock and Abstract Expressionism. In Dawtrey, Liz *et al.* (eds) *Investigating Modern Art*. New Haven: Yale University Press, pp. 109–28.

Woolgar, Steve (1980) Discovery: Logic and Sequence in a Scientific Text. In Knorr, Karin D., Krohn, Roger and Whitley, Richard (eds) *The Social Process of Scientific Investigation*. Dordrecht: D. Reidel, pp. 239–68.

Woolgar, Steve (1988) *Science: The Very Idea*. London: Tavistock.

Wray-Bliss, Edward and Parker, Martin (1988) Marxism, Capitalism and Ethics. In Parker, Martin (ed.) *Ethics and Organizations*. London: Sage, pp. 30–52.

Young, Iris Marion (1997) Together in Difference: Transforming the Logic of Group Political Conflict. In McDowell, Linda (ed.) *Undoing Place? A Geographical Reader*. London: Arnold, pp. 332–42.

# Index

Page numbers in **bold** indicate boxed text.